MENTAL ILLNESS, DELINQUENCY, ADDICTIONS, AND NEGLECT

FAMILIES IN TROUBLE SERIES

**Series Editors: CATHERINE S. CHILMAN,
ELAM W. NUNNALLY, FRED M. COX**
all at University of Wisconsin—Milwaukee

Families in Trouble Series is an edited five-volume set designed
to enhance the understanding and skills of human services
professionals in such fields as social work, clinical psychology,
education, health, counseling, and family therapy. Written by
recognized scholars from several academic disciplines, this
impressive series provides practice guidelines, state-of-the-art
research, and implications for public policies from a family systems perspective. No other book or integrated series of books
provides such an authoritative overview of information about
the wide range of economic, employment, physical, behavioral,
and relational problems and lifestyles that commonly affect
today's families.

VOLUMES IN THIS SERIES:

Volume 1
Employment and Economic Problems

Volume 2
Chronic Illness and Disability

Volume 3
Troubled Relationships

Volume 4
**Mental Illness, Delinquency,
Addictions, and Neglect**

Volume 5
Variant Family Forms

MENTAL ILLNESS, DELINQUENCY, ADDICTIONS, AND NEGLECT

Families in Trouble Series, Volume 4

Edited by:

Elam W. Nunnally
Catherine S. Chilman
Fred M. Cox

SAGE PUBLICATIONS
The Publishers of Professional Social Science
Newbury Park   Beverly Hills   London   New Delhi

#19066263

HV
699
.M47
1988

To our spouses, children, and grandchildren

For information address:

SAGE Publications, Inc.
2111 West Hillcrest Drive
Newbury Park, California 91320

SAGE Publications Inc.
275 South Beverly Drive
Beverly Hills
California 90212

SAGE Publications Ltd.
28 Banner Street
London EC1Y 8QE
England

SAGE PUBLICATIONS India Pvt. Ltd.
M-32 Market
Greater Kailash I
New Delhi 110 048 India

Printed in the United States of America

Library of Congress Cataloging-in-Publication Data

Families in trouble : knowledge and practice perspectives for
  professionals in the human services / edited by Catherine S.
  Chilman, Fred M. Cox, Elam W. Nunnally.
    p. cm.
  Includes bibliographies and indexes.
    Contents: v. 1. Employment and economic problems—v. 2. Chronic
illness and disability—v. 3. Troubled relationships—v.
4. Mental illness, delinquency, addictions, and neglect—v.
5. Variant family forms.
    ISBN 0-8039-2705-3 (v. 4) ISBN 0-8039-2706-1
(pbk.: v. 4)
    1. Problem families—United States.   2. Family social work—United
States.   3. Problem families—Counseling of—United States.
4. Problem families—Government policy—United States.   I. Chilman,
Catherine S.   II. Cox, Fred M.   III. Nunnally, Elam W.
HV699.F316   1988   88-6539
362.8′2′0973—dc19   CIP

FIRST PRINTING 1988

Contents

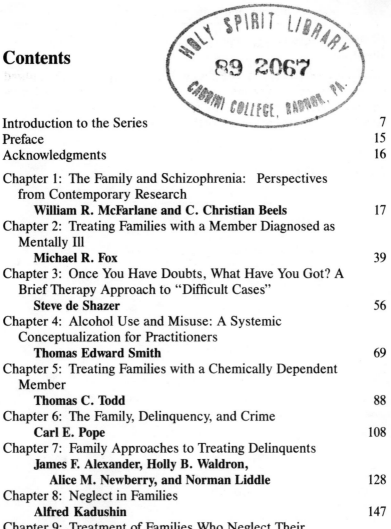

Introduction to the Series

ELAM W. NUNNALLY, CATHERINE S. CHILMAN,
AND FRED M. COX

MAJOR PURPOSES AND CONCEPTS

The major purpose of this series of books is to enhance the understanding and skills of human services professionals in such fields as social work, education, health, counseling, clinical psychology, and family therapy so that they can more effectively assist families in trouble. There is no need to elaborate here that many of today's families are in serious trouble, as rising rates of divorce, unmarried parenthood, poverty, and family violence suggest. The stresses imposed by a rapidly changing society are creating severe strains for families and their members. There are also positive aspects of these changes, however, including improved health care and freedom from backbreaking toil, as well as increasing knowledge about family-related problems and ways to minimize them.

Thus, to reduce the negatives that are afflicting families and to enhance the positives, it is important to marshal the social and psychological knowledge and practice wisdom now available to enrich professional family-related practice, policies, and programs. The editors fully recognize that current knowledge is all too meager; much more needs to be developed. However, let us use the knowledge we do have while the search for more continues.

This series proposes to function as a basic knowledge, theory, and practice resource of the highest scholarly and professional quality. It is directed to practitioners and graduate students in the human service professions who work with troubled families. It emphasizes families in trouble, rather than families in general. As far as the editors can ascertain, no other book or integrated series of books combines an authoritative overview of information about the wide range of economic, employment, physical, behavioral, and relational problems and lifestyles that commonly affect today's families.[1]

This is especially true with respect to books that link up-to-date, research-based knowledge about common family-related problems to implications both for clinical practice and for policy and program development and implementation. For the most part, publications and curricula for the human services tend to be presented in discrete, specialized units. In the family field, for instance, knowledge from the social and behavioral sciences is often presented in a separate course with its own texts that emphasize basic knowledge and theory, with little or no mention of the applications of this knowledge and theory to professional practice. Quite different courses and texts deal with clinical practice applications, often with little reference to the related knowledge and theory base. Another set of courses and texts deals with planning and policy strategies for programs to meet individual and family needs, with little reference either to clinical practice techniques or to basic knowledge and theory foundations on which program and policy development should rest.

Thus, professionals tend to have serious difficulty forming clear links along the continuum of theory, knowledge, policies, programs, and clinical practice. Yet professional services cannot be adequately designed and delivered unless these links are made and applied, in an integrated way, to meeting the needs of families and their members.

Family Systems Perspective

A family systems perspective forms the fundamental conceptual scheme of this series. Families are seen as small, open systems, deeply affected by their internal, interpersonal dynamics and by the many aspects of the external environment with which they interact. From the internal dynamics perspective, everything that happens to one member of the family affects all members. The internal systems of families can vary in a number of ways, some of them dysfunctional. For example, the members of some families are so tightly and rigidly interconnected, or "fused," that members have virtually no sense of personal identity. Flexible changes of family patterns in order to meet changing conditions from within and from outside the family then become virtually impossible. Moreover, in such instances individual family members find they cannot extricate themselves from the poorly functioning family system.

In addition, some families form dysfunctional subsystems, such as a closed partnership between a father and son in competition with a closed mother-daughter partnership. Such alignments tend to undermine the parents' marriage and the development of sons and daughters as maturing individuals.

Some families with interpersonal problems, such as poor husband-wife relationships, deny their real difficulties and displace them onto another family member, such as a child, who may then become the problem-laden scapegoat for both parents.

There are many other variations on the internal systems theme, briefly sketched here. The chief point is that efforts aimed at treating individual members of families are often fruitless unless the operation of the whole family system is better understood and included in treatment plans, as well as in programs and policies. Moreover, individual treatment, without regard to family system dynamics, may increase rather than decrease the problems of the whole system and its members.

In seeking to understand family systems, it is also important to study the many "family actors"—older, middle, and younger generations and interactive members of the extended family such as grandparents, aunts, uncles, brothers, sisters, steprelations, former spouses, and close friends.

It is also essential to consider the development of families and their dynamics over the life span, with the recognition that family interactions, concerns, and tasks vary at different life cycle stages and crucial transition points such as marriage, childbirth, launching children into schools and jobs, retirement, illness, and death.

Family structures and lifestyles vary, especially at this time in society when a variety of family forms is becoming more common, including single-parent, divorced, widowed, separated, reconstituted, gay or lesbian, extended, foster and adoptive, and two-career families; cohabiting, never-married couples who may also have children; childless couples; and, of course, the traditional two-parent nuclear family with one or more children. Each of these family forms has its own particular strengths and vulnerabilities.

When families have particular problems such as unemployment, low income, chronic physical illness or death of a member, chemical dependency, mental illness, conflict with the law, and so on, their strengths are likely to be seriously undermined. The nature and extent of the stresses they experience will be affected by a number of factors, including family system characteristics and family developmental stage. It is crucially important, therefore, to consider family-related problems, such as those mentioned above, in a family-focused context rather than in the more usual framework that seeks to treat or plan for individuals without appropriate consideration and understanding of the complexities of family dynamics, both internal and external.

External factors affecting families are all too frequently overlooked or brushed aside by human service professionals, especially those in clinical practice. Viewing families ecologically, as open systems, leads to the recognition that many factors in the environment have a strong impact on them. These factors include the state of the economy, employment conditions, the availability of needed resources in the community, racism and other forms of discrimination, and so forth. When environmental conditions are adverse and community resources are inadequate, the stresses on families escalate, especially for families of relatively low income and low educational and occupational status. It then becomes the responsibility of professionals to help vulnerable families develop strategies to deal more effectively with these stresses. Professionals may also need to serve as advocates to assist families in obtaining available resources and to work with other local, state, and national groups to promote improved conditions and resources.

In light of the above, the proposed series includes overview chapters about existing and needed policies and programs that are directed toward more effective problem management in support of family well-being. It is hoped that this material will serve as a stimulus and information base for professionals in their larger community responsibilities.

CONTENT

With these purposes and concepts in mind, the editors offer a series of five books, each of which has the following underlying structure (a) research-based theory and knowledge about each topic, (b) suggested guidelines for methods of family-centered practice, and (c) implications for public programs and policy. At our invitation, recognized specialists from their respective fields have prepared chapters dealing with particular aspects of this overall plan. Specific problem areas that are often associated with trouble for families are covered in the five books. Volume 1, *Families with Problems with Work and Financial Resources*, discusses employment and income. Volume 2, *Families with Physically Impaired Members*, deals with physical illness and disabilities. Volume 3, *Families with Disturbed Family Relationships*, covers that problem area. Behavior that the community finds unacceptable is discussed in Volume 4, *Families with Mental Disorder, Addiction, Delinquency, and Neglect*. Volume 5, *Families with Problems Related to Alternate Lifestyles*, covers participation in alternative family forms that are sometimes accompanied by difficulties for the families involved.

We recognize that not all problem topics are covered. Space

constraints require that we select a set of subjects that seem to be most widespread and most apt to be related to serious troubles for families. We also do not cover all major methods of human service delivery. Our discussion is limited, for the most part, to methods of direct practice in the provision of social and psychological services. The reasons for this limitation are (a) the editors' expertise lies in the social/psychological area, (b) we believe these practice approaches to be of major importance in assisting families, and (c) the majority of human service professionals today are in direct practice.

Although we believe the methods of social planning, administration, and legislative advocacy, to name a few, also are essential to the human services enterprise, adequate coverage of these topics is beyond the scope of the present series.

Underlying Concepts

Definition of the Family

We define a family to mean two or more people in a committed relationship from which they derive a sense of identity as a family. This definition permits us to include many nontraditional family forms that are outside the traditional legal perspective, including families not related by blood, marriage, or adoption. This broad definition is essential if we are to recognize the full variety of family forms found in modern society.

"Families in Trouble" versus "Troubled Families"

We begin with the premise that most, if not all, families are apt to encounter stresses at one time or another in their lives. Due to these stresses they may, from time to time, be "in trouble." This concept is quite different from that which proposes that some families are inherently troubled, largely because of their own internal problems.

We build on the work of such systems theorists as Bertalanffy (1968), Buckley (1967), and Bateson (1972, 1979); family stress and coping theorists such as Hill (1949), Olson and McCubbin (1983), and McCubbin, Cauble, and Patterson (1982); and such clinical theorists as Haley (1963, 1976), Minuchin (1974), Watzlawick, Weakland, and Fisch (1974), and Satir (1967, 1983). We amplify their concepts to develop a multifaceted set of interrelated principles which are reflected to one degree or another in the various chapters.

In so doing, we weave together knowledge and theory from a number of the social, behavioral, and biological sciences and integrate them within a family systems framework. Although such a complex approach may seem overly ambitious, we believe it is important, especially if knowledge and theory about families are to be effectively applied to the fields of practice, programs, and policies.

Our basic theoretical position is that the reactions of family systems and their members to stressful experiences depend on the following major interacting factors:

1. The nature, severity, and duration of the stress and its effects on each family member and the family structure.
2. The perception of each member of the family system (which often includes the extended family) of what the stress is and what it means to each member in terms of that person's beliefs, values, and goals.
3. The size and structure of the family (such as number, gender, and spacing of children); the marital status of the parents; the presence of other kin or friends in the household.
4. The stage of family development and age of each member.
5. The psychological characteristics of each family member (including personality and cognitive factors).
6. The physical characteristics of each family member (such as state of health and special physical assets and liabilities).
7. The previous life experiences that each family member brings to the present stressor event. For instance, a series of losses of loved ones during childhood and adolescence can make a parent, as an adult, particularly sensitive to another severe illness or death.
8. The characteristics of the family system, including the clarity or ambiguity of its boundaries, the rigidity or flexibility of behavioral patterns, the existence of subsystems and their nature, the degree of fusion or distancing of relationships, interaction with external systems, and patterns of communication, plus social, psychological, and material resources available from within the family and its network.
9. Social, psychological, and material resources available to families from communities. This includes not only the existence of a wide variety of community services and resources that are potentially supportive of the well-being of families and their members, but the recognition that families are apt to vary in their access to community resources depending on such factors as the degree of social stratification, racism, ethnocentrism, and power politics within the community.

In summary, the above formulation proposes that families are not inherently "stable" or "healthy" or, conversely, "unstable," "troubled," or "sick," but that most families encounter external or internal stresses at different points in the life span of each member. These stresses vary from one family to another depending on many factors in the environment and within the family. Families also differ in their capacity to cope with these stresses; their coping capacities depend on the nature of these stresses, plus a complex of family system and structure variables together with the social, psychological, and physical characteristics of each member.

To differing degrees, human service professionals can be of important assistance to families and their members at times when stressful events threaten to overwhelm their coping capacities. This assistance may consist of direct treatment, resource mobilization, or efforts to improve public policies or programs, all central topics covered in this series. These efforts are most apt to be effective if the professional approaches his or her work objectively, rather than judgmentally, and with a high level of competence solidly based on the best available scientific knowledge and skills derived from that knowledge, also a major focus of this series.

Our choice of authors was made partly on the basis of their reputations for scholarly or clinical achievements and partly on the basis of their affinity to a systems approach to understanding families and their environments. All of our invited authors were requested to relate their contributions to a systems frame of reference. We have not excluded other theoretical views, however, and the reader will find articles which contain, for example, learning theory and behavioral concepts as well as systems thinking.

We chose a systems paradigm as the orientation for these volumes for several reasons. First, this paradigm readily permits one to view the interplay of individual, family group, and community or societal factors in understanding how troubles arise for families and how families cope. Second, the systems paradigm is hospitable to developmental analyses of families and their difficulties and strengths. Third, at this juncture some of the most fruitful research studies and most exciting clinical developments reported in the scholarly and clinical literature are systems oriented.

We have asked the authors of the various chapters to pay careful attention to the available research in their fields and to view this research in a critical fashion so that they can make distinctions between what knowledge has been clearly established, what has been only partially established, and what still exists largely in the area of clinical impressions and speculation. Although much more and better research, both basic and applied, is needed on most of the topics covered in this series, the needs of families are such that it is essential for human service professionals to proceed in the most effective way they can, on the basis of what knowledge and theory is available. It is also essential for researchers to continue with the many studies that are needed, for them to disseminate their results, and for practitioners to study the research in their fields as new information becomes available. The editors have made a serious attempt to ensure that the present series brings together, in summarized and applicable form, the most pertinent, up-to-date research available on the various topics that are covered here.

Topics Included Throughout the Series: Racism, Ethnocentrism, and Sexism

As sketched above, each of the five books in the series deals with a set of issues that often cause trouble for families. Although the titles of the volumes do not include the subjects of racism, ethnocentrism, and sexism, we recognize that these factors are of central importance and have a profound impact on the whole of our society, as well as on many individual families and their members. Because these factors tend to have pervasive effects on numerous aspects of family lives, we incorporate a discussion of them as an integral part of many of the topics covered, including chapters on poverty, employment, interpersonal difficulties within families, variations in family forms, family-community conflict, and implications both for direct practice and public policies and programs.

NOTE

1. As of this writing (early 1987), there appears to be one partial exception to this statement. A recent two-volume text by McCubbin and Figley, *Stress and the Family* (1983), includes some of the topics that we have dealt with. However, the following important family-related subjects are not included in that book: poverty, long-term unemployment, alcoholism, marital and parent-child conflict, family violence, cohabitation, gay and lesbian lifestyles, nonmarital pregnancy and parenthood, chronic illness or disability of a parent, delinquency and crime, and aging. Moreover, the material on treatment in these volumes is rather sketchy and that on programs and policy almost nonexistent.

Preface

DISTURBED BEHAVIORS

Difficulties that appear to trouble families most severely include problems associated with mental illness, delinquency, substance abuse, and child neglect. These same troubles often bring families to the attention of community authorities and lead to unfortunate negative labeling of a family member as "delinquent," "psychotic," "alcoholic," "addict," or "neglecting parent." Family situations involving these problems are particularly difficult and require exceptional skill and wisdom on the part of human services professionals. These professionals as well as students preparing for the human services will find that the research-based knowledge, practice wisdom, and policy analyses contained in this volume can help them be more effective in working with this population of families.

William McFarlane, Christian Beels, Michael Fox, and Steve de Shazer describe varied approaches to helping patients and families when a member is considered to be mentally disordered. McFarlane, Beels, and Fox also present research findings on treatment outcomes; co-authors McFarlane and Beels discuss theories about causes of mental illness and alleged associations between family system functioning and mental illness of a family member.

James Alexander and his associates, Holly Waldron, Alice Newberry, and Norman Liddle, describe a research-based "functional family therapy approach" to helping families in which a child is delinquent. Alfred Kadushin surveys the research and theory literature on child neglect, and James Gaudin, Jr., outlines a research-based approach to helping families who neglect. Thomas Smith surveys the theory and research literature on substance abuse, with special attention to alcoholism, and Thomas Todd describes an approach to helping families troubled with the drug addiction of a young member. Carl Pope reviews the trends, research, and theory that link family-life factors to involvement in crime and delinquency. Two chapters on legislation and social policy relevant to these patients and their families are presented by Catherine Chilman, Mary Uyeda, and Brian Wilcox.

EDITORS' NOTE

Chapters 1, 2, and 3 in this volume focus on families in trouble with a mentally ill member. The reader will notice the great differences in viewpoints among these authors. These differences reflect the diversity of opinions among researchers and clinicians about the nature of mental illness and the relative merits of various treatment approaches. The editors of this volume think it is important for the reader to become acquainted with some of the issues currently debated among human service professionals working with families who have a mentally ill member.

Acknowledgments

We extend our gratitude to a number of people whose help has been of enormous importance in the development of this five-volume series:

To the Johnson Foundation which graciously extended the hospitality of its Wingspread Conference Center in Racine, Wisconsin, for a two-day planning meeting of most of our authors at the start of this book project.

To the Milwaukee Foundation of Milwaukee, Wisconsin, which generously provided funds to meet some of the costs of the above-named planning conference.

To MaryAnn Riggs, Word Processor Extraordinary, who, with unusual skill and pertinacity, typed many of the chapters and prepared the bibliographies in standardized formats.

To Carolyn Kott Washburne, expert technical editor, who polished the writing of each chapter promptly and efficiently.

To all of our authors who cooperated gallantly with this project and who tolerated the frequently heavy revisions suggested by the series editors who have consistently held to the ideal of a high-quality product that would be of important use to human service professionals, both students and practitioners.

To families everywhere whose strengths and whose vulnerabilities have provided the basic inspiration for this series.

ELAM W. NUNNALLY
CATHERINE S. CHILMAN
FRED M. COX

1

The Family and Schizophrenia:

PERSPECTIVES FROM CONTEMPORARY RESEARCH

WILLIAM R. McFARLANE and C. CHRISTIAN BEELS

This chapter emphasizes the findings from recent basic research on family process in schizophrenia. As a starting point it should be stated that the idea that unique family processes such as "double bind communication" or "schism and skew" cause schizophrenia has been all but discarded by most thoughtful scholars in the field. The principal arguments against these earlier concepts are powerful ones: (a) No studies have shown that any of the processes observed by early family therapists are both unique to families with a schizophrenic member and ubiquitous in all such families, and (b) there is now overwhelming evidence that schizophrenia is associated with significant and widespread impairments of brain function and structure. These alterations are of sufficient proportion to make their origination in oddities of family communication seem highly improbable. At present the likely candidates for etiologic agents are heredity, perinatal trauma and infection, and neurotoxic viruses. For these reasons we refer here to schizophrenia as an illness in the same sense as any other neurological condition that leads to chronic impairment but whose course can vary widely depending on a complex and interacting set of factors, many of them social and environmental.

However, most recent family research has focused on many issues besides that of etiology. A number of other questions, most of them of greater clinical significance, have been addressed in a systematic way using rigorous research methodology. Some of these questions include the following:

- The effects on families of having a schizophrenic member
- The effects on patients of family responses to the illness
- The degree of difference between families of schizophrenics
- The specificity to schizophrenia of factors such as "expressed emotion" (EE) and "communication deviance" (CD)
- The relative importance of these factors to the clinical status of the patient
- The factors in the family's context that might make its members more vulnerable to becoming overwhelmed or rejecting

This chapter presents a brief and highly selective survey of the more reliable research findings on these issues and a brief review of their treatment implications. These data have been important in the design of many of the therapies that have emerged recently and that are usually referred to as "psychoeducational." We have also included a proposed model for describing interactions among family variables. It may be hoped that such a model will guide the clinician in his or her thinking about the family therapy of schizophrenia.

KEY FAMILY CHARACTERISTICS

The following discussion leaves largely untouched the question of a family etiology for the disorder, a topic that has been reviewed by Liem (1980) and that Wynne (1981) has clarified. The following assumes the validity of the large volume of research pointing to a major biological contribution to, if not an etiology for, schizophrenia, as well as the validity of studies suggesting that it is a syndrome with heterogeneous forms, presentations, courses, causes, and treatments (Wyatt et al., 1982). We assume further that it is a multideter-mined phenomenon with contributing factors at the biological, psychological, and social levels of analysis, as described by Scheflen (1981).

A small number of studies, most of them recent, shed light on the question of whether there are any family characteristics that are specific to schizophrenia. At present it appears that at least four probably interrelated family processes can be correlated with chronic schizophrenia, but none of them appears to be unique or specific to the condition. The four factions we describe here seem to be influential in the course of a given case, while it remains to be demonstrated whether any are preexisting factors directly contribut-ing to the onset. We outline these factors in the order of their increasing specificity to schizophrenia.

Family-Expressed Emotion

A discussion of the importance of families in the course of schizo-phrenia should begin with the concept of expressed emotion (EE). In an original study (Brown et al., 1962), then in a replication (Brown et al., 1972), and more recently in the work of Vaughn and Leff (1976), a constellation of family interactional and emotional phenomena has been consistently correlated with the schizophrenic patients' tendency to relapse, apparent need for medication, vulnerability to "life events" and social/vocational adjustment. The primary components of high EE are criticism and overinvolvement, that is, overprotectiveness, excessive attention, and emotional reactivity (Leff et al., 1983).

The source of the parent's tendencies for overinvolved, critical behavior toward the patient is not yet identified, although disappointment, displacement, social isolation, loneliness, and marital discord have been proposed. Anderson (1983) has posited a more circular, yet parsimonious, explanation: The high-EE parents are those with high expectations and little understanding of the illness itself, whose criticism and overinvolvement can be understood as dogged, poorly informed attempts to make their patient offspring well, with alternating periods of frustration and resentment arising out of their obvious failure to succeed.

Vaughn and Leff (1981) have recently refined the concept of EE by specifying four associated behavioral characteristics: (a) intrusiveness, (b) anger and/or acute distress and anxiety, (c) overt blame of the patient, and (d) marked intolerance of symptoms, especially negative symptoms, and long-term impairment. Vaughn's content analysis of the comments of high-EE relatives in her London sample revealed that the family members' anger, in essence, was in reaction to negative symptoms. To many observers that represents an effect of the lack of information, a lack that appears as an aspect of subjective burden in many self-report studies (see "Family Stigma and Burden" below). Note that overinvolvement is still preferable to avoidance and rejection, which generally leads to an even worse course and which in a more benign form leads to the negative symptoms of patient withdrawal and apathy (Wing, 1978).

It is crucial to note that the high-EE construct is utterly nonspecific to schizophrenia. Depressed patients seem even more sensitive to the effects of these kinds of interactions than are schizophrenics (Leff & Vaughn, 1980). Further, there is preliminary evidence that EE is associated with higher risk for relapse in bipolar I major affective disorder (Miklowitz, 1985).

Family Isolation

The common observation that many families with schizophrenic members seem more socially isolated has been partially confirmed by studies of social networks. Brown and his colleagues (1972) noted that 20% of the families in their study were both extremely isolated and high on the EE rating. Another 50% were moderately isolated and showed consistently higher EE than did the 30% who seemed to have low-level isolation. Family isolation would be likely, therefore, to correlate strongly with relapse rate and need for medication.

Hammer (1963) had noted earlier that those patients whose friends and family members were known to one another tended to keep those relationships intact after hospitalizations, compared with those without such "dense" (i.e., less interconnected) networks. Tolsdorf (1976) found that schizophrenics at first admission had smaller, more family-based, and more "asymmetrical" (giving less than they received) networks than did medical patients. This tendency has been noted in several studies by Pattison and colleagues (1979), who have defined a "psychotic-level" network strongly associated with acute and chronic schizophrenia—that is, a network about half the normal size, composed predominately of immediate family members who in turn appear more involved with the patient and each other than with nonrelated friends or neighbors. Note that this apparent family isolation was not measured directly.

Garrison (1978), studying Puerto Rican women in New York City, found an inverse relationship between degree of psychopathology and the size and type of network of the patient; in the schizophrenics' families, the relatives seemed almost as isolated and withdrawn as the patients were. A related finding is that the constriction of networks noted at or just prior to the first episode is much magnified by that episode itself and by the burdens imposed by the subsequent course. There is evidence that being schizophrenic induces network contraction and condensation for the patient and, to a lesser extent, for the family (Lipton et al., 1981). In a study of EE and social networks recently completed by the senior author, we found a significant association between overinvolvement and infrequent contact with nearby friends. For family members this trend toward isolation probably results from their own preoccupation with the patient and a certain degree of withdrawal from and by friends and more distant relatives.

It seems, then, that the families with schizophrenic members are often isolated, but at present such a conclusion is tempered by at least three qualifications: (a) Direct data on the socializing of family members are quite limited; (b) not all families are isolated; and (c) some isolation certainly is a result of the onset of schizophrenia and cannot be considered an independent contributor. Family isolation probably worsens the course of illness as a result of association with higher degrees of EE. It should also be noted that family isolation is not specific to schizophrenia, but of all the syndromes studied, schizophrenia is associated with the most extreme degrees of isolation that have been observed.

Isolation of the family assumes significance when one considers the functions of a social network. Hammer (1981) has emphasized social and instrumental support, access to others, mediation of information, placing demands, and imposing constraints, all of which are essential in dealing with a chronic mental disability. Dean and Lin in their review (1977) concluded that lack of social support markedly increases vulnerability to ordinary stressors in both medical and psychiatric illness. This reflects the common clinical observation that events primarily affecting a patient's relative may be precipitants to a relapse, because that relative turns to the patient for support rather than to more intact but less available members of the network.

It is important to remember that the family is not simply a noxious influence, as many clinicians have been led to believe. Steinberg and Durell (1968) found that separation from the family, for both military recruits and college students, was the most frequent precipitant of the initial episode. Thus, the family emerges as a major source of protective support in almost all cases and of stressful interaction in a significant proportion. The *family's* social support may be one of the variables determining which families will have negative influences on the schizophrenic patient.

The social network of the family may have characteristics that have positive or negative effects on the course of illness, probably mediated through effects on the family's ability to cope. Social support also includes contributions from the culture at large, especially its expectations of the roles of work, sickness, and so on. These effects are suggested by several lines of investigation. The best evidence that the degree of social support affects the course of illness comes from cross-cultural studies (Waxler, 1979) showing that, for example, although the lifetime risk of schizophrenia is about the same the world over, its course is more benign in developing nonindustrialized cultures with a village social structure.

An American example is Christian Midelfort's work in a traditional Lutheran farming community in Wisconsin (Beels & McFarlane, 1983). He achieved high social function and a very low rate of rehospitalization in a group of schizophrenics treated with a nonspecific form of family therapy. The combination of a supportive family approach, available social and occupational roles (supported by farm life and family structure), exceptional continuity of care (provided by the low mobility of both the community and the clinic staff), and a congruent religious ideology seems to make an important difference. There are some contexts, then, where social support for the family is built into the local culture. Where it is not available, the treatment context may have to provide that support.

Family Stigma and Burden

Rabkin (1974) reviewed the literature on the stigma of mental illness and concluded that only slight progress had been made in reducing the degree of revulsion and contempt the public feels toward the mentally ill. In view of the public rejection of patients, it is remarkable that many families do not report feeling unduly stigmatized by the emergence of schizophrenia in one of their members (Freeman & Simmons, 1961). On the other hand, many family members attempt to conceal the presence of the illness from friends and more distant relatives and, in many cases, drop friends following the initial episode (Yarrow et al., 1955).

Lamb and Oliphant (1978) reported that many parents found it difficult to talk to other parents about their children's achievements—simply because the contrast was too painful—and gradually saw those individuals less often. Although the data are in some conflict, the conclusion can reasonably be drawn that a patient's family members do not automatically feel stigmatized but often behave as if they do and that friends and relatives do tend to avoid them as if they are stigmatized. Kreisman and Joy (1974) have pointed out that the discrepancy between subjective reports and objective reality may be partly explained by the length of the illness (relatives of first-break patients may feel worse and withdraw more than those of chronic patients) and by the tendency of most people to underreport negative affects. The common assumption that families play a role in causing schizophrenia is probably a significant contributor to the stigma that family members receive and feel. From these studies it seems possible to assume that every family will at some time be dealing with some aspect of stigmatization.

A related aspect of the family's situation is the burden imposed by having a schizophrenic relative. Here again it is useful to differentiate subjective and objective components. The difficulties patients pose for their families are multiple (Grad & Sainsbury, 1963; Herz et al., 1976; Hoenig & Hamilton, 1969; D. Johnson, 1986; Myers &

Bean, 1968). In general, however, most objectively burdened families complain little about their problems to researchers, and very few translate their complaints into outright rejection and abandonment. The most common elements include economic drain, sleep disruption, interferences with daily routine, tension from fear of unpredictable behavior and from difficulties in communication, and strained family relationships. Parents especially appear to resent having become captives of the situation. In poorer families the tendencies for rejection are more pronounced, apparently because they feel more stigmatized and their burden is more intolerable, given their limited resources (Kelman, 1964).

The meaning of the illness may constitute a source of subjective burden. Many families react with a sense of defeat, as if the entire family has undergone a major change in its worth as a result of the illness, accompanied by feelings of guilt, inadequacy, and anger. Disappointment and even depression follow the realization that the potential of the patient is no longer what the family had hoped. The subtly blaming treatment that relatives too often receive in psychiatric hospitals and clinics rarely alleviates any of these feelings. Further, the lack of education and guidance from professionals contributes to the family's sense of confusion and helplessness (Hatfield, 1983). Thus, a picture emerges that families may be burdened and stigmatized and may feel so as well in combinations that may be complex and idiosyncratic. These problems produce strains that are relatively specific to schizophrenia, though they are clearly and primarily consequences, not causes. When present, it is likely that they predispose the patient to a degree of increased risk of relapse and incomplete recovery.

Family Communication Deviance

A large body of research evidence has accumulated suggesting that many families, even in the absence of their schizophrenic members, tend to communicate in ways that are more fragmented or amorphous than do families without ill members (Liem, 1980; Singer et al., 1978). More specifically, many parents of schizophrenics tend to communicate with each other using odd, ambiguous, or idiosyncratic language, allowing the focus of conversation to drift tangentially, with the introduction of illogical thoughts. That is, their conversational style has a formal structure reminiscent of schizophrenic thinking and speech but to a much less obvious or pathological degree. This family characteristic is more specific to schizophrenia than those described previously but commonly occurs in the nonpsychotic, schizophrenia-spectrum disorders (Hirsch & Leff, 1975). The strong possibility that this phenomenon is a subclinical expression of an underlying heritable disorder has yet to be investigated.

For those primarily concerned with clinical practice, the complex issue of the etiological significance of communication deviance (CD) may seem less important than whether it affects course or is modifiable. As has been stated repeatedly, the answer to the etiology question depends on long-term, longitudinal, prospective studies, which are major and difficult undertakings. However, one prospective study has shown that this characteristic can be found 5 years or more before onset in most families that subsequently have schizophrenic members. The combination of CD and the presence of a poor "affective style" (which the authors equate with high EE) predicts quite accurately for schizophrenic psychosis, again 5 years in advance (Doane et al., 1981). (These are preliminary results in a large and ongoing study and could be invalidated by the outcome of other cases yet to reach the 5-year interval; they should be interrupted cautiously.) There are no data that elucidate the relationship of CD to overall course. As to whether it can be modified, only the unreported clinical experience of many multiple-family therapists and that of Falloon and Liberman (1983) suggest that one can improve or normalize CD.

Other aspects of family communication separate from the specific CD factor are relevant. It is almost a given that families with any sort of psychiatric problem have some sort of communication difficulty: blaming; double meaning, and double binding (Sluzki & Veron, 1971); speaking for others; failing to listen; distorting meaning; interrupting; and so on. Some families with schizophrenic members may suffer from these more general communication problems in addition to varying degrees of CD. Further, if one accepts that double-binding interactions can create distorted, even irrational, communication, then many "therapeutic" situations can be seen as pathogenic. For instance, covert blame of the family by professionals is often combined with overt attempts to help them, while the contradiction is denied (Appleton, 1974). Finally, Hammer and colleagues (1978) have suggested that social isolation may contribute to communication dysfunction.

INTERACTIONS OF FAMILY FACTORS ASSOCIATED WITH SCHIZOPHRENIA

Given that the research on the factors reviewed is in many cases still under way, it is too early to demonstrate any conclusive relationships among them. What is needed are multivariate studies of the family to see if there are indeed regular patterns of association. In the meantime, we are proposing here a heuristic model that at least is consistent with what is known and seems to follow from clinical experience and simple logic (see Figure 1.1.).

First, recall that there are data showing that high EE and social isolation tend to be found in the same families (Brown et al., 1972), as do EE and CD (Doane et al., 1981). Miklowitz and colleagues (1983) recently found that communication deviance, previously viewed as a nearly universal characteristic of families with a schizophrenic member, actually is clustered among relatives who are also overinvolved; low EE and critical relatives were statistically indistinguishable in their CD levels, which were significantly lower. The low EE group, in fact, was all but lacking CD. The overinvolved, high-CD subgroup

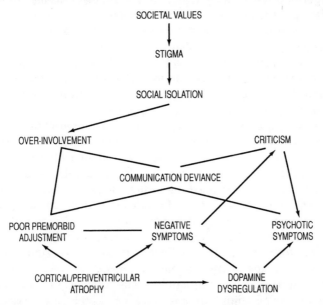

Figure 1.1 Relationships of investigated biological, family and social factors. (Lines represent correlations; arrows represent hypothesized direction of influence.)

represented only 16% of the total sample. Also, there were significant differences between relative subgroups—fathers were generally lower than were mothers or other key relatives on the sum EE score, whereas mothers were more overinvolved and fathers more critical.

That aspects of EE might be partially a reaction to symptoms is suggested by another Miklowitz study (1986) in which emotional overinvolvement was found to be associated with poor premorbid adjustment. One interpretation of this finding is that overinvolvement might result from the relative's concern about and need to compensate for premorbid disability in the schizophrenic-to-be. It is a short step to seeing overinvolvement as one, very natural, reaction to the burden of attempting to cope with a subtly and mysteriously impaired child.

There is suggestive evidence that stigma and burden tend to go with social isolation of the family. In our study of correlates of high EE, we found that mothers (but not fathers) who were isolated were significantly overinvolved, as were those with larger networks but who reported experiencing stigma and rejection from their friends and relatives. Those who had both populous and accepting social networks were protected from being overinvolved with the schizophrenic family member. We also found that cramped housing was strongly associated with overinvolvement. These observations suggest that the social and physical environment of the family plays a major role in determining responses to the patient and the illness and, thereby, in determining the course of illness.

Two sets of correlates, CD–EE and EE–isolation, tend to be associated with a poorer outcome for the patient. Although it has been suggested that CD is more severe in socially isolated families, there seems to be no direct data on the question. Thinking syllogistically, we might propose the following: If CD correlates with EE and EE with isolation, then CD might correlate with isolation.

The interactions proposed here could be seen as interacting through positive feedback processes in which an increase in one factor tends to induce an increase in the others, all in the direction of poorer functioning. Clearly, at some point an equilibrium would have to be reached, whether through a crisis and hospitalization or through stabilizing adjustments in the family, such as the patient's withdrawing from contact.

The interaction between isolation and EE, especially overinvolvement, can be seen as a manifestation of a single systems characteristic: a relatively impermeable family boundary. In everyday terms this implies that if one is preoccupied with intrafamily problems—

especially a mentally ill child—one may tend to see less of the rest of one's network. Conversely, others tend to see less of those who seem to be more involved with each other or burdened by ongoing psychosis and offer less by way of social exchange (Beels, 1981). Stigma tends to drive families into isolation especially if more peripheral members of the family's network, from feeling stigma themselves, elect to withdraw support and attention. It is a circular or, over time, a "helical" process.

The same kind of circularity describes the interaction of EE and CD. For instance, family members must be able to communicate clearly and to maintain a focus of attention in order to disentangle an overinvolved relationship. Conversely, in an overinvolved interactional process in which there tends to be high-level emotional intensity, any coexisting communication difficulties tend to be exacerbated. The interaction of both factors results in incomplete, anxious, tangential, and confusing transactions. In addition, recall that patients with a predominance of negative symptoms and asociality tend to elicit overinvolvement by virtue of their general unresponsiveness and lack of initiative.

With respect to isolation and CD one would expect that the latter tends to be exacerbated when family members have less exposure to the rest of the social network and the normalizing effects that it has on communication. Conversely, CD itself is probably a stimulus for the avoidance of and by the more peripheral members of a high-CD family. It is the authors' impression that communication patterns outside the family may be less comprehensible to some families of schizophrenics and, as a result, anxiety- and withdrawal-provoking. Anthropology provides several examples of the deviation of language and other aspects of culture in subgroups that have remained semi-isolated for a period of time.

Finally, stigma and burden, while having many effects, seem from the data to lead primarily to isolation in many families and to overinvolvement in some families. This is only stating the obvious: Most people who are simultaneously feeling ashamed, defensive, rejected, and overwhelmed are somewhat socially withdrawn as well as socially avoided.

TOWARD A SYNTHESIS

At present, an account of the relationship of each of these factors to a presumed constitutional vulnerability (i.e., an illness, narrowly defined) is quite complex and at some points speculative. Taken one by one, the following points emerge:

1. EE is a coincidental factor, completely nonspecific, yet has a powerful effect on course of illness.
2. Isolation may predate the initial episode, thus perhaps contributing in a minor way to the onset of the illness, although it is clearly exacerbated by the social processes that follow from it and seems to predispose family members to overinvolvement.
3. CD in the presence of EE may be a contributing factor to onset, although it has been speculated that it is at least partially an effect of an underlying heritable disorder; CD seems to be associated with overinvolvement.
4. Stigma and burden have to be considered effects of the patient's illness yet highly specific to it; both factors appear to be associated with and probably induce high EE.
5. Poor premorbid adjustment and a predominance of negative symptoms have been correlated with overinvolvement and criticism, respectively: It seems necessary, then, to assume that a major portion of EE may be reactive to particularly distressing aspects of the disorder.

None of these factors appears to be uniquely specific to schizophrenia, yet the convergence of all four in one family would be likely to occur in association with schizophrenia. Note that the converse is not true from research to date: Schizophrenia will not *necessarily* be associated with any one factor or even with all four together.

With reference to family therapy these factors are interrelated in a complex way. Their relationship to each other and to schizophrenia as presented here is only beginning to become clear, and the rest of the story may well emerge over the next decade. In the meantime one can readily appreciate that the corrrelation of any one factor or dimension to schizophrenia says very little about the direction of causality or even whether the concept of causation is relevant. Caution remains the best policy in this area. The fact that on the basis of existing research data schizophrenia will not necessarily be associated with any family factor or even constellation of factors seems to us to require the abandonment of the term and concept of the "schizophrenic family," because it has usually implied that an identifiable type of family will be uniquely and ubiquitously associated with schizophrenia. Our multivariate model, while more complex, seems a more accurate reflection of the situation. The trade between simplicity and accuracy may well be the price that must be paid to achieve a reliable advance in our understanding of the schizophrenic process.

DIMENSIONS OF FAMILY TREATMENT

The Object, Attitude, and Goal of Therapy

We turn now to the impact that the research reviewed previously has had on the design of family treatments. To begin with, we are faced with the fact that without a definable and predictable focus of family dysfunction, we cannot legitimately describe working with the family of the schizophrenic individual as family therapy because we are not treating the family. In this instance, the patient is the patient. As was recognized early in the history of the family therapy movement, the definition of the unit of treatment is of profound importance to formulating the problem, planning strategy and technique, and assessing outcome. We do not, therefore, lightly assert that in schizophrenia the family is not the object of treatment.

However, it seems that a major reorientation is required when attempting to design and implement a family-based treatment effort, given, on one side, the nearly incontrovertible arguments for a major constitutional vulnerability as the basis for manifest illness and, on the other, the crippling effects on the treatment system of holding the family responsible for that illness. That reorientation is at the heart of a newly arrived cadre of approaches that are loosely grouped under the term psychoeducation, which we term the medical model family therapies. Put positively, their goal is the creation of a strong alliance of therapist, family members, and functional aspects of the patient with the task of reducing to the absolute minimum the disability imposed by the schizophrenic disorder.

It must be stated at the outset that the single most frequently voiced complaint from family members is that they feel greatly demoralized by the implication, often unstated, that the clinical care system sees the family only as a pathogenic influence. This blaming process and the accompanying rejection makes impossible the creation of the *sine qua non* of any workable psychosocial therapy: trust, openness, and hope in the participants. One principal reason that family therapists must be knowledgeable about the present state of psychiatric research on schizophrenia is that to continue a causal assumption of a simple model of family etiology will all but disable any attempt to involve family members in treatment. The guilt induced by this attitude in the clinician has profound effects on the mental health of family members. Several observers have proposed that the disorganization of family interaction commonly seen is actually iatrogenic, a product of the family attempting to avoid doing anything that might seem pathological.

Beyond the attitude of the therapist and the treatment system as a whole, the other differentiating aspect of the newer, psychoeducational (PE) therapies is their research-based, targeted approach to family interaction. Rather than attempting to alter the entire pattern of family interaction by blocking maneuvers during enactments, obscure tasks, paradoxical reframings, or interpretations, the PE methods use very direct instruction, essentially training family members to adopt a quasi-therapeutic stance. The suggested intervention strategies are based on the research findings we have reviewed above. At its base, this approach assumes, until proven otherwise, that a given family's members are cooperative, competent, and well-intentioned but lack information about preferable ways of interacting with someone with schizophrenia.

More specifically, it is clear that the defective information processing and physiological hyperarousal that are at the core of schizophrenia (Neuchterlein, 1984) necessitate a low-key, friendly, somewhat distant, interpersonal style; clear, simple communication; protection from sudden contextual changes; and carefully modulated social and vocational demands. In addition, family members are asked to accept that schizophrenia means a major diminution in the patient's prospects for a full life. In essence, they may need to make a devil's pact: If one accepts the reality of the patient's neurological dysfunction, then the long-term outcome may well be superior to that which would follow from denying that dysfunction and pressing for normal behavior and the realization of normal expectations.

General Principles of Treatment

A number of other principles seem to be dictated by the research we have reviewed here. While some may be self-evident, it seems important to be explicit when dealing with such a controversial topic.

1. For patients still involved with their family of origin, family intervention is necessary, although not sufficient, to reduce risk for relapse and overall morbidity beyond that achievable with drug therapy, because (a) after the patient him/herself, the family is the entity most profoundly affected by this illness; (b) the family has the most powerful

effect on its ill member, whether that effect is positive or negative; and
(c) available medications have serious and limiting side effects, while
doing little to enhance social functioning and perhaps reducing social
responsiveness and initiative.

2. Treatment design should reflect a circular, multileveled, factor-interac-
   tional hypothesis if there is to be a reasonable chance for success. We
   have proposed a model that is punctuated thus: Illness affects the
   family, the family affects the patient, and this affects the patient's
   illness.

3. Families of schizophrenic patients are like schizophrenia itself in
   being heterogeneous along many axes, especially with respect to (a)
   the relative degree of primary versus secondary dysfunction of the
   family unit, (b) the emotional resilience and coping skills of family
   members, (c) attitudes of family members toward the disorder and
   their predicament, (d) whether the family members use the illness to
   maintain a dysfunctional homeostatic equilibrium, and (e) the total
   situation of the family with respect to income, employment, and
   housing.

4. That heterogeneity requires a variety of family approaches, the choice
   of which depends on family characteristics, phase of illness and patient factors, and availability of environmental supports to aid the
   family and patient.

5. Because family intervention does not cure schizophrenia, such work
   must be accompanied by careful diagnosis and drug management,
   social skills training, occupational rehabilitation, housing alternatives,
   and supported employment.

Core Elements of Family Intervention

The discussion to this point seems to lead to a treatment model
that comprises five core elements, all of which are present to some
degree in each of the psychoeducational approaches. These include
Goldstein's brief family treatment model (Goldstein, et al., 1978;
Kopeikin & Goldstein, 1983), Anderson's long-term psychoeducational approach (1980; Hogarty et al., 1986), Falloon and Liberman's
behavioral family management (1983), Leff and colleagues' relatives'
groups (1982, 1983), and psychoeducational multiple-family groups
(McFarlane, 1982, 1983).

Essential Components of Family Intervention

There are significant differences between these methodologies
that are of importance to the serious practitioner; limited space
requires that we refer those readers to the literature cited. What

follows are the common and essential components of all these therapies as a group.

Joining

To expect families to cooperate and extend themselves on behalf of the therapy and the patient, their members must feel that the therapist and the therapeutic organization are on their side. While perhaps seeming self-evident, it is our experience that the clinician must make a special effort to assure family members that they are not being blamed, being treated themselves, or being asked to do what is required without support for themselves.

Several elements appear critical to the creation of a therapeutic alliance. For one, Anderson has emphasized the importance of validating the family's experience of the illness rather than interpreting or ignoring it. Family members will need to be invited to share their reactions, because they may have suppressed them or be used to clinicians denying their reality. The clinical task is to reach an empathic understanding of their feelings, whatever they might be, and to communicate that empathy back to the family. A second task is to mobilize the family members' hope and energy, recruiting them as partners in the treatment/rehabilitation effort that is to follow. If the family feels validated by the clinician, it will be a rarity when a family refuses to participate in a patient-focused treatment. The goal here is to form a solid, task-oriented treatment system composed of clinician, involved relatives, and patient.

Assessment

It is crucial to evaluate the following:

1. Early signs and symptoms that portend incipient relapse
2. Precipitating life events and family reactions to them
3. Premorbid functioning of the patient and family
4. Expressed emotion and communication deviance, if present
5. Social network support
6. Objective and subjective burdens
7. Sense of stigma and rejection by friends and relatives
8. Apparent degree of investment in the illness
9. The financial and employment situation of the patient and family members

Education

This aspect has been the source of the name for the medical model therapies such as psychoeducation. Families must know as much as is known about the scientific basis for the treatment that is being offered the patient. Thus, in a straightforward manner they should be informed about the symptoms, subjective experience, usual course, role and action of medication and psychosocial treatments, and basic neurochemistry of the disorder. They should also be told about the genetic risks, which in most cases are minimal, and the long-term outcome, which now appears to be much more positive than has been assumed in the past (Harding & Strauss, in press).

Beyond the known facts families can be trained to use the seemingly reliable techniques now available for

1. Learning to recognize and handle prodromal symptoms
2. Managing crises and medication compliance
3. Dealing with paranoid ideation and delusions
4. Optimizing social activity of patient and family
5. Anticipating the effects of major life stresses
6. Learning communication techniques specific to schizophrenia
7. Using professional assistance more effectively
8. Creating the least arousing emotional climate
9. Regulating social, financial, and vocational pressures and demands

Interactional Change

Over a variable period of time almost all families can be encouraged and instructed to adjust their emotional intensity, communication, and interpersonal distance to that which is at the same time supportive but not overly stimulating or demanding. Anderson and Hogarty (1986) have contributed the clinical dictum that only one major change should occur at a time in the life space of a person with schizophrenia. These ideas can be linked directly to the available knowledge about the neurophysiology of the disorder, so that relatives and friends can learn to modulate their interactions to avoid increasing arousal and risk of relapse. What is so remarkable, in our experience and that of the psychoeducational research projects, is that these methods greatly enhance the social and vocational functioning of the patient, probably by building confidence and allowing the patients to learn to adjust the level of arousal on their own. Because criticism seems to play such a prominent role in relapse, some families may need to be taught basic communication skills, especially how to make requests for the schizophrenic member to make changes in his or her behavior without couching the request in personally critical terms. This approach will be useful specifically when the educational material fails to convince them of the reality of the patient's disability.

Structural Intervention

Although structural change is a hallmark of therapies developed by Minuchin (1974), Haley (1976), and others, it seems essential to make the point in work with schizophrenics and their families that the well members are in charge during the treatment process. The reasons are several. For one, the patient in the early phases of the postepisode period may be in dire need of protection, support, and control. Second, a clear hierarchy tends to reduce negative interaction and thereby to lower the level of the entire family's arousal. Third, the parents especially need to know that their needs will be supported and, where possible, met by the clinical team. All this translates into encouraging and backing the parents to set limits on violent, markedly bizarre, dangerous, and excessively disruptive behavior. While partly a matter of joining with the patient's family, this aspect is also part of a realistic rehabilitation process: The patient must learn that living in society requires at least a minimal effort to control symptom-driven behavior. Also, the goal of the work is to create a calm, predictable, and less enmeshed family and social environment.

Interfamily Contact and Support

Because there is so much evidence that many families with schizophrenia in their midst are socially isolated and because there is no way ultimately that clinicians can fully appreciate the family's experience, it seems essential that families have some contact with one another during the treatment process. All but Goldstein's (1978) brief intervention strategy allow families a significant measure of contact, and we suspect that a fair degree of all these methods' effectiveness derives from this aspect. Note that participation in self-help or advocacy organizations surely counts in this regard but may not be an adequate vehicle for providing the other elements described above.

One of the authors (W.R.M.) has developed a psychoeducational multiple-family group approach to encompass all the core components in one package, while providing much greater interfamily contact than the single-family methods. Because the preliminary results from that approach, judging from the present status of ongoing outcome studies, are equal or superior to that of the single-family strategies, because it affords the possibility of interfamily problem solving, and because it is so much more cost effective, it seems the most suited to use in the hard-pressed public sector. However, some families demand single-family treatment and, in many instances, know what is best for them.

Outcome Studies

The psychoeducational approaches make eminent sense once one accepts the fundamental premise of a biological disability as a major factor in the illness. What is remarkable is that they are highly effective as well. These methods have been tested more rigorously than have any class of psychosocial therapies. What emerges from the outcome research literature is that they have a profound impact on relapse and rehospitalization rates; are acceptable to families; improve patients' social functioning, work performance, and job retention; reduce familial expressed emotion; and enhance families' knowledge and coping skills. It is not an exaggeration to say that these methods were born of research and have developed entirely within that context, especially regarding rigorous testing of outcome.

The first such study was that of Goldstein and his colleagues at UCLA (1978). Focusing on the need to make families more aware of possible stresses that act as precipitants to repeated psychotic episodes, they developed a six-session, brief, inpatient-based approach that attempted to achieve four goals: (a) recognition of the psychosis and its seriousness, (b) possible stresses that preceded its onset, (c) similar or potential stressors that might occur in the future, and (d) what family members and patient might do to avoid them or, at least, to attenuate their impact. As in the research projects that followed, they compared outcome to patients given supportive individual therapy, while both test conditions received medication. Interestingly, nearly three-quarters of the sample were recruited during their first episode. At 6 months, 0% of the family-treated group and 17% of the individually-treated group had relapsed.

Falloon and colleagues (1985) reported similarly impressive results in a longer-term study of a family approach in which formal education of families was followed by 9 months of in-home behavioral training for family members, focusing on communication skills and problem solving. Some cases were then referred to multifamily groups, while the remainder were followed in a single-family format, but less intensively, until a total treatment period of 2 years had elapsed. The patients in the family-treated group achieved a relapse rate of 11% at 9 months and 17% at 2 years, compared to 50% and 83%, respectively, in a randomly assigned and individually treated control group. Schizophrenic symptomatology, community tenure, medication dosages, and episodes of other symptoms were significantly more favorable in the family-based treatment condition.

Leff and colleagues (1982, 1985) tested a relatives-group approach, in which high-EE relatives were helped to change by low-EE peers in a 2-year treatment model. This approach included education of relatives as the initial intervention. In a study nearly identical in design to Falloon's, relapse rates were 9% at 9 months and 20% at 2 years in the relatives groups, while individually-treated patients relapsed at rates of 50% and 78%, respectively. Relapse only occurred among families in which relatives were high on the EE measure and remained high through the course of treatment. Most relatives were able to reduce their levels of criticism and/or emotional overinvolvement.

Anderson and colleagues (1980, 1986) developed another long-term approach based on the attention-arousal hypothesis (Tecce & Cole, 1976) and the EE research. Their approach stresses gradual recovery from an episode, followed by carefully regulated increases in expectations and functioning. The family work is collaborative, with family acting as ancillary rehabilitation workers, in exchange for generous support and relief from the clinicians.

Seemingly the most ambitious of the new methods, their relapse outcome was numerically less dramatic—19% at 1 year, 32% at 2 years, vs. 41% and 67% in the comparison group—but functional outcome at 2 years included at least part-time, out-of-home occupational activity in over three-quarters of the cases.

In a study being conducted by the first author in which families and patients are seen together in psychoeducational multiple-family groups for a minimum of 2 years, outcome compares favorably with the other studies. This is true despite a generally more relapse-prone sample and treatment by junior or in-training therapists. Relapse outcome at the time of this writing, stands at 12.5% at 1 year and 25% at 2 years in the multiple-family groups, while the results in a single-family version of the psychoeducational approach are 25% and 53.5%, respectively. Relapse at 4 years stands at 50% to 62.5% in the multiple-family group cell and 55% to 94.4% for the single-family treatment. Because no interfamily contact was arranged by the single-family clinicians, this study also represents an attempt to estimate the therapeutic effect of interfamily social support. Because this like all the studies to date includes a small sample, it is being replicated at six sites with a total sample of 194, with closer supervision of senior staff clinicians.

In reviewing this body of evidence, one is struck by the consistency of outcome and study design across research teams, all of whom are largely independent, if not competitive, in relation to each other. It is difficult to discount such evidence. For the clinician the implications appear unusually clear for the mental health field: If one cares about results, these models offer a high probability of success, on the same order as neuroleptic medication. Questions that remain to be investigated empirically include: What are the characteristics of patient and family that best fit various models? What kinds of functional outcomes may be possible, whether the results are replicable with larger samples and in other hands and whether the results persist after the treatment is discontinued or attenuated? Of course, a larger question also lingers: Would tests of other approaches based on entirely different theoretical premises, for example, systemic or structural models, do as well in equally rigorous evaluation experiments?

CONCLUSION

What we hope has been communicated here is a perspective that varies from previous family systems teaching about the families of individuals suffering from schizophrenia. This perspective includes a substantial, if not dominant, contribution of biological dysfunction and deficit in the generation of a serious and unrelenting illness. This does not negate a systems view but rather expands an overly narrow *family* systems paradigm to include interactions of family process with verifiable neurophysiological disease. Further, it is our contention that in schizophrenia especially family interactions are also heavily contingent on extrafamily factors such as economic resources, community tolerance of stigma, conceptual orientation of the extended kin and neighborhood network, and other specific aspects of the family's social network.

Further, if we listen to what families themselves are saying, misinformation, insensitivity, causal blaming, and outright rejection of families in and by the treatment system must be included as powerful disabling influences on family functioning. These biological and extrafamily factors, from the perspective of both an enlightened systems theory *and* empirical research, produce very complex effects, which in turn affect the functioning, symptomatology, and course of illness of the person with schizophrenia.

This view does not deny that family dysfunction exists and induces effects on the patient. Rather, we start from the point of view that families of schizophrenic patients vary in their level of functioning in the same way as all families do and that the effects on different families of a catastrophe such as schizophrenia vary widely and somewhat unpredictably from family to family. If one then includes differences in severity of illness and characteristics of the family's social network and surrounding community, a complex but more comprehensive view of family process in this illness emerges.

This newer systems perspective is of great significance for treatment. As the educational and behavioral family strategies have shown, seemingly conclusively, the conceptual orientation and attitude of the therapist toward family members makes an enormous difference in clinical outcome and family morale. It is our view that these approaches do improve family functioning as well, probably by eliminating the iatrogenic effects of a destructively blaming treatment system and also by training families in coping strategies that protect them from excessive stress and preoccupation with the patient and the illness. These approaches are inconceivable without the joining efforts made by the therapist, efforts that communicate support, validation, and empathy of and toward the family and the patient. These joining techniques, we believe, are impossible to implement effectively without taking into account the research findings presently available and translating them into an attitude of acceptance and collaboration with family members in a long-term but optimistic approach to the rehabilitation of the person with schizophrenia.

Treating Families with a Member Diagnosed as Mentally Ill

2

MICHAEL R. FOX

I will present my therapeutic approach with persons diagnosed as having a long-term mental illness. While not necessarily the best approach, it is simply my best effort but not, perhaps, the best way for others to proceed. Given our present state of knowledge, there can be no one *right* approach in the treatment of such complex and multidetermined problems. In this chapter I will sketch the major features of my approach and present the results of an uncontrolled outcome study of 35 schizophrenic patients in my private practice.

Advances in psychoparamacology and in psychoeducational methods, along with the emergence of family advocacy organizations such as the National Alliance for the Mentally Ill, have brought deserved critical scrutiny of traditional family therapies and their results. Although most therapists acknowledge the importance of family involvement, there is little research data to support the claims of effectiveness for traditional family therapy methods.

PRINCIPLES OF PLANNED CHANGE

I call my treatment method "Planned Change," a term taken from Ortiz (1985), because it requires a therapist to actively plan interventions to change the present context of the illness. It is based upon the principles of strategic therapy and the work of Haley (1963, 1976, 1980), Madanes (1981, 1984), Fisch and colleagues (1982), Watzlawick and colleagues (1974), de Shazer (1982, 1985), and others. My interpretations of their work should not be construed as representing their thoughts.

The principles of strategic therapy are sometimes assumed to constitute a theory of causality or, worse, a set of very manipulative techniques. But in fact they are a theory of change, a conceptualization of problem definition and resolution. They are a theory of how to go about changing a problem once it has become a problem, not a theory of what caused the problem.

My approach is based upon considering the solution to problem behavior as involving three or more persons in addition to the

therapist and help-giving system, the interruption of habituated sequences of interaction between those persons dealing with the problem behavior, and the reestablishment of an appropriate hierarchy
within the entire family and help-giving systems, not just the family
system. I assume that the problem includes not just the disturbing
behavior but also the previous assumptions about the problem held
by all and the unsuccessful attempted solutions based upon those
assumptions.

Because the disturbing behavior and the changing of it occurs in
the present, I must plan a change in the present situation. I must
especially change the interactions between all involved, both family
members and therapists as well as other helpers. The method should
allow alternative interactions to occur despite past experiences that
have shaped family perceptions of what is possible in the present and
future. Thus, I prefer the term "Planned Change" to that of strategic
therapy.

I view therapy as strategic and planned only if the therapist
initiates what happens during therapy and designs a particular approach for each problem. My approach is active and process-ori-
ented, with little reliance on both an assessment of problem content
or insight. The initiative is largely taken by myself because I am
responsible for creating a context in which change can take place.

My method assumes change is not only possible but inevitable
and that it occurs in stages. A small change is better than no change
and better than a large change that is not sustained. A small change
usually leads to larger changes, and minimal changes are needed to
initiate a solution to the disturbing behavior. Once change begins,
further change ripples throughout the system, which includes the
patient, other family members (including those not present), and all
helping persons and agencies.

One must remember that even small changes can be very disruptive to all involved, and the therapist must always be readily available
to capitalize on any crisis, for example, by interrupting repetitive,
unhelpful interactional sequences (attempted problem solving) in
order to facilitate new solutions and thereby further change.

The disturbing problem should be defined in "action language"
terms, that is, behavior that the patient is doing or not doing that the
family disapproves of and behavior he or she should be doing instead. The therapist's responsibility is to arrange a situation in which
all family members are empowered by having clear role definitions.
The disturbing member should be given clear behavioral expecta-

tions and consequences from which to choose, and other family members are helped to uphold these expectations consistently and administer consequences predictably in helping the disturbing member.

Symptoms are seen as arising simultaneously with an inability to make a family life-cycle transition. It is especially difficult that just when other family members are experiencing stress from their own life-cycle transitions, the disturbing family member experiences symptoms from the stress of his or her own unique life-cycle transition. Just helping the family help the disturbing member get back to doing what he or she should normally be doing at this age and stage of life is not enough. One must also facilitate the helping family members to make their own developmental transitions. Therapy should be a process of introducing variety and richness into the entire family's life, not just removing noxious behavior.

OUTCOME RESEARCH

There are only a few rigorously designed, controlled-outcome studies on treatment of families with a schizophrenic member. There are several studies of treatment outcomes (e.g., Falloon et al., 1984; Goldstein et al., 1978; Leff et al., 1982) that combined an educational and crisis model of family intervention with neuroleptic medication. These reported significant decreases in relapse rates.

Hogarty and colleagues (1986) reported on the results of a psycho-educational program combining family education with individual social skills training and medication for the patient. After 1 year posthospital, 19% of those receiving family psychoeducational intervention and medication relapsed, whereas none of those receiving family psychoeducational intervention, medication, and social skills training relapsed. A cautionary word was included in their report, however, indicating that continuing study suggests a delay of relapse rather than prevention. From the same project Anderson and colleagues (1986) noted that relapse rates continued to rise in all treatment conditions as patients neared the end of their second year of treatment although an effect of the family treatment was still present.

The results of the small number of clinical studies suggest that no treatment method is successful with all patients over a long period of time. Findings to date lead to the tentative and common-sense conclusion that a combination of correct medication and psypchotherapy with both patients and their families leads to a higher success rate than any single intervention strategy (Falloon et al., 1982, 1984; Goldstein et al., 1978; Leff et al., 1982).

COMMENTS REGARDING PSYCHOEDUCATIONAL APPROACHES

There is evidence that psychoeducational approaches significantly reduce relapse rates and especially that these approaches result in delays in relapse. Nevertheless, I have several concerns with these approaches.

I have very grave concerns about the reliance on medication that distinguishes psychoeducational approaches as well as traditional psychiatric practice. I notice that in Hogarty's review (1984) 68% of placebo patients relapsed, which means that *32% did not relapse*. If one out of three needed no medication to avoid relapse, a routine and continuing use of neuroleptics is hard to justify when viewed in the context of the risks of serious neurological damage. Tardive dyskinesia occurs in one out of five patients treated with neuroleptics over 5 years. So, then, what is the effect and personal cost to a person who is encouraged to take medication unnecessarily over a period of years?

I believe that providing information to patients and their families is helpful; however, close attention must be paid to *what* information is given and *how* it is provided. Given our present stage of knowledge, I do not find it in the best interest of families to authoritatively educate them to believe that their member's disturbing behavior is exclusively an illness, requiring life-long treatment with medication, frequent hospitalization, and a high risk of permanent incapacitation.

I agree with psychoeducational therapists (Anderson et al., 1980) that families have the power to influence the course of schizophrenia, especially through diminishing their emotional reactivity to each change in the patient's behavior. Dealing with overstimulating family responses, even though they may be understandable, is a crucial factor in the treatment of any family with a disturbing member, not just in mental illness (Vaughn & Leff, 1976). But rather than educating families about the cause of mental illness, I find it more helpful to educate them about alternative problem-solving strategies, especially those regarding how to make and implement decisions differently.

THE PLANNED CHANGE APPROACH

I accept that certain persons behave in disturbing ways that meet DSM III criteria; however, systems theory suggests that interpersonal problems develop within a multidetermined, biopsychosocial process. The multitude of contributing factors, all relating to each other, make identifying the cause of the problem a futile endeavor and akin to affixing blame.

My therapeutic responsibility is to promote change in the family's problem-solving processes, regardless of whether family members played a role in the development of the disturbing behavior. After a thorough medical evaluation for any demonstrable physical abnormalities, I assume that understanding the cause of the problem has little to do with changing catastrophic behavior and how it affects all family members. This is especially true of exploring family causality factors because there is no data to support the now-outworn argument that family members cause major mental illness (or any other form of disturbing behavior for that matter).

It is important to note that I am not responsible for making change happen. Rather, I am responsible for creating a situation where change can occur. I arrange the treatment context differently, thereby allowing family members to do something different. Change is seen as the result of altering how people (including myself) do what they will do rather than resulting from an understanding of what various family members are doing.

The best plan addresses a change in the process by which rules governing behavior are made, enforced, and changed. It is not just a change in what the rules are, as assumed by many therapists. Frequently a change in how decisions are made and enforced in the entire system is needed, even though what is done may often be the same. Such changes must not reinforce sexist, stereotyped gender roles, nor reduce, humiliate, or embarrass anyone within the system.

Similarly, if we assume context effects outcome and the "helping" agents and their agencies are part of the system, then the agency context within which therapy takes place may also need to be changed. The agency context includes the written and unwritten rules governing how and what a therapist can do. Although it is possible for some skillful therapists to change how and what they do without changing their agency's rules, if therapy with a specific family or type of problem has not been effective, then the focus must also be on changing the agency's rules governing therapy. This is particularly important in psychiatric clinics and hospitals, as will be discussed later. When you change the context of the situation within which therapy takes place and change the content of the system's response to disturbing behavior, you change the behavior, usually for the better.

Therapy need not be complex or difficult, but it must treat all involved with respect. It focuses on the positive assets of all family members and their situation rather than limitations. It must empower all family members and lay a foundation for new roles in the family. How to empower all family members, including the patient, is the question.

Empowerment requires a therapist to help an individual, family, or group to assume or reclaim more control over their lives, that is, over the process of what is or will be happening to them. Empowerment focuses on increasing the capacity, or as I prefer, actualizing the capacity of individuals to function on their own behalf. In my opinion this is rarely pursued vigorously in working with long-term mental illness.

The following questions are useful to assess the level of empowerment present in any approach. To what extent is the approach

1. Based on what the disturbing persons and their family members indicate as *their* needs?
2. Based on a positive, expectant attitude toward the disturbing persons and their family members, focusing on strengths rather than limitations, and accepting patients and their families as resources for enriching the process of change?
3. Allowing the disturbing persons and their family members to play a leadership role in their treatment by being given active decision-making authority?

THE FOX SYSTEM

My task becomes how to contruct a situation in which I can place the responsible family members in charge of changing the disturbing member's behavior. Keeping in mind that power, and therefore empowerment and disempowerment, are always relative, I primarily empower families by disempowering myself vis-à-vis the responsible family members. Instead of accepting the role of being the "expert," that is, "I know best what decisions should be made," I define my expertise as deciding how therapeutic decisions can best be made differently so that what is done and the results will be different from previous attempts.

In the consultation sessions I prescribe a new process of how the family members and I will relate to each other in making decisions, but I will leave to the family what the decision will be. I maintain responsibility for the therapeutic process while they have responsibility for the content of the therapeutic decisions. I prescribe how they are going to decide what they and I will eventually do in therapy. They are informed that I will support whatever decisions they make as long as they are within the prescribed process and not physically harmful to anyone. I have never had to overrule a family's decision. Simply giving appropriate authority and control to the family mellows the most difficult family members.

As a result, I function as a consultant to the family by advising members about alternatives available and by supporting their decisions, while the family simultaneously functions as my consultant because I retain my medicolegal responsibility and control over the treatment process.

Placing Family Members in Charge Differently

My prescription (Fox, 1985) as to how the family will make their decisions is based on an assessment of the cyclical interactional sequences involved in the family's previous problem solving and the disturbing member's developmental needs. The process is derived in part from Stuart's (1980) five levels of decision making in a marital relationship but is applied to any two caregivers.

In a parent–child case it is crucial that both parents be experienced as coequal authorities by their disturbing child, that is, coequal to each other and not with the therapist who is one down in relationship to the parents. Contrary to the public myth I believe most parents rarely make and enforce decisions by mutual agreement. Usually responsibility is divided. One parent more so than the other has responsibility for making the rules, and the other parent has more responsibility for enforcing those rules. Therefore, I divide the parental decision making into rule making and enforcement.

I place one parent in charge of making all rules but only after obtaining input from the disturbing child, other relatives, myself, and the second parent. The second parent becomes responsible for enforcing the "rule-making" parent's final decisions. Thus, they are experienced by the child as having very different functions, yet coequal to each other.

The decision of who will be placed in charge of which role should not be based on stereotypical gender-role ascriptions. It should allow each parent an opportunity to develop different role interactions with the child and participate differently in problem solving, based on what change is needed in the cyclical sequence of interaction between the parents during their attempted problem solving.

How does one determine which parent does what function? Both parents frequently feel powerless but usually one more than the other. Usually one is more active, loud, and critical and attempts to *do* something, whereas the other is more quiet and empathic and tends to talk rather than do something.

Which parent during a crisis is more prone to engage in rapidly escalating emotional cycles out of a sense of powerlessness and frustration? In moments of crisis just before considering hospitalization or medication, which parent is more prone to argue, berate, physically fight, totally withdraw, or threaten to eject the disturbing member from the home? Although appearing very controlling, this parent is feeling the least influence with all members of the caregiving system and naturally responds with massive emotional and coercive maneuvers in the hope of having an effect. I marvel at how often a previously "out-of-control" parent regains control, cooperates, and becomes a nurturing person once he or she experiences having influence and being supported by other family members and myself.

The more quiet and empathic parent is traditionally accused of being overly protective, overinvolved, or overenmeshed. Despite the intense involvement forced upon the parent by the situation, I find this view not helpful. It is more helpful to consider parents' involvement as a reasonable outcome, given the trouble at hand and the strongly negative position of the other parent. When the parents find themselves working together differently and the previously negative parent becomes more available and less threatening, one begins to find both the other parent and the parental relationship changing.

In marital cases frequently the "ill" spouse's behavior is in part clearly the result of sexist oppression and neglect. Even so, the "helping" spouse makes all therapeutic decisions, but only after getting the "ill" spouse's input, and enforces those decisions. The "helping" spouse must also comply with specific behavior changes defined by the "ill" spouse in areas of family living and work. Thereby, the process empowers each spouse to achieve changes in areas where he or she previously experienced powerlessness.

Connecting with Families

Joining the family before attempting a major intervention is crucial. While attempting to change the family's interaction, I must accept and adapt to the family's way of relating to each other and myself in order to increase their comfort. Even when not cooperating with interventions, I do not assume the family is "resistant." There is good reason for the family's refusal when this occurs. At this time the members know best what is possible and not possible in their family. They are attempting to cooperate with the therapy, to which I must adapt my style (de Shazer, 1982).

While overtly accepting the family's definition of the problem or the situation, I simultaneously and slowly introduce new perspectives that will facilitate my accomplishing what the family has asked. This is done directly through changes in the decision-making processes, using specific directives. It is done indirectly through embedded metaphors, stories, subtle reframes, and microstructural shifts during the session.

Interactions between family members with a disturbing member are often called undifferentiated or overenmeshed. I prefer "negatively differentiated." Statements are commonly communicated in a negative context, either describing what is not happening that should be happening or what is happening that should not be happening. This occurs even when expressing caring and concern for the patient or describing how family members are attempting to be helpful. It is still unclear whether this is a response to a mental illness catastrophe or an antecedent pattern. Recent studies have suggested this phenomenon occurs prior to the onset of the illness (Goldstein, 1985). Regardless of its origins the negativistic context creates great impediments to increasing the positive sense of attachment to one another, which is so necessary for growth and development in family members.

Typically almost all positive caring expressions and actions done for, with, or to the disturbing member are expressed by family members in relation to the "disease" metaphor or a somatic concern. They are expressed through questions and discussions about the diagnosis, medication, symptoms, side effects of medication, hospitalization, lack of appropriate community resources, and so forth. Because most disturbing persons experience discussions about the "disease" as negative, the principal way family members attempt to express their caring positively is experienced by the disturbing member as negative.

How does one bridge the gap that develops where despite good intentions the family's efforts fail and increasing emotional detachment occurs? Unfortunately, the emotional detachment frequently is dealt with by family withdrawal in defeat, community placement, or chronic rehospitalization. I do not believe the solution lies in attempting to increase positive connectedness through a discussion of the "disease," as in the psychoeducational approach.

During the initial sessions I join the family by increasing the sense of positive attachment among all members by using a modification of Stuart's "Caring Days" list technique (1980). This provides for the increase of simple, small, specific, positively experienced caring acts among all members, not just directed toward helping the disturbing member. As a result, the expression of "positive" caring through the disease metaphor diminishes, and this is followed by a diminution in the use of the disease metaphor. Subsequently, the disturbing behavior often diminishes.

Dealing with Violence

Some say violence is rarely an issue in treating family members with long-term mental illness. I disagree. Violence or a fear of future violence by the patient directed toward self, others, or property is always in the mind of family members. I have never seen a case of severely disturbing behavior where violence was not either a past, present, or future concern in therapy. It cannot be ignored.

The concern may be a specific previous violent action or it may be a very controlling perception, a worry or a fear that violence will erupt, and this controls the flexibility of the family to do something different. In fact, this very predictable response pattern by family members rigidifies the family's problem-solving abilities and may precipitate violence.

I am not interested in who is responsible for causing the violence. Rather, I am interested in stopping future violence by holding all members responsible for changing the violent pattern. Those members who commit criminal actions must always be held responsible for their actions.

One must find a way of enhancing the power of the seemingly less powerful members of the family. This means holding the batterer and the battered person both responsible for change. The batterer, and not the battered person, is clearly responsible for his or her brutal actions regardless of the situation. However, the battered person must also be held responsible for changing his or her role in the violent sequence.

I assume that changing the context within which violence takes place will force all family members to change their behavior. I inform *all* members that they must make a commitment to nonviolence: to not resort to violence themselves and to respond to violence as an act of criminality and *not* as an act of mental illness. (I know many seriously "ill" persons who go out of their way to avoid injuring any animate thing, and I have also evaluated many violent criminals with no trace of mental illness. Yes, there are some who are violent and mentally ill. It is they I am addressing.)

If any family member, including the disturbing member, becomes violent, the family must go through a clearly defined response. This includes seeking a safe place, calling the police, filing criminal charges (not an emergency petition for hospitalization), allowing the person to return home if the judicial system refuses incarceration in jail or hospital, and following through with the court trial and sentencing. If the family does not pursue charges and/or the trial, I terminate my treatment.

Ideally, I want the family to file charges and not an emergency petition for hospitalization; then it appropriately becomes the judge's responsibility to decide whether it is best to place the violent person in custody and await trial or to order commitment to a hospital. If the family insists on signing an emergency petition for hospitalization, they must also file charges and follow through in court after hospital discharge.

I do not believe the best treatment for mentally ill persons is in jail. They are treated poorly, if at all. However, it is necessary for the judicial system and family members to take a congruent position vis-à-vis the patient and society, that is, a violent act is an act of criminality and not an act of mental illness. For the disturbing member to achieve independence, all family members must learn to internalize impulse control and take responsibility for their thoughts and actions, regardless of the situation or coexisting mental illness. The commitment must be made in the spirit of positive caring and responsibility to the disturbing member, not out of anger and vengeance.

Thus far I have never had a family get up and leave, although they may verbalize agreement and later not follow through. I show respect for their judgment that my approach is unwise or inappropriate for them at this time, and I terminate without malice or blame. They may test me by balking but then follow through when I am firm. Thus, the family either risks leaving a therapy that has already given them hope for the change they desire or risks having to do the hardest thing in their lives, arresting one of their own members.

I will never ask family members to do anything that I would not do myself in my role as therapist or family member. They are informed that I will follow the same prescription if violence is directed toward myself or my property. (Only once have I had to file charges against a patient.)

DEALING WITH THE MEDICAL CONTEXT

A most neglected issue in family therapy with severely disturbing persons is how to effectively use the power of the medical context, that is, the physician, medication, and hospitalization. Most family therapists either pretend the medical context is not an issue or adopt it as the solution when feeling powerless to promote change without medical treatment.

Because therapy is focused on changing the context within which the problem is manifested, we must accept that disturbing behavior is usually treated within the medical context, whether we agree with it or not. To ignore the medical context, the effects of medication, or the physician and hospitalization is to treat families noncontextually and doom treatment to failure. Ignoring it is equivalent to ignoring a powerful grandparent.

The therapeutic problem becomes how to use its existence to advantage. How can the medical context be used to empower family members? While many use medical treatment with little regard for its systemic effects or espouse it as a solution for *the* cause, I prefer to use its power to create a context for systemic change.

While the concept of "illness" is often used to alleviate family guilt, using it makes it hard for a therapist to justify family involvement in therapy other than for continuing "illness" education and for informing the therapist of changes in mental status. It becomes hard to justify asking all family members to participate or asking family members to change how they relate to all the other family members, not just the patient, as a way of helping the patient. Within the "illness" metaphor I can ask for the family's involvement only by couching it as a way of helping an "ill" person, which solidifies them in the powerful one up/one down position.

Using the illness metaphor, medication, and hospitalization suggests that the power for change lies with the expert helpers, that is, the physician, hospital, and staff. However, using hospitals and medication is not in itself a problem. It is how they are used that has serious systemic effects.

The best way to change a destructive process is to arrange for those persons or elements involved to become part of the therapy.

Usually my first step is not to reframe the problem out of the illness metaphor. It is more successful to accept the problem definition as an "illness" and begin changing how the solution deemed appropriate by the family and the medical context is carried out.

As the first stage I do not change the content of the problem or the solution, that is, *what* the problem and solution are; rather, I change *how* the solution is implemented, as shown below. I change how the family and psychiatrist make decisions regarding the medication and hospital treatment. By changing how decisions are made, even when what the decision is remains unchanged, I will have introduced a systemic change. There is less chance of alienating the family and my medical colleagues because I appear to have not changed what the decision was.

Medicating Decisions

Because families suffer the consequences when medication or a change in medication is not helpful, they should be in control of those decisions. The same manner of making behavioral management decisions is applied to medication decisions. At no time will I prescribe or change medication without obtaining a consultation from involved family members. Unless harm will occur, I follow the "decision-making" member's decision. In order for the medication to be changed or discontinued, that member must define specific objective behavioral criteria that the patient must achieve as well as consequences for medication noncompliance. The "enforcing" member monitors compliance and implements consequences. Only when behavioral criteria are met, will I change or discontinue medication.

Most clinicians agree that families are appallingly uninformed about medication and its side effects. I explain how psychotrophic medication functions from a "nondisease" perspective, its potential side effects, and the incidence of side effects. All family members must sign an informed consent form allowing prescription of medication.

EFFECTIVE USE OF HOSPITALIZATION

Hospitalization in this approach (Fox, 1985) is used sparingly and differently. When used, it is seen as an opportunity to achieve a structural change in the family's method of decision making and enforcement. While I maintain ultimate medicolegal responsibility for how and what is decided, the nonhospitalized family members are delegated authority to make all decisions regarding the patient's individualized milieu treatment plan and medication.

I prescribe how the family will develop the plan, that is, how decisions will be made and enforced and who will do this, but the decision of what the patient's milieu expectations and consequences will be is decided by the family in the manner described above. One person makes the final decisions, and the other enforces. The staff and I function only as consultants, with no authority to change any decision made by the family. We provide them information, choices, and rationales. We are responsible for enforcing their plan. When a family member is present, he or she must enforce the plan, with the staff providing emotional support. This agreement is broken only if there is grave risk to someone in the total system.

Hospitals primarily focus on compliance with medication and the hospital's behavioral standards and control methods, which are usually different from the family's. Often there is very little change during a hospitalization, and very little learning is permanently transferred into the home.

My approach forces all, including the therapeutic team, to work together and change in a way that is congruent with the family context. My purpose is not to bring the family into the hospital in order to be more easily changed. Rather, it is to allow the hospital staff to change and treat the patient in a manner that is congruent with the standards of the family to whom she or he will return.

This applies even when the patient has alienated his or her family and lives in a community therapeutic setting. If the patient is returning to the community setting and the family is unwilling to be involved, the community authorities are required to function in place of the family. If the family is willing to reengage with the patient, whether members will accept him or her at home or not, they are given control over the plan. I have been amazed by the eagerness of previously burned-out, disengaged parents to become involved when this approach is offered. No one has refused.

If asked to accept a patient's treatment on discharge, I must meet with the family as many times as needed *before* discharge to arrange an appropriate plan. If the hospital refuses, the hospital must either find another therapist or be willing to continue medicolegal responsibility while I continue as a consultant until a plan is completed. I refuse to take responsibility for a lack of responsible discharge planning.

To the family I say, "My goal is that this will be the last hospitalization. In the future we will be dealing with disturbing behavior in a more family way. Failure to achieve this goal is my responsibility, not yours."

A FOLLOW-UP STUDY

Description of Sample

From 1979 through 1985, 35 patients diagnosed as schizophrenic according to DSM III criteria were treated with this approach. All but two cases were from private practice, with most having failed with traditional approaches. All cases were followed up by contacting the family members. I included all cases seen after two initial consultations, even if they terminated therapy soon thereafter.

There were 9 subchronic patients (26%), with 7 having one prior hospitalization each, and 26 chronic patients (74%), with an average of 3.5 hospitalizations each. The average age of subchronic patients was 20 years, while that of chronic patients was 27 years. I hospitalized only 7 patients, 6 chronic and 1 subchronic.

The families were of lower- to upper-middle-class, all with insurance benefits. All families had two biological parents, except for one single-parent family and two stepparent families. Six patients were married (4 chronic and 2 subchronic), with the patients having in part become psychotic around unresolved marital conflicts.

Success Criteria

In this day of cost containment a successful treatment must not only be helpful but also cost effective. It must interrupt patterns that contribute to expense, primarily the use of hospitalization and medication. It must reduce the time that the patient is unemployed and promote employment, thereby decreasing disability payments and also increasing available taxable and spendable income. It should do so with the fewest treatment hours necessary.

In this approach success is defined as follows:

Level O: Following treatment, the disturbing person became worse.
Level 1: Following treatment, no significant change, positive or negative, in the disturbing person or the family's problem-solving approach.
Level 2: Following treatment, significant change in the disturbing person

and/or the family's approach but not enough to meet the criteria for higher levels, or the family terminated therapy.

Level 3: Treatment was ongoing at least 12 months, with continuing medication use; no further hospitalizations and not working or attending school.

Level 4: Same as Level 3, except the person is working or attending school.

Level 5: Treatment has been discontinued for at least 12 months and the person is working or attending school, is taking no medications, has had no further hospitalizations, and is positively involved with family.

The cost of psychotherapy includes only the fees charged by myself, not the cost of medication or per diem hospital charges. For comparison purposes, it is prorated into the costs at my 1985 fee of $100.00 per 60 minutes.

Results

Levels 3, 4, and 5 are reported as successful treatment. Eighteen of the 35 cases (51%) were successful, 4 being Level 3, 2 being Level 4, and 12 being Level 5. Seventeen cases (49%) were unsuccessful, with one being Level 0, 7 being Level 1, and 9 being Level 2.

Chronicity and Outcomes

Of 26 chronic cases, 12 (46%) were successful, with 4 being Level 3, 2 being Level 4, and 6 being Level 5. Fourteen chronic cases (54%) were unsuccessful, 1 being Level 0, 4 being Level 1, and 9 being Level 2.

Of 9 subchronic cases, 6 (67%) were successful, all being at Level 5, and 3 (33%) were unsuccessful, all being at Level 1.

I consider only Level 5 cases truly successful. These totaled 12 cases (34%), with 6 chronic and 6 subchronic cases. The time since ending therapy for the Level 5 cases ranged from 22 to 94 months, with an average of 46 months. Therapy lasted from 2 to 24 months, with an average of 11 months. Total therapy hours ranged from 5 to 52 hours, with an average of 27 hours, making the average *total* cost of psychotherapy $2700.00 per level 5 cases.

The pattern of using rehospitalization as a solution to disturbing behavior was interrupted in most cases. Out of the 35 cases, 22 cases (63%) had no further hospital admissions.

Costs and Outcomes

The 8 Levels 0 and 1 cases were seen an average of 7 months, for an average of 20 hours of therapy ($2000). The nine Level 2 cases were seen an average of 8 months, for an average of 19 hours of therapy ($1900). The four Level 3 cases have now been seen an average of 42 months, for an average of 124 hours ($12,400). The two Level 4 cases have now been seen an average of 27 months, for an average of 53 hours ($5300). The 12 Level 5 cases were seen an average of 11 months, for an average of 27 hours ($2700).

Summary

Although the sample was small and the research design quite simple, the results suggest the efficacy and cost effectiveness of an approach based on strategic therapy principles in the treatment of schizophrenia.

This approach successfully interrupted the massive costs of life-long medication maintenance in 34% of cases and rehospitalization in 63% of cases. While psychoeducational approaches report impressive outcome results (Anderson et al., 1986; Hogarty et al., 1986), no data are presented regarding cost, which I must assume is high considering the intensity of treatment and cost of medication.

This approach demonstrates a method of treating families that, while neither ignoring nor espousing the medical context, is able to work with it. It focuses on changing how decisions are made and therefore how power is distributed and caring shown. As a result, some families are empowered to change their disturbing member. Our job is to create a situation that increases everyone's fulfillment and an enhanced sense of power over his or her destiny, including our own as therapists.

Once You Have Doubts, What Have You Got?

3

A BRIEF THERAPY APPROACH TO "DIFFICULT CASES"

STEVE DE SHAZER

Psychiatry spends time trying to unravel the correct, clear cause of the problem with a crystalline analysis devoid of inconsistencies and pure in its structural flow, [however] the brief therapist will settle for any dirty little solution that works. The flow of the structure can be marred, illogical, and inconsistent as long as the solution works (Norton, 1982, p. 307).

Therapists and their clients often make the assumption that a complicated problem needs a complicated solution. Or, to put it more exactly, they assume that their complicated description (or analysis) of a problem means that the problem is complicated; therefore, it needs a complicated solution. Also, therapists and clients alike often assume that a problem's duration is directly related to its severity and intractability, thus unnecessarily complicating the situation.

Brief therapists, however, think differently. No matter how complicated the problem (or the description of the problem), and no matter its duration, a small and simple change often leads to unpredictably large changes. A simple doubt can be enough to begin changing a lifelong pattern or way of thinking.

> The centipede was happy, quite
>> Until a toad in fun
>> Said, "Pray, which leg goes after which?"
>> This worked his mind to such a pitch,
>> He lay distracted in a ditch,
>> Considering how to run.

AUTHOR'S NOTE: The author wishes to thank Elam Nunnally and Calvin O. Chicks who were the other members of the team involved in treating the cases described in this presentation and Insoo Kim Berg, Eve Lipchik, and Wallace J. Gingerich (of the Brief Family Therapy Center, Milwaukee, Wisconsin) who, together with the author, developed the conceptual framework.

FRAMES

The cases discussed in this chapter are usually described as "difficult cases." "Difficult cases" is simply a name for the frame therapists often use to define what it is that is going on in certain cases. There are many reasons for this "difficult case" ascription, but it boils down to this: Strange ideas and bizarre behavior seem to demand complicated descriptions and elaborate explanatory metaphors, that is, a "difficult case" emerges. This seems somehow to be the nature of things. Following from this is the not-very-useful idea that a complex description means that there is a complex reality underneath, and therefore therapy must be equally complicated. This idea results from a breakdown of the distinction between "map" and "territory." Simply, a map is not the territory. A description is not the problem it describes. When a distinction breaks down, concepts become reified. That is, the complicated descriptions are thought to be necessary in order to match an equally complicated reality that is "out there," which necessitates an equally complicated therapeutic intervention.[1]

Any map only must be "good enough" to be useful, "good enough" to get the users where they want to go. For instance, to go from Illinois to California, all you need is a map that says: Find and follow Interstate 80 west. You do not need to know that you will pass through Omaha on the way, and you do not need to know about the rivers and mountains. Of course, you might miss a lot of interesting things if your travels are built on following this kind of map, but you will get where you want to go. From a brief therapists' perspective, that is all you want from a map.

Another of the reasons for the ascription "difficult case" is that the clients' frames (Goffman, 1974), or how they define what it is that is going on, seem rather global. Any frame can be described as if it at least helps to determine the person's behavior. In these cases, however, the clients frame their difficulties and problems in such a way that the frames become "facts of life." For example, someone might blame all his or her difficulties on the sun's rising in the east. This may seem absurd to an observer, and it could lead the owner of the frame to unusual and bizarre behavior. As long as that premise helps to determine how the person sees things and therefore how the person behaves, then beneficial change is unlikely. But once the person comes to doubt that premise, then an expectation of change is created (de Shazer, 1985), and different behaviors and different ideas are likely.

Frames color how their owner (creator) behaves toward other people and therefore how they behave toward him or her. Mead (1934) suggested that a person's self-image is based on how that person sees other people seeing him. If a therapist frames a case as a "difficult" one, then he or she is on the way to behaving toward the client in ways deemed appropriate for dealing with difficult cases. Frequently people who behave in strange ways and/or who have bizarre ideas are experienced in dealing with therapists who think of them as "difficult" cases. Thus, if the client sees the therapist treating him or her as a "difficult case," then the client will come to see him- or herself as a "difficult case," and consequently a difficult case develops. The ideas about self-image suggest, however, that when the therapist frames things differently and responds differently than the client expects, then the client will come to see him- or herself differently. Thus, the client's frame may be placed in doubt, and more useful behavior might follow.

At first glance the idea of helping the client develop some doubt about how he or she frames situations may seem absurdly small and simple given the "traditional" ideas about these "difficult cases." However, general system theory has long held as axiomatic the idea that a change in one part of a system will lead to repercussions (and changes) in other parts of the system. This simple idea forms the foundation of brief therapy (de Shazer et al., 1986; Weakland et al., 1974) in general and the approach described in this chapter in particular.

FLUKES, EXCEPTIONS, OR ANOMALIES?

One must be careful in drawing conclusions from single-case studies or even from the study of three cases illustrating the same point: They may just be exceptions to some general rule, or they may even be flukes. But they may also be important: They may be anomalies that lead to some new theoretical understanding and/or new intervention techniques.

A four-step, research-and-theory-construction method, developed at the Brief Family Therapy Center in Milwaukee, Wisconsin, has been applied to "difficult" cases where the therapist searched for ways to introduce doubts, and these doubts have rather quickly and rather strikingly led to a solution:

1. The first step of the method involves attempting to build a thick description of what happened in these cases that seems to have contributed to their unique solutions. (A "thick description" involves the researchers in describing the observed events from as many different points of view as possible and then searching for commonalities.)
2. The second step involves attempting to figure out how we might operationalize that description in such a way that we can try to prompt a similar solution deliberately.
3. The third step involves actually trying the procedure developed in Step 2. When it is effective in prompting a solution, then we will continue using the procedure under conditions where we think it might prove to be effective.
4. The fourth step (which depends on and evolves from the third) involves rigorously defining the conditions under which the procedure will not work.

The approach described in this chapter is in Step 3. At this point we still cannot say whether these cases are (a) flukes, (b) exceptions, or (c) anomalies. We cannot define the conditions under which the procedure is likely to be effective or the conditions under which it is not likely to be useful. Thus far the only tentative idea we have is that the doubt needs to be prompted early in therapy, probably in the first session. When we have been unable to prompt doubt in the first session, cases seem to follow a different pattern (potentially, a different branch of solution-focused interviewing), or they evolve into a different sequence of events.

Even if these cases eventually come to be seen as flukes or exceptions and therefore the approach's usefulness is more or less a matter of chance, it does not mean that we should ignore these cases. It may simply mean that our description does not include all the salient factors. Before Step 4 is completed, the first two steps might have to be revised and redone. Finishing Step 4 might take another 10 years, and it might take yet another unique event to provide us with the key.

CASE EXAMPLE

> Therapist: "I bet you that most people don't believe you're really the devil."

A unique event, such as described in the following case example, provided us with a point of departure. Although rapid change is not unusual in the practice of brief therapy, the simplicity of the approach to what is traditionally seen as a "difficult case" did suggest to us that we were in unexplored territory.

A 28-year-old man, Paul, claimed to be the devil, specifically, the serpent from the garden of Eden. (His medical records indicated that this was not a new idea. He had been making this claim since he was 8 years old.) Therefore, he claimed to be the prime cause of all the evil in the universe.

At this point he was in a halfway house after having been in the hospital. He had not held a job for more than a week in the previous 4 years. Now he wanted a job and did not want to go back to the family farm, because he had been alienated from his family for 4 or 5 years. Throughout the previous 20 years he had been in and out of therapy, in and out of hospitals, and frequently on medication. He wanted to break that pattern but saw little hope of that, but he saw the first step as getting off medications and then out of the halfway house.

Paul readily agreed that most people did not believe he was really the devil. The therapist suggested that if he were in Paul's shoes, this lack of belief would really anger him. Paul agreed. Again, if he were in Paul's shoes, the therapist thought that he would want to prove it to all those doubters. Paul agreed that he wanted to prove it to people, particularly his family. The therapist wondered how Paul was going to go about it. Paul said that the ultimate evil was nuclear holocaust: This would be the proof. The therapist agreed that nuclear holocaust was certainly evil enough to qualify as the ultimate evil.

However, the therapist saw one problem. Again, if he were in Paul's shoes, he thought that he would want people to grovel and to acknowledge the truth: Paul was indeed the devil and the cause of all the evil in the universe. But after the holocaust, there would be nobody there to acknowledge this truth. What good would it do?

Throughout this statement (which is only summarized above), Paul sat motionless, eyes wide open and unblinking. The therapist stood up, and so did Paul. The therapist shook hands and scheduled the next appointment.

Obviously, arguing with Paul about his claim to be the serpent has not worked during the previous 20 years, and so the therapist needs to make sure that he does not let that happen. The therapist must accept the client's premise. The conversation flowed naturally until the therapist was able to develop something "wrong" about the conclusions following from Paul's beliefs or how he framed his situation. In this way some doubt could be introduced.

During the next two sessions Paul talked exclusively about the steps he was taking to get out of the halfway house. With his physician's approval he had gradually stopped his medications and was beginning to look for a job. He had applied for several and had enlisted the help of an agency. During the two weeks following the first session he had not felt "weird" at all (and he had not behaved "weird" according to the halfway house staff). There was no devil talk during either session.

Within a few weeks Paul found a job as a live-in companion to an elderly man. He was responsible for shopping, cooking, laundry, cleaning, and giving the employer a bath, helping him dress, and driving him. Paul's only contact with the therapist during this period was over the phone when he reported doing well. During the third month of this job Paul called on a Monday for an appointment, which could not be scheduled until Friday of the same week.

Paul said that he had originally called to get some medication but that he no longer felt that need. On the previous Saturday he had started to feel "weird" again, thinking about being the devil, and so on. But he had to continue giving his boss a bath. So he gave him his bath. Then, even though feeling "weird," he had to help him dress, fix the evening meal, do the dishes, and clean up. By the time he was finished with his chores, he was so tired he went to bed and to sleep immediately. The next morning, though still feeling weird, he had to help the man dress, drive him to church, and then drive him home again. Grocery shopping had to be done, the house had to be cleaned, and dinner cooked. He continued his work while continuing to feel weird. By Monday he was simply tired but no longer felt weird.

Previously when Paul had had attacks like this, he had ended up in the hospital by the end of the first day. He would have been heavily medicated and would have lost his job, because getting out of the hospital had always taken 4 to 6 weeks. But this time he just forced himself to continue working. On Sunday he had made an interesting discovery: He was not the source of all evil—God was. In fact, as he saw it, he had actually been protecting the universe from the evil God. He went into this scenario in detail and at great length. At the end of the session the therapist shook Paul's hand, saying, "Hang in there. Lord knows we need all the protection we can get." Paul smiled broadly and said nothing.

Paul was not seen in therapy again. When over the course of a year he made payments on his bill, he reported the following. He continued to hold his job and felt good about it. Over the previous 4 years his visits to his family had all ended up with hospitalizations. However, since getting this job, he visited his family twice, and neither time did he find himself feeling weird. He had taken no medication and had not been in the hospital. He also reported feeling "somewhat weird" now and then, but he ignored it and continued doing what he was doing.

CASE EXAMPLE

Therapist: "How come the CIA sent such incompetent killers?"

The apparent success of the approach in the first case led to the following experimental approach of attempting to help the clients develop doubts about how they are framing their situation. At this point a tentative rule was followed: Accept the client's frame as logical up to the point where it produces troublesome behaviors. Then question the logic of the behavior within the person's frame.

Therapy began with Ron, a Vietnam veteran and a former CIA operative, complaining about the plot against him. The plotters had recently escalated by having someone accidently ram into the rear end of his new van for the second time in 6 weeks. His wife, Dorothy, came to therapy complaining about Ron's having recently purchased a side arm, which he carried in the car. She was afraid for her life and the lives of their two children and had notified the police.

Ron tried to reassure her about her safety as well as the children's, but his violent attacks on her in the middle of the night prompted doubts. She saw Ron's behavior and fears as "getting worse, day by day." She was concerned when he took apart the television and the telephone looking for bugs and when he took sentry duty around the house through much of the night. She did not mind his not sleeping, and he usually did nothing during his patrols to disturb her or the children until the previous four nights when he had carried a loaded automatic.

Ron defended himself by saying he was protecting her, the children, himself, and their home. Because he had worked for the CIA, he knew how "they" worked, and that was why he took apart the television, the telephone, and the radios and hunted for bugs throughout the house. He knew that the accident with the car was not an accident; it was, in reality, an aborted atttempt on his life.

Throughout the previous 18 months Dorothy had tried to logically convince Ron that he was imagining things: The CIA was not out to get him, and the accidents were simply accidents. However, her approach did not work. All Ron did was talk less to her in general and keep quiet about the plot while thinking more and more about it. Recently, in fact, Ron had begun to withdraw and was hardly talking to her at all about anything.

Being realistic and trying to talk Ron out of his beliefs had been Dorothy's approach but that did not work, and it is important for the therapist not to do something that has already not worked. Therefore, the first step in this case was to accept Ron's beliefs at face value: Behave as if there were a CIA plot against him. Then, think about what was wrong about the details of Ron's description of the CIA's plot. Most simply, what was wrong with Ron's details was that the two attempts on his life had failed miserably: The CIA had not even come close to killing him. How come? When the CIA plans to kill someone, they do it. Therefore, the question was: Why would the CIA send incompetent killers? What's wrong with the CIA?

Following this line of thought, the therapist asked Ron such questions as, "How come the CIA sent such incompetent killers?" "Don't CIA operatives usually know what they are doing?" "If you wanted to kill someone in your situation, couldn't you do a better job?" "Wouldn't the guy already be dead?" "What's wrong with the CIA?" Ron agreed that if he had wanted to kill someone like him, he would already be dead. He could not figure out why the CIA had sent such incompetents, and the therapist asked him to think about this puzzle.

The therapist switched topics, suggesting loaded guns were not a good way to protect his family. What if there were an accident and the gun went off and he accidentally killed one of his kids or his wife? This Ron did not want, and he agreed to think about unloading the guns around the house.

Then, the therapist asked to speak to Dorothy alone for a minute or two. He suggested to her that because pointing out logic to Ron had not worked, she ought to stop trying it. Repeated attempts to convince him that he was wrong would only make him think she was part of the plot and was trying to get him to let his guard down. Dorothy verified that Ron had recently started accusing her of being in on the plot. The therapist suggested that whenever she thought Ron was thinking about the plot, she should quietly get next to him and without a word give him a hug. She should not argue with him about the plot, and she should not walk away when he withdrew.

Ron interpreted Dorothy's disbelief as proof that she thought he was crazy. Ron also interpreted her "just letting him brood" as further proof that she did not believe that the CIA was after him. Therefore, if Dorothy avoided walking away from Ron when he was thinking but gave him a hug instead, then, because that was rather different behavior, Ron could interpret it as she no longer thought he was crazy. This interpretation would be strengthed by her no longer arguing "logically" about the situation.

Thus, the first principle: If the client is sure, introduce doubts. Ron's central premise (i.e., how he framed or defined what was going on) was that the CIA was after him. He had no question about that. By accepting that premise, the therapist was able to introduce doubt by questioning the CIA's behavior and thus Ron's central premise. Similarly, the suggestions to Dorothy were intended to introduce doubt about Ron's idea that she thought he was crazy. In both of the cases discussed here, doubts are essential to successful therapy because the client needed to "see through" the frame he or she has given the situation and thus develop options.

The therapist maintained his frame in subsequent sessions. Whenever the topic of the CIA came up, he wondered about its incompetent operatives. Ron would share in this puzzle. The therapist would then switch to wondering about what Ron had done that was good for him, and Ron would then describe his efforts to fix up their house so that they could sell it. After the fifth session Ron dropped his ideas about the plot. Or, he at least stopped talking about it and stopped acting as if he believed in the plot's reality. Once in a while he still heard voices from the television but now he knew they were not real and therefore did not act on them.

Dorothy reported following the suggestions and discovered that Ron was extremely responsive. When she resisted the urge to be logical or to walk away and hugged him instead, he would snap out of his "bad mood" and return to his tasks.

During the seventh session (3 months after the first), Ron reported planning to go back to full-time work because the house was now completely ready to sell. Ron and Dorothy reported increased teamwork and improvement in their sex life. (Six months later, Ron was still talking about going back to full-time work, but he had not done anything about it. He continued to occasionally hear things over the television, but he no longer paid attention to what was said. The marriage continued to go well.)

Once some doubts were introduced in session one, the therapist focused on what Ron and Dorothy were each doing that was good individually and for their relationship. Once these activities were described, he encouraged them to do more of the same. That is, the therapist concentrated on working with Ron and Dorothy to build a more satisfactory marriage based on what they did that was good for them (de Shazer, 1985).

Simply put, on one hand, "doubt" can be seen as a way of introducing a small change or an exception to the rules of the complaint, while on the other hand, "hugs" can be seen as introducing a small step toward the solution. As the hugs increased, Ron, Dorothy, and the therapist talked more about what they were doing that was good for them. As the doubt increased we talked about the CIA less and less. Hugs and doubts together allowed Ron and Dorothy to construct a more workable view of reality.

CASE EXAMPLE

> Degas: "One sees as one wishes to see. It's false; and it is that falsity that constitutes art."

In the following case the therapist and client were able to identify some exceptions or times when the complaint did not happen. These exceptions were then used to build the foundation of the solution (de Shazer, 1985). However, the client did frame her complaints as a "fact of life," so that introducing some doubt seemed necessary to enable her to see through the frame and thus behave differently.

A 56-year-old woman, Mrs. J, came to therapy because her paraplegic husband had been increasingly irritated by her being distracted when he needed her. Although she heard nagging voices, what currently distracted her most, she said, was "naked people that were not really there." She had not been in a mental hospital for over 13 years but was afraid that things were getting worse, and she certainly did not want to go into the hospital again. She saw naked males and naked females who generally were just "standing there, doing nothing." When she tried to ignore them, more would appear. Then she would not hear her husband when he called.

The therapist's first step was to find out when Mrs. J did not see imaginary naked people. She reported that she did not see them throughout most of the day except when she sat down to relax. In the evenings she would see them more frequently, because, she thought, she was more tired. This coincided with periods when her husband demanded more from her even though their son was home and helped her.

Offhandedly the therapist wondered why seeing naked people bothered her so much. After all, being naked is just the first step in getting dressed.

In the following session Mrs. J reported that she had started to dress the naked people as soon as they appeared. Interestingly, they would then disappear. Mrs J continued to find this a useful tactic when she thought she saw naked people. Instead of trying to ignore them or pretend she did not see them, she had started to pay attention to them, which seemed to break the troublesome pattern.

Several months later Mrs. J returned complaining that she was arguing more and more with her voices. She continued to dress all the naked people who appeared, and they would simply go away. But she had not found anything that would make the voices go away. The therapist explored with her the times when she did not hear the voices or did not pay attention to them, or did not argue with them even though she paid attention to what they said. She was only vaguely aware that there were times when she did not hear the voices or did not argue with them but agreed to keep a detailed log for 2 weeks.

Mrs. J was asked to carefully note what she was doing (a) when she did not hear the voices, (b) when she did not pay attention to them, (c) when she did not argue with the voices and (d) how she knew her husband knew that she was not paying attention to her voices.

For the therapist it was a question of, "What was Mrs. J doing that was effective or useful or good during those periods when the voices did not disturb her or did not distract her?" Once this was determined, then she could be encouraged to do more of the same things or the same type of things. Hearing the voices of people who were not there was simply accepted as part of the way Mrs. J viewed the world. For the therapist it was not a matter of trying to stop the voices but rather to increase the times or the proportion of time when she was not bothered by the voices.

Mrs. J reported that she seldom argued with the voices before noon. During this period she was busy doing housework and taking care of her husband. She discovered that by not arguing with the voices, they would sometimes become silent for a period while she was busy. But the moment she sat down, she found herself arguing with the voices. She also discovered that she did not argue with the voices when the visiting nurse made her daily visit to her husband. Mrs. J and the therapist explored in detail what she did when she was "busy." Once these details were known, the therapist simply suggested that Mrs. J needed to do more of the same sort of stuff. She agreed.

In the following session Mrs. J reported that she had been able to not argue at all before 5:00 p.m. throughout the 2-week interval. She was busier and felt better. Offhandedly she said that she had become aware she was smoking too much.

The therapist again suggested that Mrs. J continue to do more of what worked for her, and she agreed. Then the therapist told her he had an idea that he thought would be very helpful to her, but it required her agreeing to it before she knew what it was. He assured her that it would be good for her and that it was something she could do, but it would be very difficult. She agreed to "give it her best effort" if it would help. But the therapist thought it was too much to ask of her to agree to it without a lot of thought. So he asked her to think about it for 2 weeks, warning her that her voices would probably try to get her to argue with them about it, and they would probably try to talk her out of agreeing.

Two weeks later Mrs. J appeared eager to hear what the therapist had in mind. Indeed the voices had picked it up and had been telling her not to agree. She had dismissed them as often as possible, but she did argue with them now and then. She thought she had argued less during the 2-week interval. Once again the therapist questioned her willingness to follow through, and she insisted that she would follow through. He again pointed out that it might prove difficult, but it would be good for her. Mrs. J once again promised. The therapist then told her. What she had agreed to was that now and forever, on any particular day, once she had argued with the voices, she could not smoke anymore that day. That is, when she argued, she would not smoke, which would be good for her. When she did not argue, she could smoke, and not arguing was good for her—that is what she wanted out of therapy. She agreed that it would be rough at times. The therapist wondered if her voices had already tried to talk her out of sticking to her word. Mrs. J said, "Loudly and clearly, but I won't listen."

One month later Mrs. J reported both arguing less and smoking less. She had stuck to her word, which meant at least once she did not smoke all day and for 3 days in a row she did not argue at all. The voices, it turned out, tried to convince her that not following their directions was a form of arguing, but she dismissed that as crazy.

Over a period of time the voices diminished as Mrs. J no longer argued with them, and Mr. J's complaints diminished in both frequency and intensity.

CONCLUSION

Even though these cases may be flukes and not anomalies demanding a revision of theory, they suggest that reality is constructed out of some rather flimsy stuff, not concrete and stone. For therapists this is good news. Even problems that are traditionally seen as "difficult" are subject to rapid change—under the right conditions. At this point we do not know what the "right conditions" are exactly. (If they are flukes, then the right conditions are beyond the therapist's control.) Therefore, although we do not know when to use this approach or when not to, we will continue to use it experimentally with those cases traditionally seen as "difficult" ones.

NOTE

1. The philosophical premises behind this point of view, called radical constructivism, are beyond the scope of this chapter. The interested reader is referred to Watzlawick (1984), in particular the first two chapters, "An Introduction to Radical Constructivism" by E. von Glassersfeld and "On Constructing a Reality" by H. von Foerster.

Alcohol Use and Misuse:

4

A SYSTEMIC CONCEPTUALIZATION FOR PRACTITIONERS

THOMAS EDWARD SMITH

Alcohol use and abuse has stirred public interest for decades. Few social issues have commanded more attention. The rhetoric's fury has led to developments such as changes in state statutes regarding the legal age of use, increasingly severe penalties for driving while intoxicated, and attempts to limit the distribution of alcohol. There have also been strident public education campaigns as well as efforts to severely curtail advertisements of alcoholic beverages.

This chapter is designed to be a primer on the characteristics of alcoholism. It is neither comprehensive in its discussion nor its coverage of relevant issues. Rather, it attempts to present a brief, analytic synthesis of some of the major scholarly writings on the topic as they relate to marital and family functioning.

Alcohol is a drug whose use is variously legally permitted for most individuals past 18 to 21 years of age. Its use is largely unregulated although there is a certain amount of statutory control over consumption in public places. Unrestrained use is also forbidden before or when driving motor vehicles. For most people how much, when, with whom, where, and why they consume alcohol depends on personal norms and beliefs. Reliance on personal control of alcohol use makes this drug different from others such as marijuana and cocaine, which are clearly proscribed by lawmakers, and amphetamines and barbiturates, which can be prescribed only by physicians. Alcohol belongs to a class of drugs that includes tobacco products and caffeinated beverages: legal, relatively uncontrolled, and with varying levels of toxicity. Alcohol was chosen as the subject of this chapter because of its widespread use; its massive impact on individuals, couples, and families; and the increasing public interest in moderating its costs to the public.

The resource materials on alcoholism are bewildering in their number, complexity, and level of sophistication. This chapter limits itself to three aspects of alcohol use: medical and physiological, marital, and familial.

DEFINITIONS OF ALCOHOL MISUSE

Definitions of alcohol misuse are highly variable and controversial. Practitioners and theorists make numerous assertions about how to recognize alcohol dependency, assertions that differ in philosophical assumptions about the problem, theories of causation, stringency of diagnostic criteria, treatment prescriptions, and policy recommendations resulting from the definitions (Fonaroff et al., 1980). Reviewing past efforts to derive a definition of alcohol dependency may provide clues as to why there is so much confusion on this topic.

In an influential article that has shaped much current thought, Jellinek (1952) proposed that there are different patterns of alcohol use and misuse. He was careful to note that alcohol use and abuse are two different things and that it is essential to recognize the differences. Pattison and Kaufman (1982) note that Jellinek's taxonomy of alcohol use and abuse has been largely abandoned because of its imprecision and that more reliable and empirically derived definitions are needed.

Numerous studies have failed to isolate a single, unidimensional concept that could reliably differentiate "alcoholics" from nonalcoholics. Personality tests have attempted to test out traits that could be used to establish predictive profiles of those who would misuse alcohol. Neuringer (1982) reviewed efforts to establish psychometrically sound measures of alcohol addiction and concluded that past studies have not isolated any single personality variable or single personality constellation that reliably predicts alcohol misuse. He observed that "Alcohol is a topic that lends itself to emotional overreaction" (p. 518) and that researchers' contributions to the literature are polemic in nature.

The failure to locate a "disease entity" and a common pathway by which individuals contract and experience alcohol disorders has led theorists to adopt a "multivariate–multimodal model." A major proponent of this model has outlined 11 propositions that describe this approach (Pattison, 1982).

Pattison proposes that alcohol dependence includes a number of "alcoholisms," each with different drinking patterns and adverse consequences, as follows:

1. Alcohol use falls on a continuum from nonuse to use to varying degrees of abuse and dependency.
2. Different alcohol misuse patterns have different courses.

3. Abstinence and rehabilitation are independent of each other.
4. Psychological and physical dependency on alcohol are independent variables.
5. Continued use of large quantities over extended time periods will result in physical dependency on alcohol.
6. People who abuse or depend on alcohol do not share any single characteristic or cluster of personality traits.
7. Life problems are interrelated with alcohol abuse, especially if physical dependency is present.
8. Treatment should include a differential diagnosis that takes into consideration individual and environmental characteristics of the alcohol misuser.

If these propositions are empirically validated, and there is increasing research to support them, they challenge common assertions that there is a single process by which individuals become addicted to alcohol, that alcohol misuse is confined to any one subpopulation, that there is any inevitable outcome for alcohol misusers, and that any one treatment is effective for all alcohol-dependent individuals. Thus, it is reasonable to question to what extent assertions about "alcoholism" and "alcoholics" are overgeneralizations. Sweeping claims about the superiority of any single treatment appear at best to be premature and at worst exploitative of alcohol abusers and their families.

Available research on alcohol misuse to the contrary, predominant theories rest on the assumption that it is an illness (Dreger, 1986; Peele, 1984). Many clinicians believe that alcohol misuse is a disease. Campbell and colleagues (1979) found that 85% of general medical practitioners considered alcohol to be a disease but that only 50% of medical school professors concurred. A recent study by Zygarlicki and Smith (1986) found that 60% of marriage and family therapists believed that alcoholism was a disease; this same sample reported that previously in their professional careers only 49.7% had espoused this belief. What seems apparent from reviewing the literature on alcohol misuse as a disease is that clinicians and academicians (especially researchers) will continue to disagree on the matter. There are many reasons for this disagreement, and a complete discussion of it is beyond the scope of this chapter. Listed below is an example of the arguments that have been proposed and rebutted by practitioners and scholars.

Vaillant (1983) reviews both sides of the controversy on alcohol misuse as a "disease." Condensed below are both sides of arguments that have been advanced for and against accepting alcohol misuse as a disease.

First, a commonly believed aspect of alcohol misuse as a disease is that an alcohol-dependent person does not have control over its use. Yet misuse requires that an individual drink enough quantities to experience the ill effects. For use to approach misuse, an individual must purchase liquor, prepare it for consumption, consume it, and repeat this pattern many times. In short, it can be argued that alcohol misuse apparently *is* under an individual's control. Further, Pattison and colleagues (1977) noted that many studies reveal that a significant proportion of alcohol-dependent patients are able to regain control of their alcohol use.

In providing a persuasive counterargument to the concept that alcoholism is a disease, Vaillant argues that the term "disease," traditionally applied, may be misleading. He argues that alcoholism and hypertension are comparable as "diseases." Both are caused by some somatic pathology; both defy precise assessment; and both have significant physiological and psychological determinants. In addition, the reluctance to label both disorders as diseases is largely determined by the fact that these disorders fluctuate in intensity and therefore vary from time to time and will result in differing diagnoses when the physician examines the patient.

Second, the traditional disease model predicts that individuals either have or do not have a disorder. This prediction is not borne out with respect to alcoholics because it is difficult to discriminate between alcohol users, occasional abusers, and frequent severe abusers. If the disease model were to hold true, observers should be able to readily separate use from abuse. To rebut the foregoing argument, Vaillant again uses the example of hypertension. The diagnosis of hypertension also defies a dichotomous decision. Because social, cultural, and interpersonal factors are critical in a diagnosis of hypertension, he asserts that it is a mistake to assume that the disease model implies dichotomous decision making. The same is true with respect to alcohol.

Third, the disease model does a disservice by ruling out problems in the larger environment that may stimulate alcohol misuse. For example, surveys by Jacobson (1976) and Smith and Bauer (1986) of public assistance populations show disproportionate numbers of alcohol-dependent clients receiving aid. Depending on one's political views, this situation may be construed as being primarily a result of poverty and unemployment or that alcohol dependency leads to poverty. Thus, it can be argued that defining alcohol dependency as a disease focuses on only one aspect of the context that may give rise to problems. Vaillant once again uses the example of hypertension in dismissing the idea that alcoholism is not a disease; if hypertension can be considered a disease, then alcohol misuse can also fit the label in that both are affected by environmental factors.

Fourth, a function of the disease model is to provide a diagnosis of "alcoholism" to someone who is dependent on alcohol. This labeling process may be iatrogenic—a process that in itself causes more problems than it solves. Essentially, Vaillant counters this fourth argument against the disease model by stating that public knowledge and admission of alcohol misuse is necessary for clients to accept their "disease" and to seek medical treatment. He asserts that acceptance of the label frees clients from a belief that they have a characterological deficit and teaches them that the drinking behavior is beyond their control. Vaillant continues that this labeling process in turn provides clients incentive to receive treatment; the label provides a rationale for accepting help, much of which can be obtained through health insurance. Vaillant suggests that the diagnostician should in fact make the diagnosis and work toward changing society's views of the disorder.

Finally, Vaillant argues that alcohol misuse is a behavior disorder but that alcohol-misuse-related somatic complications require that medical attention be given and that third party payment will not be readily forthcoming for behavior disorders, a critically important point. Thus, Vaillant defends the practice of labeling alcohol misuses as a disease for pragmatic reasons—insurance companies and other organizations are likely to assist individuals with diseases but not those with behavior problems. Another pragmatic aspect of the disease or behavioral-disorder definitions involves the question of what kind of professional can be considered qualified to treat alcoholics and receive third party payments. If the disease definition is accepted, only physicians would be considered qualified. If a behavior-disorder definition is used, other human service professionals might be considered qualified. Thus, pragmatics for the various treatment professions are heavily involved in the not-completely-scholarly arguments regarding definitions of alcoholism.

Though persuasive, Vaillant's presentation is not conceptually compelling. His rebuttals rely on comparing alcohol with other disorders that do not meet the formal criteria of "diseases." Second, he concurs that alcohol misuse is more akin to a behavior disorder but that it has medical complications and that it is pragmatic to understand alcohol misuse as a disease. His solution is specious—to accept alcoholism as a disease, one need only broaden the definition of what constitutes a disease.

Nonetheless, Vaillant represents a moderate position among those who argue that alcohol misuse is a disease. Popular literature on alcohol misuse states without equivocation that it is a terminal medical illness. For example, Dr. Vernon Johnson, in the widely used book *I'll Quit Tomorrow* (1980, p. 1), states, "Alcohol is a fatal disease, 100 percent fatal," and "The most significant characteristics of the disease are that it is primary, progressive, chronic, and fatal." Thus, among proponents of the disease model are writers like Vaillant who defend the use of the disease model for pragmatic reasons; others like Johnson have taken a far more extreme position.

However, to fully accept the concept that alcohol misuse is a disease may do a disservice to the public, to other professionals, and to clients themselves. Individuals who are reluctant to believe in a disease-model interpretation of their condition may be refused adequate treatment on the basis that they are dissembling (i.e., "denial"). In sum, though a disease-model treatment is used widely, it is neither the only one nor in many cases the best one available (Zweben, 1986). For a more complete review on alcohol misuse as a disease, readers are referred to Hill (1985).

To maintain the pragmatic benefits of classification as a disease (such as insurance), one partial solution is to classify alcohol misuse as a mental disorder and comment on its etiology, physiological bases, and interactional implications. Perhaps it is for this reason that the most widely used diagnostic manual, the third edition of the *Diagnostic and Statistical Manual of Mental Disorders* (DSM III) has three categories of alcohol misuse: alcohol intoxication, alcohol abuse, and alcohol dependence (American Psychiatric Association, 1980).

The first category intoxication primarily refers to the reversible somatic effects of alcohol. The second category includes "pathological use patterns" (i.e., disruption of work habits, legal difficulties, interpersonal conflicts, and violent behavior attributable to alcohol use) as criteria to use in deciding whether abuse is present. The third category alcohol dependence is identical except that either overtolerance of large amounts of alcohol or withdrawal symptoms must be present.

Other popular definitions of alcohol misuse include many of the same distinctions as those of DSM III. The prototype of recent definitions of alcohol misuse derive from the diagnostic schema proposed by the National Council on Alcoholism (NCA) in 1972. This schema included a listing of sociobehavioral (i.e., nonmedical) consequences of alcohol misuse as well as medical complications of alcohol misuse. In reviewing this model, Pattison and Kaufman (1982) noted many of its deficiencies. The 86-item measurement instrument proposed by the NCA is still undergoing modifications to give it better psychometric properties. Until these changes are widely developed and used, definitions based on the NCA scale will remain problematic in their sensitivity and specificity and their inability to distinguish between prodromal-stage (i.e., early) drinkers and late-stage, alcohol-dependent individuals (Pattison & Kaufman, 1982).

The NCA schema also has a major premise that may seriously limit its usefulness—it forces diagnosticians to state that an individual is either "alcoholic" or "not alcoholic." This forced choice may lead to large errors in specificity, so that individuals who have occasional problems in drinking may be labeled as alcohol-dependent. In this regard DSM III, with its diagnosis of alcohol intoxication or alcohol abuse, may provide diagnosticians with more flexibility and precision in examining clients who misuse alcohol. Further, the decision on whether to label alcohol misuse as a disease becomes unnecessary so long as the DSM III diagnosis is used. Whether it is useful to convince clients that alcohol is a disease becomes a therapeutic issue with each client: This metaphor may prove useful for some clients and less so with others.

EPIDEMIOLOGY

Partly because of definition problems and partly because of social sanctions against alcoholics, it is difficult to arrive at an accurate statement concerning the rate of alcoholism in the population. A national sample survey in 1982 revealed that 11% of older adults and 7% of younger ones reported daily use of alcohol, but this clearly does not indicate alcoholism rates because many people use alcohol daily without overusing it or becoming addicted. In the same survey about 8% of adult male respondents and 4% of females said they had been at least partly dependent on alcohol in the preceding year—again not synonomous with being an alcoholic but perhaps coming close to that condition (Anderson, 1987).

As far as can be determined, Jews have low to moderate rates of alcohol dependence, whereas rates are considerably higher among Roman Catholics, Protestants, and the unaffiliated. Adolescents rarely show symptoms of physical dependence on alcohol, although 70% of the sample surveyed in 1982 reported that they drink at least occasionally. Factors most closely associated with drinking by adolescents include: peer and parental drinking and approval, a predisposition to nonconformity and independence, poor academic performance, and minor delinquent acts (Polich et al., 1984).

Alcoholism rates appear to be higher among widowers, single adults, and perhaps the elderly. Whites and blacks seem to have about equal rates, but alcoholism is found to be especially high among American Indians and to a somewhat lesser degree among Hispanics. Few Asian-Americans appear to be heavy users of alcohol or to be alcohol-dependent (Anderson, 1987).

THE CAUSES OF ALCOHOLISM

Single-factor theories regarding the causes of alcoholism are apt to be fallacies. There is considerable research support for the concept that genetic and biophysiological variables account for much of this condition (Goodwin, 1976; Murray & Stabenau, 1982) but not for all of it. The proposal that there is a typical alcoholic personality has been disproven by research, which fails to show that alcoholics have personality traits that are distinctive from those of other people. The same might be said of psychodynamic theories that hold that alcoholics have typical and different developmental life experiences. Then, too, sociocultural contexts have been shown to play a part in a person's drinking values and attitudes, but obviously not everyone in a particular cultural group behaves in the same way in his or her use of alcohol.

All in all, it appears most likely that a combination of biological, social, psychological, and situational factors interact in complex and variable ways to affect an individual's drinking behavior and whether this behavior will lead toward alcohol dependence and alcoholism itself (Anderson, 1987; White, 1982).

MEDICAL AND PHYSIOLOGICAL CONSEQUENCES

Any discussion of the consequences of alcohol use and misuse are laden with inherent difficulties. At one extreme, one person can argue that any use of alcohol is potentially problematic; on the other hand, it can also be argued that only unwise use has untoward effects. To better understand the physiological impact of alcohol, some attention to its biochemical effects on the body is necessary.

Alcohol's principle ingredient is ethanol; it is present in all alcoholic beverages in different concentrations. Ethanol is a central nervous system depressant whose effects resemble those of general anesthetics. When individuals say that they are using alcohol to "deaden pain" or to "anesthetize their feelings away," their statements have physiological and emotional accuracy.

Such potency, however, makes extensive use of alcohol especially hazardous; Tewari and Carson (1982) discuss physiological consequences of ethanol consumption. First, they discuss the metabolism and metabolites of ethanol. The consequences of how ethanol is metabolized can be seen dramatically in its effects on the liver. Though ethanol directly and indirectly affects all bodily organs, the liver is probably most commonly identified. Segal and Sisson (1985) discuss several complications of alcoholic liver disease. It occurs because a significant presence of ethanol disturbs the liver's regular metabolic processes. Segal and Sisson write, "Metabolizing alcohol is always a priority liver function. Hence when alcohol is present, the liver is distracted from other normal and necessary functions." This is in part due to ethanol's toxicity; in short, the liver's capabilities in breaking down wastes or detoxifying substances are called into action when ethanol is introduced into the body. Further, ethanol's potent toxicity is the primary reason that the liver reacts so strongly. In increasing order of severity, the liver diseases most commonly associated with alcohol misuse are fatty liver, alcoholic hepatitis, and alcoholic cirrhosis.

An enlarged liver with abdominal tenderness or pain is characteristic of alcoholic-related liver diseases. Weight loss, loss of appetite, nausea, and fatigue are other common symptoms of alcoholic hepatitis and alcoholic cirrhosis. With alcoholic cirrhosis or end-stage liver disease, widespread destruction of liver cells has resulted in subsequent replacement by a fibrous scar tissue. Although its hampered effectiveness may not be immediately noticeable, the consequence of this damage is a greatly reduced functional capacity of the liver. "Portal hypertension" may result from the impeded blood flow through the liver and result in serious physical conditions. Segal and Sisson (1985) provide a useful discussion for nonmedical practitioners regarding these and other alcohol-related complications (e.g., susceptibility to infections and malnutrition) that arise from impaired liver functioning.

Alcohol use and misuse also have significant short-term and long-term effects on the brain. Because of ethanol's toxicity, brain cell loss is almost certain; whether the cell loss is irreversible is another question. With Wernicke's syndrome the nerve damage is hypothesized to result from thiamine (vitamin B[1]) deficiency. Failure to receive treatment for this condition may result in Korsakoff's syndrome, characterized by widespread brain cell loss. Wernicke's syndrome is characterized by nystagmus (i.e., jerky, unstable eye movements), appearance of being cross-eyed, and ataxia (i.e., uncoordinated gait). In contrast, Korsakoff's syndrome is identified by significant memory loss, generalized disorientation, and overall cognitive deterioration. The significant memory loss often results in individuals dissembling events to conceal their dysfunction—this behavior can confuse friends and relatives who are puzzled by the apparent lack of candor.

A second type of brain damage is chronic brain syndrome (CBS). This dysfunction has been difficult to detect in the past using traditional assessment techniques. Because CBS is a form of nonspecific brain damage, early diagnosis is difficult. Segal and Sisson (1985) state that EEGs, intelligence tests, and other tests of brain dysfunction do not readily reveal the existence of CBS. Neuropsychological tests suggest that CBS involves widespread brain cell loss, and computerized axial tomography (CAT) scans show that the brain size has decreased by nearly 50% in long-term alcoholics.

Segal and Sisson do state, however, that this diminished brain volume is reversible. Further, Tarter and Edwards (1986) note that fully 25% of chronic alcoholics fail to display cognitive deficits. They caution that neuropsychological deficits have a multifactorial etiology, and it is premature to assume that all alcoholics share the same cognitive deficits.

Other forms of brain damage experienced by alcohol misusers include subdural hematomas and peripheral neuropathy. The first refers to a hemorrhage within the brain; its symptoms may, however, be hidden by alcohol intoxication or withdrawal problems. The symptoms include confusion, dizziness, headaches, and a unilateral dilated pupil. This form of brain damage most often occurs as a result of a fall or some other blow to the head. The other form of injury, peripheral neuropathy, refers to damage to nerve tissue other than those in the brain, and it usually results from nutritional deficits.

Clients report numbness, tingling, or burning sensations in extremities (e.g., hands and feet). As with most nutritional deficits, an enhanced diet can remedy many of the symptoms.

Other types of alcohol-related medical complications are easy to find. Various kinds of heart diseases have been noted in individuals with a high intake of alcohol, such as diseases of the heart muscle, hypertension, coronary artery disease (Segal & Sisson, 1985). Other medical complications include the heightened incidence of cancers of the head and neck (Lowenfels, 1979), pancreatitis and diabetes (Korsten & Lieber, 1985), and cancer of the esophagus and other abnormalities in the gastrointestinal tract (Mezey, 1982).

The medical complications are important indicators of alcohol use and misuse. However, the most commonly used physiological indicators of alcohol misuse are alcohol tolerance and withdrawal symptoms (American Psychiatric Association, 1980; National Council on Alcoholism, 1972). Tolerance and withdrawal symptoms represent the central nervous system's (CNS) accommodation to the continued introduction of a depressant—alcohol. When an individual withdraws from alcohol use, the CNS must readjust to its absence. Thus, withdrawal represents the period of time after alcohol is no longer consumed but before the body has become accustomed to its absence.

Withdrawal can represent a serious medical crisis. Although the reaction of individuals differs with their age, metabolic rates, size, and amount of alcohol normally consumed, the symptoms of withdrawal range from sweating, insomnia, and anxiety to seizures and delirium tremens. The term "detoxification" is frequently used to describe an inpatient hospitalization for an individual who is beginning to withdraw from active alcohol use. The inpatient setting may be required to monitor the individual's withdrawal symptoms.

Tolerance is also an example of CNS adaptation to the presence of alcohol. It refers to the use of ever-increasing quantities to achieve the same pharmacological results. Gitlow (1982) states that tolerance can be conceptualized as resulting from CNS adaptation and from changes in metabolism. As discussed above, after the CNS has adapted to the presence of alcohol, its absence results in an agitated state; an individual must drink more alcohol to feel relaxed. After the CNS becomes accustomed to the presence of a certain level of alcohol, ever-increasing amounts are necessary to achieve the same pharmacological effects. Cross-tolerance to sedatives (e.g., benzodiazepines, meprobamate, and barbiturates) is also seen in individuals who demonstrate alcohol tolerance. Sedatives can have the same physical effect that alcohol has on alcohol-tolerant people. Once they develop tolerance to alcohol, people feel relaxed after they drink alcohol or take sedatives. Similarly, tolerance to sedatives can also occur to clients who are alcohol-tolerant.

As the preceding discussion has suggested, there are many direct and indirect medical complications arising from alcohol misuse. These medical complications are understandably more visible and severe after many years of alcohol use. Because these medical complications are serious and in most cases attributable to alcohol use, it is easy to diagnose such clients as "alcoholics." Conceptual problems arise, however, when such medical complications are not present, for the absence of such complications does not rule out alcohol misuse. An individual can easily experience significant social problems in drinking without sustaining medical complications. Further, the puzzle of alcohol misuse lies not with the amount of drinking or the pharmacological dependency but with alcohol misusers' pattern of relapsing despite the consequences of such behavior. The importance of nonmedical complications is dramatically illustrated in definitions of alcohol misuse that rely heavily on the existence of alcohol-related interpersonal, social, legal, and employment difficulties. One such nonmedical complication concerns disturbed marital relationships when one individual misuses alcohol.

CONSEQUENCES FOR THE MARITAL RELATIONSHIP

Commentary on the consequences of alcohol misuse on interpersonal relationships has come from many writers (Bateson, 1971; Bowen, 1974; Davis et al., 1974; Elkin, 1984; Stanton, 1975; Zweben, 1986). How alcohol misuse affects interpersonal relationships has been examined in numerous studies using diverse methodologies. Unfortunately, much of what has been written in this area must be viewed cautiously because it is not based on adequate research studies. Rigorous studies with adequate study samples, control groups, well-established instruments of measurement, and careful statistical analyses are the exception rather than the rule. Typically, clinical studies with small sample sizes are the norm. To examine all or even a significant number of the publications would quickly numb the mind; thus, this section seeks to integrate and help organize some of the different writers' conclusions on the topic. Readers are warned that the conclusions in this section represent clues for further inquiry rather than solid generalizations.

In a summary of the available, often weak, research, Jacob and colleagues (1978) observed that many difficulties experienced by spouses of alcoholics are also experienced by other clinical populations. They caution, however, that very few studies could be construed as rigorous research. Studies that did, in fact, attempt to collect data did so from small samples with numbers of less than 30. In another review of the literature, this observation was also made by McCrady (1982, p. 602);

> It may be that the concept of the so-called alcoholic marriage has outlived its usefulness. To date, the data do not find patterns of interaction that characterize all or even the largest majority of subjects in studies. Findings are hard to replicate and vary greatly with sample characteristics.

In a rigorous study Jacob and colleagues (1983) found that marital satisfaction was positively correlated with alcohol consumption among "steady" drinkers. In contrast Zweben (1986) found that marital satisfaction was inversely correlated with the number of "sociobehavioral consequences" of drinking. In his study "sociobehavioral consequences" referred to alcohol-related difficulties experienced by the nonusing spouse. His study was notable because it was well-controlled, had a relatively large sample ($n > 100$), and used well-established measures. Zweben posited that differences among alcoholic and nonalcoholic couples were reduced when alcohol-related difficulties were introduced as control variables. In short, marriages involving an alcoholic spouse may experience stress because of associated factors such as poor sleeping habits, refusal to participate in family activities, inadequate hygiene, and erratic behavior (i.e., jealousy and aggression).

Zweben (1986) suggests that individuals who steadily consume alcohol, while their spouses do not, may not experience severe marital disruptions if the drinking spouse does not engage in negative social behaviors. On the other hand, individuals who sporadically consume alcohol but who misbehave at these times are likely to report marital difficulties associated with alcohol use. In short, the alcohol use itself, even its abuse, will not present sufficient reason for people to seek treatment. The critical element is the effect of alcohol on the individual's social behavior.

This research predicts when marital problems might occur if one spouse or another is actively using alcohol. It is not altogether clear why couples often continue to experience problems once both parties are no longer using alcohol. Several hypotheses are possible. One, the couple might still be experiencing the aftermath of a long period of abusive use of alcohol. Legal, employment, and health problems related to a person's alcohol use may exist even after both spouses are sober. Zweben's "sociobehavioral consequences" may haunt the couple after sobriety and thus create tension.

A second and more elusive reason that couples may continue to experience problems is suggested by a number of writers. Nurse (1982, p. 23) summarized past research by stating that:

> Findings suggest that while alcoholic couples have much in common with the interaction problems of other couples, it is alcohol abuse that helps the couple relationship survive by maintaining two sets of behaviors: one sober and one inebriated.

Elkin (1984) asserts that alcohol use enables individuals to relax "boundaries" and to assume "power." He defines boundaries around an individual as personal space and power as the ability to "dictate the context in which behavior occurs" (p. 21). He goes on to reason that intoxication allows individuals to reduce acceptable limits of personal space as well as ignoring others' demands for its maintenance. Ironically, this pattern of behaviors also allows individuals to temporarily increase their sociability.

Thus, alcohol consumption allows a temporary breaching of boundaries that promotes perceived sociability among users. Elkin goes on to explain that social gaffes committed when inebriated are quickly forgiven or forgotten when apologies are given by the user. In intimate relationships, however, the repeated cycles of sobriety and inebriation, each with their distinctive behavioral sequences, render such apologies ineffective. In time the use of alcohol mediates the marital relationship, or as Nurse (1982, p. 23) states, the " . . . couple 'triangulates alcohol'."

Johnson (1980) defines alcohol as a potent drug that allows individuals to consciously alter their mood (i.e., "self-medicate"). He further explains that problems arise when enough alcohol is consumed such that its pharmacological effects as a CNS depressant become dominant. In short, disinhibition gives way to depression, self-doubt, and anger. He presents alcohol use as a normative activity that exacts an increasingly high price, depending on the purpose of use and misuse. When used consciously and chronically to alter moods, Johnson argues that this is when alcohol use as a "temporary" solution has become a problem.

Johnson's concern about how alcohol misusers define their use has also interested other writers. Christiansen and colleagues (1982) found from their research that adolescents have deeply ingrained, preexisting expectancies concerning alcohol use before their first drink. The researchers observed that adolescents perceived pharmacological effects as confirming their expectancies. The implications are, of course, that misusers may not need to experience alcohol's potent pharmacological effects to exhibit behaviors that are societal indicators of use and misuse. (See, for example, Hull & Bond, 1986). The discussion of Christiansen and his associates appears relevant to what Spradley (1980, p. 37) called the "contextualization of substance use." An anthropologist, Spradley examined substance use in terms of its symbolic meaning and concluded, "Use is related to cultural recipes, group membership, learning processes, eligibility requirements, social sanctions, and the very expedience that results from the dynamic pattern of use."

The context of an "alcoholic couple" may determine the character and duration of a spouse's alcohol misuse. Though there is no consensus on how chronic alcohol misuse is viewed by the nonusing spouse, it is clear that over time the behavior assumes heightened importance. Thus, although the "sociobehavioral consequences" may predict the functionality of the marital unit, the alcohol misuse becomes the symbol of dissatisfaction. The couple may ritually battle over who will prevail. The nonusing spouse will seek to control the amount of alcohol consumed, and these attempts to limit use or even comment on use patterns create marital tension (Bateson, 1971; Wiseman, 1980). If Spradley's analysis is correct, how this battle is conducted will be determined by the couple's informal norms. This suggests that single-factor attempts to characterize "alcoholic marriages" are futile and that researching the couple without including their cultural context will be at best misleading. One consequence of this "contextualization" is that most psychological research on "alcoholics" should be integrated with research from sociology, anthropology, social work, and other social sciences. A logical focus of attention would be to determine the immediate context of marriage and the family.

CONSEQUENCES FOR FAMILY RELATIONSHIPS

Davis and a team of researchers (Davis et al., 1974) propose an intriguing hypothesis: Drinking behavior is maintained by operant consequences within a family. The notion that behavior is maintained by its operant consequences is hardly novel; however, Davis and his colleagues suggest that alcohol misuse has "adaptive" consequences. Alcohol misuse by one family member in some sense is assisted by and in turn provides assistance for other family members. To discern the motivation of individual family members, however, would be difficult. Heath (1975) observed that alcohol use has no universal meaning or function for any one person at any one time. However, it is possible that each family has its own understanding of the "function" of alcohol use and misuse. Although cultural patterns may give a general sense of the why and how people use and misuse alcohol, each family is left to derive its own explanation of its experiences.

Davis and his colleagues suggest that a person would not continue to drink (and experience sociobehavioral consequences) without reason. One possible explanation is advanced by Hull and Bond (1986) who reviewed studies on alcohol consumption and expectancy and differentiated the expectancy of the effects of alcohol and the actual pharmacological effects. They concluded that the users were able to engage in novel social behaviors and attribute them to the effects of alcohol. Whatever a person's idiosyncratic reason, the result is that alcohol misuse may become a stable characteristic of the family and that the misuse may result in secondary gains or rewards for each family member.

Hill and Bond (1986) theorize that the precise pattern of adaptive capacities relies on each family's shared understanding of its interpersonal and social world views. Reiss and Oliveri (1980) have linked families' internal adaptive capabilities to their idiosyncratic response to stress. They suggest that how family members respond to the stress engendered by an alcoholic parent may not overtake their coping abilities; indeed, the alcoholic parent's use and misuse may be well incorporated in the family's "normal" life-style. Reiss and Oliveri urge caution in prematurely rejecting the conceptual utility of each family's individual responses to alcohol misuse. On the other hand, one could urge caution against a ready acceptance of this theory as to how it might apply to *all* families.

In a popular book, Wegscheider (1981) asserts that the alcoholic behavior of one parent resulted in children assuming "survival" roles for which they receive secondary gains. The typology derived from her clinical work but not from formal research includes the "enabler," "family hero," "scapegoat," "lost child," and "mascot." She proposes that each role is a response to the stress created by the behaviors of the alcohol misuser. It seems reasonable, however, to also propose that the children's behaviors as typified in these roles influence parents to maintain their folie à deux. In short, it is theorized that members of an alcoholic family system assume their roles as part of a reciprocal, coercive process: Supposedly, each person shapes the other persons to respond in kind (Patterson, 1982).

What is not immediately clear is why the family would not simply disown the alcoholic misuser after a long series of disappointments. The behavior of an alcoholic misuser's spouse may reflect the coercive, interactive sequences that may bind a couple together in an implicit marital quid pro quo (Lederer & Jackson, 1968). The children, of course, have fewer options; they do not enter contracts in the same manner that their parents do. Patterson (1982) found in his extensive clinical analyses of children in these families that parents and children shaped each other to behave in specific patterns. Thus, it is reasonable to assume that Wegscheider's roles may well result from this coercive process. A caveat, of course, is that these roles may not occur in all families, may not be stable across the life cycle, and may take varying forms in different subcultures or that the roles may be perceived differently by different family members (Heath, 1975).

All in all, the Wegscheider (1981) typologies are attractive in their pat and dramatic proposals but must be viewed warily because they represent clinically derived opinions and have not been adequately supported by research. An easy adoption of these concepts by practitioners can have damaging effects on alcoholics and their families in that strongly held assumptions of these kinds can become self-fulling prophecies, thereby adversely affecting family behaviors.

Bowen (1974) takes a different approach, suggesting that alcohol is used by individuals to regulate their emotional closeness to their parents. This concept, derived from his clinical work, agrees with the observations made by other observers who note that people under the influence of alcohol can dramatically change their social behavior (Hull & Bond, 1986). How Bowen's ideas coincide with

Wegscheider's family roles concept is not clear. However, both agree (perhaps erroneously) that the children of alcoholic parent(s) experience emotional difficulties when they become autonomous.

Many books and articles describe the behavior patterns and beliefs of the adult children of alcoholics (e.g., Kellogg & Hunter, 1986; Woititz, 1985). However, research findings are at best equivocal about the existence of specific behavior patterns and attitudes among these children (e.g., Jacob et al., 1978). Jacob and Leonard (1986) compared the psychosocial functioning of the children of alcoholic fathers, depressed fathers, and control-group fathers and did not find significant differences. It seems more likely that children adopt individual coping strategies that are congruent with their familial and cultural milieu. Because clinicians are most familiar with the most severe alcoholic populations and because these populations are exactly those that are most memorable, the conclusion that adult children of alcoholics all experience a specific pattern of problems is understandable but clearly inaccurate. Such an approach is unfortunate and may do a disservice to those children who are not impaired as a result of their parents' alcohol misuse (Werner, 1986).

A prudent conclusion to be made is that children of alcoholic parents are more at risk than children who did not experience the problems frequently associated with alcoholism in the family: chaotic homelifes, financial difficulties, legal encounters, and so on. The question that can reasonably be asked is whether it is the alcohol misuse or whether it is the sociobehavioral consequences that is the key to difficulties that the child may encounter. Neither alternative convincingly answers the question. Further studies that include a focus on family members' interactive patterns are needed to understand more clearly the contribution of alcohol misuse to family disruptions.

CONCLUSIONS

This chapter has touched on some of the complex debates on the topic of alcohol use and misuse. The debates mirror the confusion and controversy that surround professionals and lay persons' concern over how best to approach the topic. The frustration experienced by clinicians in treating alcohol misuse has led to the frequent introduction of panaceas at workshops, conferences, and case conferences and in the classroom. This outpouring of interest has not, however, led to any coherent decisions on what constitutes alcohol misuse, what causes it, and how best to remedy it.

Perhaps the most notable conclusion that can be drawn is that practitioners and policy makers should be cautious in accepting any group's prescriptions on the nature of alcohol misuse. Practitioners are confronted by the need to verse themselves in how to best assist individuals and families in resolving difficulties posed by alcohol misuse. Whether this means becoming knowledgeable about Alcoholics Anonymous or reframing clients' difficulties in a way that is acceptable to third-party payors, responsible treatment may require that alcoholism treatment personnel become heavily versed in case management and less in direct-treatment paradigms.

Given the relatively high incidence of alcohol use and misuse, the challenge for treatment personnel interested in the welfare of children and families is to mobilize all the resources within systems— individual, marital, familial, organizational, and community—to help family members better manage the situation. Given the confusion and misinformation in the popular and professional literature on alcohol use, proceeding cautiously and devaluing false promises becomes essential. At the same time, more experimentation and research is needed to further explore ways that may be more effective in both preventive and treatment approaches to reducing the severe effects of alcohol abuse on individuals, their families, and the larger systems with which they interact.

Treating Families with a Chemically Dependent Member

5

THOMAS C. TODD

The purpose of this chapter is to provide human service professionals with general guidelines for conducting treatment with families of substance abusers from a structural–strategic orientation. In this introductory section a brief review of the structural–strategic model is presented, followed by specific modifications for the treatment of substance abuse. It is recognized that there are a number of other treatment modalities employed with substance abuse, but the family-systems approach is the sole focus of this chapter.

OUTLINE OF STRUCTURAL-STRATEGIC FAMILY THERAPY

The following review of structural–strategic family therapy is adapted from Stanton, Todd, & Associates (1982). While the structural and strategic approaches differ to some extent, they share important commonalities. As a rule both schools subscribe to the following view of the family or couple:

1. People are seen as interacting within an interpersonal context—both affecting it and being affected by it.
2. The family life cycle and developmental stage are important both in diagnosis and in defining therapy strategy—a problematic family is seen as being stuck at a particular stage in its development.
3. Symptoms are maintained both by the family system and tend to maintain the operation of that system.
4. The family or couple can change, allowing new behaviors to emerge, if the larger context is changed. Further, for individual change to occur, the interpersonal system itself must change. This would permit new aspects of individual family members' styles of interaction to emerge.

Both schools also agree regarding therapy and therapist in the following ways:

1. Treatment is viewed pragmatically, with an eye toward what "works."
2. Emphasis is on the present rather than the past.

3. Problematic repetitive behavioral sequences are to be changed.
4. While structural therapists may not be as symptom oriented as strategic therapists, both are much more symptom oriented than psychodynamic therapists.
5. Process is emphasized much more than content. This includes interventions that are nonverbal and noncognitive—in a sense, "doing away with words." Such interventions are derived from viewing the system from a "meta" level and recognizing that verbalizations per se by therapist or family are often not necessary for change and that new patterns of interaction may be initiated and maintained without "insight."
6. The therapist should direct the therapy and take responsibility for change.
7. Diagnosis is obtained through hypothesizing, intervening, and examining feedback from the family system.
8. Therapeutic contracts, which relate to the problem and the goals of change, are negotiated with clients.
9. Interpretation is usually employed to "relabel" or "reframe" rather than to produce "insight."
10. Behavioral tasks (homework) are routinely assigned.
11. Considerable effort may go into "joining" the family positively and reducing apparent "guilt" or defensiveness of family members. This is more than simply "establishing rapport"; rather, it is done selectively with particular family members and in line with specific therapeutic goals.
12. Therapy cannot usually progress from the initial dysfunctional stage to a "cure" stage without one or more intermediate stages, which, on the surface, may appear dysfunctional also. For instance, a therapist may have to take sides with a spouse, thereby "unbalancing" the couple in a way opposite to the balance existing before the couple entered treatment in order to restabilize the couple's relationship at a level of enhanced equality between the partners.
13. Therapy tends to be brief and typically does not exceed 6 months.

Structural therapy (see Minuchin, 1974; Minuchin & Fishman, 1981) tends to place more emphasis on change within the session and on straightforward requests for change made by the therapist. The therapist focuses on "restructuring" the family by changing the patterns of communication, establishing or loosening boundaries, differentiating enmeshed members, and increasing the involvement of disengaged members.

Techniques that are characteristic of the structural approach include unbalancing the system, intensifying patterns of interaction, and enacting important interactional sequences. (See Glossary for the definitions of all techniques mentioned in this chapter.) While tasks and directives are used in both structural and strategic therapy, in structural therapy they are usually assigned to consolidate changes made during the session (rather than the tasks and directives being seen as the primary vehicles of change.)

Strategic therapy also makes heavy use of directives but of a less straightforward nature. These directives can take many forms, including but not limited to the following: (a) replacing one "abnormal" situation with another, such as putting a "one-down" spouse in a completely "one-up" position; (b) reframing interactional patterns with new labels that are expected to change the interaction; (c) restraining the couple or family from changing "too fast" by warning of the dangers of change; (d) assigning "pretending" tasks or rituals to break up repetitive patterns of interaction; and (c) paradoxically prescribing the symptomatic behavior and the responses of family members.

The strategic approach developed by Haley (1980) has several other distinctive characteristics. He emphasizes that the problem must be put in solvable form. It should be something that can be objectively agreed on, something that is counted, observed, or measured, so that one can assess whether the problem has actually been influenced.

Haley also places considerable emphasis on the consideration of power. This includes avoiding power struggles with the patient or other family members and using techniques to deal with resistance. Both Haley (1980) and Madanes (1981) view symptoms as correcting power imbalances, particularly in the relationship between spouses. For example, the nondrinking spouse often appears to be overadequate, yet on another level the drinking behavior may demonstrate that this spouse has little power over the drinker, balancing the relationship.

Haley believes that it should be possible for therapy to progress through a planned series of stages. In developing these stages, he places particular emphasis on correcting aberrant hierarchies (such as cross-generational coalitions) and other problems of family organization.

Other strategic approaches, while less central in the development of the Stanton and Todd model, have also been influential in the development of the present approach. The first of these strategic approaches was developed at the Mental Research Institute (MRI) in Palo Alto, California (Fisch et al., 1982; Watzlawick et al., 1974). In the MRI model the "solution" is often the "problem," that is, family members or professional helpers may unwittingly make "helpful" interventions that actually perpetuate the problem. The task of the therapist in such situations is to prevent "more of the same" interventions, possibly by reframing, overloading, and suggesting competing activities.

Most examples of "enabling" behavior readily fit the MRI conceptual framework because they are intended to help the substance abuser and the family yet have the unintended effect of perpetuating the situation and even allowing it to get progressively worse. A wife who continually covers up for a drinking husband, thereby protecting him from the consequences of his behavior, might have the consequences of her behavior pointed out to her in a straightforward manner. If the pattern is quite entrenched and straightforward efforts are not successful, a situation of overload could be created by asking her to do *more,* suggesting that he needs full-time surveillance and protection, until she finally rebels and accepts that he needs to face the consequences of his behavior himself.

The Milan Associates (Selvini-Palazzoli et al., 1978) have placed heavy emphasis on the importance of developing and testing hypotheses. These hypotheses are not seen as "true" in any objective sense but rather as alternative views of reality that may be useful in freeing a family system to change. In this model the task of the therapist is to expand the view of the family rather than insisting that the family change. For example, a substance-abusing adolescent might be praised for self-sacrificing efforts to protect the family. The assumption is made that when the family sees the behavior of the adolescent in a new way, possibilities of change are created.

A STRUCTURAL–STRATEGIC APPROACH TO SUBSTANCE ABUSE

Similar to the model developed by Stanton, Todd, & Associates (1982), the approach outlined in this chapter is "structural–strategic." This means that the overall approach is "strategic" in Haley's sense, including the focus on the symptom and behavior around the symptom, the planned progression of stages of therapy, and the use of directives. Many of the moment-to-moment interventions during sessions are more structural, such as the use of enactment within sessions and the focus on intensifying and resolving interpersonal conflicts between family members. Other "micromoves" are more strategic in the paradoxical sense, such as the use of restraining and prediction of relapses and the use of paradoxical or Milan-style final interventions.

The therapy is goal oriented and short term. Data are gathered early in therapy, particularly concerning drug use and family interaction related to drug use. As data accumulate in early sessions, the therapeutic team attempts to formulate hypotheses linking the substance abuse to the family system. Based on these hypotheses and data, the therapist develops outcome goals and intermediate goals and negotiates explicit goals with the couple or family. (All these points are discussed in greater detail later in this chapter.)

Goals should be consistently related to the drug abuse, but they should also relate to broader issues, particularly to interpersonal issues. Marital and family issues should be linked to the overall goal of reducing drug abuse. For example, as Haley (1980) has emphasized, early sessions should focus on parental teamwork. Marital problems should rarely be addressed as such but rather seen as obstacles to this teamwork. When symptomatic improvement occurs, it is crucial to shift the emphasis away from drugs to other issues but to anticipate possible relapse. Finally, when symptom-reduction has been initiated and is supported by important changes in the system, the therapist should gradually withdraw, giving appropriate credit to the patient and family system.

COURSE OF TREATMENT

For the sake of simplicity treatment can be divided into early, middle, and late stages. In the initial session the therapist attempts to obtain a clearly defined statement of the problem in concrete, behavioral terms and investigates the family's previous attempts at problem solution. It is also important to get a sense of the family members' expectations for treatment. In the early stage of therapy the operative style, arrangements, and structure of the family are identified and a sense of movement is or is not established. The therapist seeks to identify early those aspects of family life in which the instigation of change will have wider repercussions. He or she looks at all of the following: family alliances, parental relationships, filial relationships, peer relationships and family rules, mythologies, and history.

By the middle phases of treatment the therapist already knows the degree to which the family will cooperate, what function the symptom may serve for the family, what typical patterns of behavior can be expected, and what avenues of change may be profitable. Behavior related to the symptom reveals characteristic family defensive styles and reactive patterns. By this time it will be fairly obvious where the strengths and weaknesses lie. Meanwhile, there is a constant evaluation of therapeutic tactics and strategies and negotiation with the family concerning goals for work that remains to be done.

In the late stages of treatment, the last two months or so, the therapist has either made progress or has not. If the former, he or she then summarizes the gains and looks for ways to deal with unfinished business. He or she also reinforces new patterns, styles, or behaviors directly or indirectly. Finally, there is a move to terminate, with plans for follow-up contacts in the future.

If there has been little or no progress in the sessions, then the therapist looks for possible flaws in the treatment plan and implementation. Because this lack of progress should have been evident during the middle phases of treatment, presumably adjustments already have been made and new tactics and strategies tried. Finally, there is a move toward termination, probably with a referral for further treatment if there has been little or no progress. At times the move toward termination in itself may cause a family reevaluation, which the treatment alone did not accomplish.

RESEARCH EVIDENCE

In general there is an almost complete lack of evidence of the effectiveness of treatment of drug and alcohol abuse. This is particularly deplorable when one considers not only that substance abuse is a multimillion dollar problem but also that alcohol and drug treatment is a multimillion dollar industry.

One of the few studies cited by reviewers as having adequate research controls is the Stanton, Todd, & Associates (1982) project using structural-strategic therapy with heroin abuse, referred to extensively in this chapter. This study employed brief (10 sessions) family therapy with 118 adult male heroin abusers in Philadelphia (48% black and 52% white, with 40% of the latter Italian and 25% Irish). To summarize briefly the outcome data presented in more detail in Stanton, Todd, & Associates (1982) and Stanton and colleagues (1979): (a) given considerable effort by clinicians, families can be engaged in treatment (71% of the eligible families were engaged, 88% of all of the families in which the addict allowed the therapist to contact the family); (b) once the families engaged in family treatment, they usually continued in treatment (74% attended at least four sessions); (c) depending on the outcome criteria used, therapy was successful in 49% to 79% of the cases, with results significantly different from nonfamily treatment; and (d) results were maintained over a 2-year follow-up period. This pattern of results is especially noteworthy because (a) these were young adults for whom parental influence might be expected to be weak; (b) the heroin abuse was chronic; and (c) in roughly 80% of the cases, one or both parents had his or her own substance abuse problem.

Szapocznik and his colleagues in Miami (1983) have evaluated the use of one-person brief strategic family therapy with Hispanic adolescent substance abusers and their families. Both one-person and conjoint family therapy were effective, with one-person therapy showing slightly greater effectiveness.

Alcoholics Anonymous (AA) groups, as well as more recent adaptations such as Narcotics Anonymous and Cocaine Anonymous, are ubiquitous throughout the United States and abroad. In addition, the AA philosophy forms the cornerstone of many residential rehabilitation programs. Although AA is generally credited with saving millions of lives, there is little systematic investigation of the effectiveness of AA and a general climate that is antagonistic to such efforts. This is particularly unfortunate because there may well be certain subgroups of patients with substance-abuse problems who are not reached effectively by AA.

Hospital and residential programs are used extensively in the treatment of chemical dependency. Although research evidence is sketchy, some tentative generalizations can be made:

1. It is generally conceded that short-term detoxification from drugs or alcohol has little permanent effect. Although detox may be medically necessary, it must be followed by longer-term treatment to have any lasting value.
2. Residential treatment probably is effective in the short term. Interestingly, this is even true of involuntary patients such as the vast majority of hospitalized adolescents.
3. The obvious problem with any residential program is what happens on discharge. Unless the environment has also been changed, the probability of relapse is quite high.

ALTERNATIVE APPROACHES

A number of conventional approaches to the treatment of chemical dependency have been discussed in the above section on research. This section focuses on a variety of family and quasi-family approaches other than the structural–strategic model, which forms the bulk of this chapter.

One highly influential model has been the family communication model of Satir (1983), particularly as embodied in the work of Wegscheider (1981). Satir has identified a number of family roles such as "blamers," "placater," and "distracter," which Wegscheider has applied persuasively to the families of alcoholics. In this view family members adopt increasingly rigid and stereotyped roles, particularly when faced with stressful situations such as drinking. Thus, the placater predictably tries to make peace, the distracter clowns or responds tangentially, and so on. All these roles are viewed as reducing the stress of alcoholic behavior and also decreasing the likelihood of the family doing anything effective to combat the drinking. Family members seem to understand these concepts readily when explained to them in family education programs. While the author believes that therapy must also focus on behavioral change, such education is at least a useful adjunct.

Multiple-family therapy is also widely used. Again, the author regards such groups as useful adjuncts to other, more intensive forms of treatment, especially with adolescent substance abusers. Reportedly, many parents find them to be extremely positive sources of support. They also seem to learn from the adolescents in the group, who are usually much more effective in confronting each other than the parents are at confronting their offspring.

Some mention should also be made of Tough Love, a movement that has been enthusiastically received by many desperate parents. They find it very supportive, particularly for the difficult task of enforcing a "bottom line" position with an adolescent substance abuser. When the "toughness" and "love" components receive equal emphasis, this approach can be quite helpful. The danger, when the approach is misapplied, is that parents can encourage each other to scapegoat the adolescent, blaming the teenager for the parents' longstanding failure to set appropriate limits. In such circumstances it is not unusual for a teenager who has previously had few limits to suddenly be kicked out of the house, with little transition between these extremes.

It may seem surprising to think of long-term residential programs such as Synanon as included under the general rubric of family and quasi-family approaches. Yet such programs see themselves as providing an alternative "family" for the substance abuser, who often has come from a severely dysfunctional family and an environment generally conducive to drug use and criminal activity. There is some evidence that those patients who complete such a long-term program (the majority of patients do not last the recommended 1-to-2-year period) do benefit significantly. Most of the highly successful patients seem to achieve continued success, however, by remaining in this new "family" through becoming counselors or other employees.

DETAILS OF THE STRUCTURAL–STRATEGIC APPROACH

Techniques for Initiating Treatment

The Relevance and Role of Family Members

Stanton, Todd, & Associates (1982) have emphasized the importance of the "non-blaming message" recruiting the families of drug abusers into treatment. This message should be tailored to the particular clinical situation, depending on the information that is known about the case, and may involve any of the following elements. First, it is always safe to stress the need for a maximum, coordinated helping effort on the part of everyone involved in the life of the substance abuser. While the therapist conveys the expectation that therapy can be helpful, the therapist should also make it clear that he or she "needs all the help he can get."

Second, the therapist should be careful to imply a belief that the spouse and family members have a genuine desire to be helpful to the substance abuser. The therapist also notes that, despite this desire, they may not know the best way to be helpful or they may try to help in ways that turn out to have the unintended effect of promoting drug abuse or undermining abstinence. (This is similar to the idea of "enabling," where a family member may, for example, make excuses for the drinker, with the intention of saving his job, maintaining his relationships, and so on, but with the unintended result of protecting the drinker from the consequences of his behavior.)

Third, similarly, the therapist should not imply an underlying motivation on the part of the spouse or family members to see the patient fail and use drugs. Instead, it is better to imply that significant others learn to accommodate to drug use and its consequences over a period of time and that they may be unprepared for the upsetting effects of abstinence. The analogy is made to a broken leg or physical disability—no one wants such a handicap and anyone would like to get rid of it, yet the person having the handicap and those around him or her may be unaware of the complex accommodations that have been made to the condition, which will be upset by a return to normalcy.

The abuser, spouse, or family member may offer some alternative basis for involvement in marital or family therapy, such as improving communication, dealing with sexual problems, or deciding whether to remain married. The therapist should accept such contracts cautiously and regard such goals as secondary to the primary goal of reduced drug involvement. If difficulties develop with these goals or they seem to be overstressing the abuser at an inappropriate time in relationship to the drug treatment, the therapist should always be ready to abandon or postpone the pursuit of such secondary goals.

While the degree of resistance to conjoint therapy varies from one substance abuser to another, the therapist must be prepared for resistance and should take responsibility for recruiting the family or spouse directly. If the abuser offers resistance to family involvement, the therapist should offer to contact the family, explaining that this will remove the abuser from a position of having to "sell" something that he or she doesn't fully understand. Of course, this also prevents the abuser from presenting the idea to the spouse of family in a distorted or self-serving way, but the therapist avoids mentioning this aspect. If the therapist obtains permission to contact the other parties and then encounters resistance from them, he or she should ask only for an initial contract for a single visit to assess the whole situation with the family and "see what the best treatment plan would be." Particular emphasis should be placed on the importance of obtaining more than one version of the situation in order to help the substance abuser more effectively.

The following case example is presented in some detail because it illustrates many aspects of the application of this therapeutic model in actual practice. Following each stage of the therapy model, illustrative case material is presented that is relevant to that stage.

> Fred, a 35-year-old heroin addict, was referred to the author for outpatient treatment. He was living with his parents at the time, although he had lived on his own for a considerable time previously. An older sister who worked in the social service field had been very involved in investigating alternative treatment resources for him. The father was involved with the patient in an unusual manner: Fred would buy a 2-day supply of heroin and give the envelopes to his father, who then would dole them out on a regular schedule.
>
> Fred was quite reluctant to involve his family in the treatment,

maintaining that he had caused them enough trouble and also emphasizing how much he valued autonomy. While there was abundant
evidence of the family's role in his addiction, that was not emphasized
in the initial effort to "sell" family therapy. Instead, emphasis was
placed on Fred's inability to achieve stability on his own. (He had been
through two detox programs in less than a month and was frantically
seeking still another program.) The parents and the sister were therefore portrayed by the therapist as potential stabilizing influences, with
this stability presented as a necessary short-term goal to enable him to
ultimately achieve autonomy.

Data Gathering

The guiding principle in data gathering is that the therapist is
constantly trying to understand the interpersonal significance of the
substance abuse. It is, therefore, important to obtain data that would
allow the therapist to develop and test hypotheses concerning the
role of substance abuse and factors that may maintain the abuse.

Initially, much of the data concerns the drug abuse itself. The
therapist should take a careful drug history, being alert to time
periods in which there were marked changes in amount or kind of
drugs used. Building on this base, he or she attempts to obtain
information that offers clues about interpersonal factors. What
effects have there been on others? In what ways have the spouse,
family members, and others tried to help? What shifts in relationships have occurred?

The therapist will attempt to obtain illuminating data in each of
three major areas:

1. *Function of the symptom.* What has happened in the family or marriage during periods of accelerated drug use, during financial or vocational crises, and so on? What has happened when the abuser has tried
   to reduce his or her level or use of "go straight"? In addition to the
   spouse or family, what other people seem to play crucial roles?
2. *"Solutions" that become the problem.* On a day-to-day basis, what do
   the abuser, the spouse, and others do in an effort to reduce drug
   abuse? What is the usual effect? What previous treatment efforts have
   there been? What was the outcome?
3. *"Organizational" issues.* The therapist should learn what other helpers, formal or informal, are currently involved with the patient and the
   family. This is especially important when the patient has recently been
   discharged from an inpatient treatment program. If other treaters are
   involved, what sort of "program" has the abuser been given? What is

the program ideology, and how easy will it be for the marital/family therapy to co-exist with the other facets of treatment?

Important data are also obtained that suggest possible treatment goals that the patient or spouse may desire. Adult substance abusers usually have problems in the areas of their finances, marital relationship, or job, all of which may have been further complicated with legal difficulties. With adolescent abusers problems with peers, school, and family are typical, again with possible legal complications. Whatever the problem area, the therapist attempts to ascertain what the current situation is and what the impact of substance abuse has been.

Finally, the therapist should not forget the other key figures who are not in attendance but who may be important. If the interview is with an adolescent and the parents, how do the siblings and the extended family fit in? If the interview is with a couple, how are their children involved? What do they know or sense about the drug abuse? With respect to the families of origin it is helpful to obtain basic information about who comprises the families and where they are. How are they involved with the couple? Is there any current or past history of substance abuse or other addictive behavior in other parts of the family?

Forming and Testing Hypotheses

When developing hypotheses, it is important for the therapist and any team members to remember constantly that the crucial issue is for hypotheses to be useful therapeutically as opposed to being "true." Hypotheses can always be generated on several levels and with different time frames, but many possible, interesting hypotheses have limited therapeutic value.

The most important hypotheses therefore are those having to do with the current role of the chemical dependency in the family or marital system and in other interpersonal systems. Next in order of importance are those hypotheses having to do with other factors that may be maintaining the drug abuse. These hypotheses may include the role of other helpers, the role of friends and the work environment, the role of economic issues, and so forth.

None of this is meant to imply that hypotheses having to do with historical factors are useless. Always, however, they need to be connected with current reality and current therapeutic strategies and goals. If, for example, there are issues surrounding the death of a significant family member who was linked to the abuser, which Stanton (1981) has frequently found to be the case, the issue for the therapist is to bring this event and connection into the present and find some way to deal with it, even symbolically.

> In the previous example of Fred the heroin abuser, it appeared that there had been previous periods during which he functioned at a high level. His drug usage had accelerated during the past few years, which coincided with the forced retirement of his father at age 62. His mother was making a successful transition to being a grandmother to two grandchildren belonging to one of her daughters, but his father seemed to feel totally unemployed.
>
> The preliminary assessment was therefore that the father had found a new purpose in life through dealing with Fred's drug problems. This was further supported by the observation that he drove Fred everywhere and maintained tight control over his son's finances. It was clear therefore that therapy would need to develop a central role for the father to play in Fred's recovery. Ideally, it would also be desirable for the father to develop interests that did not center on Fred. Early indications were that this would be difficult, perhaps because the father felt guilty and responsible for Fred's drug usage.

Goal Setting

The process of establishing and refining therapeutic goals is crucial to the structural–strategic therapy of substance abuse, a process that should begin with the first session. If the abuser, spouse, or other family members are demoralized, it may be necessary to "sell" them on the possibility that therapy will make a real difference. Typically, however, it is better in the first session for the therapist to take a more neutral and pessimistic position, especially if the abuser is newly abstinent and seems optimistic about therapy. Under these circumstances, the therapist (or, even better, the team behind the mirror, if one is available) usually expresses some doubts about whether therapy will be helpful and sends the family or couple home to think and talk about it before the second session.

Typically, the formal goal-setting process begins in session two. The stated goal of the couple or family is usually quite clear: to have the drug abuser stop taking drugs and stay off drugs. The therapist, on the other hand, wishes to establish goals in two major areas—the area of drugs and the area of interpersonal relationships, with a clear connection between the two sets of goals.

As therapy progresses, it usually develops that the couple or family has difficulty translating their goals into action. The abstract idea of abstinence may be fine, but the realities of confronting the abuser or setting limits may be more difficult to achieve. Furthermore, as abstinence is achieved, other problems typically surface and may develop into important new goals of treatment.

> George, a 40-year-old man, sought individual therapy because of an incident related to drinking. One evening after having a few drinks, he was driving a teenaged babysitter home, stopped the car, and made a pass at her. She fled from the car and nothing happened, but the incident left him badly shaken. He had sworn never to drink again and had been sober for 5 days at the time of the first psychotherapy session.
>
> It was difficult to develop a workable therapeutic contract with George. He did not see himself as an alcoholic and refused to attend AA. He saw drinking as his only problem and believed that he had already stopped. The only leverage was his fear that he might drink again. He was assigned the task of developing a list of "pros" and "cons" of giving up drinking. At first his list consisted only of reasons for giving up drinking, and he resisted looking at the factors that might make drinking attractive. The author insisted that he do so, on the grounds that otherwise these factors might catch him by surprise. If they could be identified, alternative strategies could be developed for achieving the same purposes without alcohol.
>
> On closer examination George revealed that his drinking was confined almost exclusively to a single situation. Following a high-stress period at work, he would purchase liquor on the way home and drink it in the car. He never threw away the "evidence," waiting for his wife or one of his sons to catch him. This suggested that he needed alternative mechanisms for dealing with job stress and that his wife and possibly his children might need to be involved in the therapy.

Dealing with Symptomatic Improvement and Relapses

Although structural–strategic therapy is definitely symptom-focused, the handling of either symptomatic improvement or relapse is far from simple. Changes in either direction must always be evaluated in terms of previous patterns of improvement or lack thereof, the stage of therapy, and the ideal stance of the therapist and other team members. Only after all these factors have been considered can an appropriate therapeutic plan be developed.

When therapy is proceeding well and there are no exacerbating circumstances, it is reasonable to expect significant improvement as early as session three or four. When this improvement occurs "on schedule," it is crucial to do two things: consolidate the changes and shift to interpersonal issues. To consolidate positive therapeutic change, the therapist should usually adopt a stance of guarded optimism—that the changes appear desirable and real but they may not last.

As symptomatic improvement occurs, interpersonal issues typically emerge. It is crucial for the therapy to begin to focus more directly on these issues. If the spouse or family members are allowed to maintain an exclusive focus on the abuser and the possibility of a return to drug use rather than focusing on more basic interpersonal issues, a relapse typically occurs.

The therapist has considerable latitude in influencing the stance taken by the spouse or family when a relapse or slip occurs. At one extreme it may be appropriate to treat an early relapse as a major crisis, mobilizing the resources of the couple or family to meet this challenge. Usually such a relapse has already been anticipated and planned for, and the relapse is the occasion for activating this plan.

In contrast, late in treatment it is often desirable to treat a relapse more casually, as a temporary slip rather than a permanent reversion to drug use. When the couple or family has made solid progress, the therapist should convey the attitude that they already know how to cope with this temporary setback. Usually the relapse comes when the couple or family is facing an interpersonal crisis such as marital friction, with the relapse functioning to divert attention away from the interpersonal issues. The therapist must recognize this pattern and prevent this diversion from occurring, even though it may also be necessary to deal with the relapse directly.

> George had two relapses during therapy which were handled very differently. His first slip followed his classic pattern—he worked too hard and felt sorry for himself, so he "couldn't resist" buying some beer. After drinking it, he felt guilty and left the bottle in the car. The ensuing scene with his wife created two opportunities for therapy: (a) Obviously, the problem was not "cured," so more aggressive measures were needed; and (b) his wife was brought in for conjoint sessions, which alternated with his individual sessions. The content of the conjoint sessions was unremarkable. What seemed significant was that these conversations would previously only have taken place after George had been drinking.
>
> Following this slip, George was much more willing to look at the attractive aspects of drinking. He began to attend a therapy group for

alcoholics and also to look at his difficulties in asserting himself at work. The marital relationship also began to improve. A few weeks later he again stopped and bought a bottle. Uncharacteristically, he had one taste, realized he didn't want it, and then threw the bottle away. His wife did not learn of this episode until the next session. Her tendency was to treat this as a major slip, but in the session the author was able to relabel this as major new behavior on his part. This was the last such relapse, at least over the next year in which the author had contact with the couple, and it marked the transition to real marital work with them.

Techniques for Ending the Treatment

Reviewing Goals and Giving Credit for Change

Structural–strategic therapy is typically brief. Whether or not it is formally time-limited, it usually lasts 10 to 20 sessions over a period of 4 to 6 months. Within the context of such brief therapy, it is particularly important for the therapist to review goals periodically and be prepared to terminate when goals have been achieved. Even when goal achievement is less than perfect, the therapist may wish to move toward termination when therapy has reached a point of diminishing returns or when there is a danger of excessive dependence on therapy.

Stanton (1981) has argued that it is important that the patient and family receive most of the credit for change. This is particularly consistent with the assumptions of structural–strategic therapy. The therapist should only take credit as a facilitator or catalyst, making it clear that the couple or family has done the real work. It is also dangerous for the abuser to get too much credit for change because this lessens the commitment of the spouse or family members to maintaining the changes and preventing relapse. In this respect it is important to link drug improvement to changes made in interpersonal areas.

The couple or family should be warned in advance that life may not go smoothly and future problems can be anticipated. It is useful to review the problem-solving skills they have learned in the course of therapy to create confidence that they can deal successfully with future problems or crises.

As termination has been approaching, the therapist has been spacing out the sessions with longer intervals between sessions. Usually the final sessions are treated more as extended follow-up than as therapy sessions, such as coming together at monthly intervals to review progress and ensure that there has not been any slippage. If therapy has ended ahead of schedule, the family or couple can be told that they have a few sessions "in the bank" should any problems appear during that period.

Summary of the Structural–Strategic Approach

1. The spouse or family members are recruited into therapy as "helpers" to the therapy of the drug abuser, with the therapist careful to avoid blaming.
2. Short-term treatment is emphasized, with an expectation that treatment might last 4 to 6 months.
3. Data are gathered to develop hypotheses concerning the interpersonal significance of the substance abuse.
4. Goals are developed in drug-related and interpersonal areas, with a connection made between the two.
5. Abstinence from drug use continues to be the primary criterion of success of the therapy. Other goals and contracts are secondary and should always be clearly related to the drug problem.
6. The possibility of relapse should be anticipated and specific plans made to handle a relapse. Different plans will be appropriate at different stages of therapy.
7. When progress has been made in the drug area and interpersonal issues surface, it is important not to allow a relapse to divert attention from these issues.
8. Termination should be anticipated and planned from the beginning of therapy. Patient, spouse, and family members should receive credit for change so that they are invested in maintaining the change and so that they will be optimistic about handling future problems and crises.

GLOSSARY: DEFINITIONS OF KEY TECHNIQUES

Boundary Making. The therapist acts through directives and the use of the therapist's role in the communication process to change the membership of subsystems or the relationship between subsystems. For example, the therapist may reinforce boundaries that differentiate the roles of parents and children or strengthen the alliance between parents or among siblings.

Complementarity. The therapist attempts to counter stereotyped perceptions held by family members of themselves and others by placing them in a larger context, emphasizing the complementary nature of relationships and the circular, reciprocal process that maintains this complementarity.

Deliberate Splitting. The therapists or therapeutic team members deliberately adopt extremely polarized, opposing positions to influence and moderate a similar split in the couple or family. This can be serious or playful to fit the clinical situation. Ideally, the position taken should relate to real opinions or behavior of the team members but exaggerated to make the positions flexible and keep the conflicts among the therapists from becoming problematic.

Enactment. The technique whereby the therapist constructs an interpersonal scenario in the session in which dysfunctional transactions among family members or spouses are played out. (For example, parents of an anorectic might be asked to get her to eat.) This transaction occurs in the context of the session, in the therapist's presence, and in relationship to the therapist. While facilitating this transaction, the therapist can observe the family's behavior and the range of transactions the family can tolerate. The therapist can then intervene in the process to increase its intensity, involve other members, and indicate alternative transactions.

Intensifying. These interventions on the part of the therapist increase the intensity of an interactional situation to take the couple or family beyond their usual threshold of tolerance, creating a crisis that demands new patterns of interaction. Depending on the therapist and the family, these interventions may be loud or soft, dramatic or low key. Examples include repetition of a message from the therapist, extending the duration of an interaction, using confrontation by the therapist, or dramatizing a situation by making it more real (such as the family lunch session for anorexia).

Joining. A group of techniques and an overall attitude on the part of the therapist that lets the couple or family know that the therapist understands them and is working with them and for them. The therapist activates and adapts aspects of self that stress similarity to the family members. This includes a whole spectrum of actions, including body language and nonverbal behavior, the use of humor and self-disclosing stories, and so on.

Positioning (see also Restraining). The deliberate adoption of an attitude by the therapist or team that is more negative than that of the patient or family or is the opposite of what they would normally expect from a therapist. Examples include seeming more hopeless than a depressed patient, being skeptical about the desirability of a drug-free life, or suggesting that clear communication and honesty may not be wise.

Prescribing. This is usually considered in its more paradoxical sense of prescribing the symptom. This can include therapist directives to increase the symptom or to schedule its occurrence. It is more effective to prescribe the behavior of the marital or family system rather than the behavior of one person in isolation. Rituals may also be prescribed that are not paradoxical themselves but that have the effect of removing the participants from a paradoxical bind (Selvini-Palazzoli et al., 1978).

Pretending. The therapist prescribes behavior of the couple or family often in the form of a ritual, in a way that asks them to pretend, rather than giving "real" behavior. The behavior prescribed typically centers around the symptom and its consequences, although it may either represent the symptom literally or metaphorically. This intervention is intended to block or change the usual transactions around the symptom, often providing a substitute that has a similar function.

Relabeling (also called reframing, positive connotation, or positive interpretation). This involves attaching new labels to behavior to facilitate change. When used more strategically, it particularly involves labeling symptomatic behavior or other "undesirable" behavior to attribute positive qualities to the behavior. The therapist suggests underlying motivation for behavior that is positive, such as protectiveness or loyalty. It is the "benign" quality of the relabeling that makes it difficult to resist in the ways that a more conventional interpretation would be.

Relabeling can also be used to change the meaning of positively valued qualities such as honesty and openness when it is desirable to counter their usage in the typical pattern of interaction. It is also an oversimplification to think of relabeling as simply positive or negative; even when relabeling has an apparently positive tone, it usually has an underlying "sting." For example, the drug abuser may be praised for his or her loyalty and self-sacrifice but with the thinly veiled implication that he or she is a "sucker."

Restraining. This refers to interventions made by the therapist that appear to advocate that change should not occur or at least that it should only occur slowly. These techniques can range from simple "go-slow" admonitions from the therapist to more complex interventions advising the patient and family to consider all the possible dangers and consequences of change. (See Haley, 1976, pp. 142–150.)

Unbalancing. The therapist uses a variety of techniques with the goal of changing the heirarchical relationships between the couple or family members. During unbalancing the therapist may temporarily join one individual or subsystem at the expense of another, maintaining this "unfair" alliance until the family system has shown the desired shift in response. Other techniques may be milder, such as deliberately violating family communicational rules or ignoring particular family members.

The Family, Delinquency, and Crime

6

CARL E. POPE

Traditionally we are conditioned to think of the family unit as a healthful and nurturing environment in which children prosper and parents realize their full potential. Unfortunately, for many families this represents a myth, not reality. In many instances families are disorganized and unable to cope with the complexities of modern-day living, including the stresses of poverty, racism, lack of education, and the like. Many family members suffer from various maladies of the modern society, including heroin, cocaine, and alcohol addiction, and are increasingly likely to come in contact with the criminal justice system.

To think of the family as a potential cause or correlate of crime is not something that society as a whole is conditioned to do. Although not ignoring the family environment, many criminologists have tended to seek explanations for crime in contextual conditions such as poverty, inequality, school failure, discrimination, and the like (Straus & Lincoln, 1985). For example, Staples (1986, p. 150) argues that behavioral scientists traditionally have neglected violence in family relationships as an area of study. He concludes that

> A primary reason for this void in the family literature on family violence has been the prevailing ideology of the family as a unit characterized by affection and cooperation among its members. Yet, it has been known for quite some time that the largest group of homicides in the United States involves spouses, kinsmen and close friends.

Family life may actually be hazardous to one's health, as some data indicate. An examination of homicide in Philadelphia conducted by Wolfgang (1958) in the early 1950s was one of the first studies to examine specific patterns associated with this offense. The results indicated that in about two-thirds of the homicides alcohol was present in the victim, the offender, or both. About one-quarter of all homicides were victim-precipitated in that the victim appeared to initiate the situation that led to his or her own death. More importantly, 65% of all victim-offender relationships involved primary contacts such as a close friend, family member, or lover. One-quarter of all the homicides examined by Wolfgang involved family associations and were more likely to occur in the home. Furthermore, the motives behind these homicides often seemed to be trivial in nature in that about 35% of the cases involved minor altercations (insult, cursing, or jostling, and the like). Thus, an impressive amount of criminal violence in the form of homicide was found to originate within family settings, suggesting that the family itself should be one of the focal points of criminological inquiry.

TRENDS IN FAMILY VIOLENCE

Recent national crime statistics confirm Wolfgang's (1958) earlier findings for Philadelphia in that approximately 60% of all homicides cleared by arrest include victims and offenders who were in primary relationships (McGarrell & Flanagan, 1985). As opposed to other violent index offenses (rape, robbery, and aggravated assault), homicides are typically not stranger-to-stranger crimes. In 1982 of those murders and nonnegligent manslaughters where the victim/offender relationship was known, only 17% involved killings among strangers. Over one-half of these incidents involved immediate family members, acquaintances, and friends (McGarrell & Flanagan, 1985). Conversely, families may not only be dangerous to themselves but to others as well. For the same year approximately 34% of all police officer injuries occurred when responding to domestic disturbance calls such as family quarrels (McGarrell & Flanagan, 1985). These data underscore the actual and potential violence that can erupt within the family setting.

A recent U.S. Department of Justice special report on family violence provides some additional insight on both the nature of the problem and the difficulties in trying to measure it (Klaus & Rand, 1984). Currently there are two national statistical series that measure criminal incidents. The Uniform Crime Reporting System compiled by the FBI enumerates crimes known to the police and crimes cleared by arrest. The National Crime Survey includes incidents reported by victims of crime and hence is independent of police arrest statistics. Neither of these measures, however, gives complete estimates of crime and family violence (McNeely & Pope, 1981). As Klaus and Rand (1984, pp. 2–3) note, incidents of family violence are likely to be significantly underreported for the following reasons:

> Many victims of family violence do not perceive their experiences as crimes.

Although interviewers are encouraged to interview each respondent privately if possible, there may be other family members present during the survey interview. If the offender is present, the chances diminish that the victim would feel free to describe the event.
Many victims of family violence are reluctant to speak of their experiences because of the shame and revulsion they feel about the matter.

Even given these limitations, however, approximately 450,000 incidents of family violence are reported annually (Klaus & Rand, 1984). In addition, the National Crime Survey of victims reveals some interesting findings regarding the nature of family violence. Of those crimes committed by relatives, the majority are committed by spouses or ex-spouses. Over four-fifths of these incidents involved assaults, whereas less than one-tenth were robberies and rapes. (The National Crime Survey does not measure homicide.) Of the assaults, one-third were aggravated. Serial victimization was also relatively common. Those attacked by spouses, for example, reported similar attacks within the past 6 months. Women were substantially more likely than men to be the victim of family violence. In those incidents involving spouses, 91% of the women were victimized by their husbands or ex-husbands. Those in the lower income groups and those aged 20 to 34 were the most likely to be victimized. About three-quarters of the incidents of spouse abuse involved divorced or separated persons. Weapons, most often a gun or a knife, were used in approximately 30% of violent crimes committed by relatives. Forty-nine percent of all family violence incidents resulted in injury of some type, with the injury rate for spouse abuse being somewhat higher. Resistance to an attack was not uncommon (in about three-fourths of the incidents) but tended to be passive in nature such as trying to obtain help (Klaus & Rand, 1984).

In a nationally representative survey of 2143 couples, Straus, Gelles, and Steinmetz (1980) found spouse abuse to be quite extensive, ranging from relatively minor incidents to attacks involving the use of guns and knives. Aside from spouse abuse, mistreatment of children is not a recent or unusual phenomena. Further, there is evidence to suggest that child abuse within the home is related to later incidents of aggression, delinquency, crime, and mental health problems (Hirschi, 1983; Wilson & Herrnstein, 1985; Zingraff & Belson 1986). With regard to abuse and delinquency, Steele (1976), Gelles (1972), and Reidy (1977) all report a strong relationship in that those youths who were abused as children were more likely to engage in delinquent and violent behavior. Although the majority of research in this area has found a relationship between child abuse and later pathology, there are, however, some exceptions. Kratcoski (1982), for example, reports that those youths abused as children were no more likely to engage in violent behavior than those who had not been abused, whereas another study found that abused children were less likely to be incarcerated for a violent offense than those who had not been abused (Zingraff & Belson, 1986).

It should be noted that research focusing on both spouse and child abuse has suffered frequently from numerous methodological limitations such as limited sample sizes, lack of random selection, lack of generalizability, definitional problems, and the like. Abuse, for example, can take many forms ranging from psychological to physiological, and the degree of physical injury can vary greatly, sometimes culminating in the death of the child or spouse. In addition, most of this research is retrospective, asking people to recount earlier events in their lives. Thus, errors in recall may produce misleading results.

When one looks at general crime patterns, it is evident that youthful involvement in criminal activity is a serious matter. For example, data derived from the Uniform Crime Reports (McGarrell & Flanagan, 1985) indicate that youths under 15 years of age accounted for 12.1% of those arrested for index offenses in 1983 (homicide and nonnegligent manslaughter, forcible rape, robbery, aggravated assault, burglary, larceny–theft, motor vehicle theft, and arson). With regard to the total number of arrests across the United States, those aged 13 to 15 accounted for 6.7% of all arrests, although they constituted only 4.7% of the resident U.S. population. Those aged 16 to 18 accounted for 13.3% of all arrests while constituting 4.9% of the resident U.S. population (McGarrell & Flanagan, 1985). These data suggest that the problem of delinquency, including violent criminal acts, is a serious issue facing the United States and one that cannot be easily dismissed. It may well be the case that the conditions for delinquency and other forms of maladjusted behavior originate, in part, in the context of family life, and, further, that criminal and delinquent behavior, in turn, combine to produce detrimental results on the family itself.

THE IMPACT OF CRIME AND DELINQUENCY ON THE FAMILY

In discussing the relationship between crime and the family, Fox (1981, p. 255) notes that:

. . . First, antisocial behavior or incarceration may, in itself, precipitate a crisis for the offender and his or her family; second, crisis itself
may precipitate delinquency or other behavior by which the individual
becomes an offender with all the concomitant problems and stigma
which occur for the family.

Thus, while familial and societal conditions may lead to delinquent
and criminal behavior, such behavior, especially in the context of
criminal processing, may produce a series of crises with which both
the offender and his or her family must learn to cope. Among these
are included separation from spouse and children due to arrest and
possible incarceration; economic hardships inflicted upon families of
prisoners; adjustment difficulties facing children left behind, including possible termination of parental rights or placement in foster
care; potential dissolution of the marriage; and lack of adequate
services to families of prisoners.

Most citizens, especially those from lower-income groups, are
woefully unaware of their constitutional rights and have little understanding of the machinery of criminal justice. The system is complex, gives out little information, and often presents at least the
appearance of injustice. However, recent attempts have been made
to rectify some of these problems. For example, in most cities victim/
witness assistance programs have provided encouragement, information, transportation, and similar services. Programs have also been
developed to service offenders, especially those incarcerated in
penal institutions and after their release. Until very recently, however, there have been few programs and services provided for the
families of those being processed and incarcerated. As Weintraub
(1976, p. 28) has pointed out,

> A family member of an incarcerated individual may indeed receive
> social work services from one of a number of agencies but it is rare
> that the special problems arising out of the incarceration of the family
> member will be recognized and dealt with properly. In addition, there
> is no formal mechanism to deliver basic information about the jails,
> the courts, the prisons and what is happening to the individual who
> passes through them. It is therefore necessary to identify the families
> of incarcerated individuals as a distinct client group with specific
> problems and to have the appropriate agencies assume responsibilities
> for dealing with these problems.

Weintraub (1976) identifies four crisis points in criminal processing that have direct implications for the family. These include arrest

and arraignment, sentencing, initial incarceration, and immediate/ pre/postrelease. At each of these stages there is an immediate need for both information and services (Fishman & Alissi, 1979). When an offender is arrested and remanded into custody, he or she is temporarily removed from society and the family. Within a relatively short period of time, the offender is taken before a magistrate, at which time a bail determination is made. Although in some unusual cases bail is denied, it is typically set at a sum that more often than not the offender is unable to raise. In the latter case the offender is held in pretrial detention until either bail is raised or trial commences. During these proceedings, the family is often confused, unaware of what is taking place and unsure of what to do about it. If the offender is held in pretrial detention, it means continued separation from the family and community, loss of job if previously employed, and difficulty in putting together an adequate defense.

After trial, or more commonly after a plea of guilty, for most defendants comes the moment of truth—sentencing. If the sentence involves incarceration, and for most serious offenses it does, this represents a major crisis for the family unit that now must redefine itself in the absence of the incarcerated individual. Incarceration itself represents a stressful period, including for many families problems of economic hardship and coping with the institutional regime with its bewildering array of rules and regulations. Such factors as transportation to the institution and the many restrictions on visitation may become insurmountable hurdles. In most cases the eventual return of the prisoner to the family creates serious problems of adjustment. As Weintraub (1976, p. 30) notes:

> The incarcerated individual has adapted to existence in prison society. There is presently minimal attention given to preparing the incarcerated individual to return to his family or preparing the family to receive him. There is little or no continuity between planning which may be done for the individual in the institution and agencies which may have been working with the family in the community and the field parole office.

Perhaps one of the major "pains of imprisonment" for those incarcerated in both men's and women's penitentiaries is that of separation and loneliness. If nothing else, "a prison sentence serves to disrupt an individual's participation in a social network of friends, relatives and associates" (Jones & Schmid, 1987, p. 12). Recent research conducted by Flanagan (1980) provides support for this observation. Flanagan interviewed a sample of inmates from five maximum-security prisons, all of whom had served at least 5 years of continuous confinement. His research suggests that problems relating to the deprivation of liberty (severance of ties to the outside world) were consistently ranked as the most severe problems facing these inmates. "Missing somebody" was consistently ranked as the most severe problem, followed by missing "social life" and "worrying about how you will cope when you get out." As Flanagan notes, often times these feelings become exacerbated, resulting in severe behavioral problems within the institution. These results are even more alarming when the increasing lengths of time inmates are now serving across the United States are taken into consideration.

Separation from husband or wife poses even a greater strain for the married inmate. As Hinds (1981, p. 8) has observed,

> Although a number of researchers have found that there is a clear and positive correlation between the maintenance of family ties during incarceration and the success of a released prisoner upon his return to the free society, the destruction of the marriage is almost inevitable.

In reviewing those programs designed to aid an offender's reentry into society, Curtis and Schulman (1984) argue that social networks, marriage, and the family are critical to the counseling and treatment of ex-offenders. Frequently marital strain is related to the economic problems facing the families of incarcerated individuals (Struckhoff, 1979). The vast majority of those being processed through the criminal justices system and ultimately found in penal populations are drawn from the ranks of the poor and underprivileged. Because the families of prisoners are often poor to begin with, incarceration serves to increase their poverty level (Hinds, 1981).

Aside from financial problems, separation due to incarceration may be related to behavioral problems in those children left behind. Fritsch and Burkhead (1981) reported a variety of behavioral problems associated with the children of incarcerated men and women. These included disciplinary problems, withdrawal, continuous crying, poor school performance, medical problems, and aggressive behavior. They also found that the sex of the parent was correlated with specific types of behavior. In general, acting-out behaviors were associated with the absence of the father, whereas acting-in behaviors (e.g., withdrawal) were associated with the absence of the mother. Further, the conditions found in most penal institutions and the skills needed to adjust and survive therein are not generally considered to be conducive to family life. There is the distinct possibility that the negative aspects of imprisonment may carry over after reentry (Hairston & Lockett, 1985).

There is evidence to suggest that the difficulties experienced by women in prison may be more pronounced than those for men (Sobel, 1982). Given the fact that many imprisoned women are mothers, maintaining contact with their children often becomes a very serious problem (McCarthy, 1980). Sametz (1980) argues for prison reform such as maternity centers, relocation of prisons near city limits, and increased use of work-release programs. McCarthy (1980) suggests the increased use of home visits to maintain the inmate mother's ties to her family and children.

In sum, criminal processing and the process of imprisonment itself imposes severe strains on offenders and their families. As noted above, these strains are exacerbated by the fact of separation and financial hardship and often manifest themselves in dissolution of the marriage and behavioral problems in the children of those incarcerated. It has also been noted that family variables play a critical role in treatment programs geared to the reentry into society of ex-offenders (Marsh, 1983).

FAMILY CORRELATES OF DELINQUENT AND CRIMINAL ACTS

Social science research has examined various characteristics of family life that may be associated with future delinquent activity and adult criminal behavior. These have included such factors as divorce, single-parent homes, parental attitudes toward children, family cohesiveness, parental discipline, family size, and degree of supervision. Although none of these factors may be directly linked to criminal behavior, they may play an important role in aiding our understanding of this phenomenon.

For example, while it is true that not all delinquent youths come from single-parent homes, this does not mean that single-parent homes are unrelated to our understanding of crime and delinquency, especially because such homes frequently have incomes well below the poverty line. For some youth, the trauma surrounding the breakup of the parents' marriage may, in conjunction with other factors, provide a needed push toward delinquency. Research conducted during the first half of this century frequently noted that delinquents compared to nondelinquents were more likely to come from homes with only one parent (Breckinridge & Abbott, 1912; Glueck & Glueck, 1930; Healy & Bronner, 1926; Shaw & McKay, 1932). While more recent research is less consistent in reporting a relationship between delinquency and single-parent homes, the majority of studies still support these earlier findings, although the relationships are often weak (Dentler & Monroe, 1961; Hennessy et al., 1978; Hirschi, 1969).

Some research has suggested that the effects of a disrupted home may be more detrimental for female compared to male youths (Austin, 1978; Chilton & Markle, 1972; Datesman & Scarpetti, 1975; Gold, 1970; Toby, 1957). Datesman and Scarpitti (1975) found that females were more likely than were males to be charged with ungovernable behavior when coming from a single-parent home. These researchers also found that those females charged with ungovernability and running away were referred to the court more often by parents and relatives than were their male counterparts. On the other hand, research reported by Wilkinson (1980) and Canter (1982) found few differences between male and female youth when examining their family structure and delinquency.

With regard to race Monahan (1957) reported a higher proportion of single-parent homes among black delinquent adolescents as compared to whites, a condition that seems to be increasing at the present time (Lehman, 1986a, b). Generally, however, the family situation has been found to be less important in generating serious misconduct among black youth, especially males (Chilton & Markle, 1972; Hraba et al., 1979; Willie, 1967). This finding requires further study with adequate samples and research designs.

With regard to race and type of offense, Austin (1978) found no relationship between father absence and type of delinquency for black males. However, Austin (1978) did find that black males and white females coming from single-parent homes were more likely to be arrested for crimes against the person than were their respective counterparts. Willie (1967) reported that both family situation and economic status were associated with delinquent behavior. Among those families characterized as affluent, single-parent homes were associated with higher rates of delinquency for white youth compared to nonwhite youth.

One problem with research linking single-parent homes to delinquency is the possibility that the relationship may be an artifact of criminal processing or reporting of criminal events. That is, parents or neighbors may be especially likely to complain to the police regarding incidents of children from disrupted homes (Nye, 1958). Further, the juvenile justice system may be more responsive to acts committed by youths from these homes and thus more likely to institute formal proceedings against them (Smith, 1955). There is some research that suggests that this may well be the case in at least some jurisdictions (R. E. Johnson, 1986; Paquin et al., 1976; Pope et al., 1984). Fenwick (1982), in examining official records and conducting systematic observations of intake hearings, discovered that family disaffiliation (including nonintact homes) greatly influenced the extent to which a youth was defined as delinquent and held for court action. Similarly, research by Kruttschmitt and McCarthy (1985) lends partial support to the premise that family status affects case processing.

Overall, research conducted over the past 80 years on delinquency and single-parent homes is inconclusive, inconsistent, and ambiguous (Wilson & Herrnstein, 1985). Given differences in methodology, sample size, jurisdiction, time frame, and the like, this is not unexpected. Wilkinson (1980) notes that research employing self-report techniques has generally not shown the single-parent home to be a major factor in the etiology of delinquency, whereas studies using official statistics have. Type of measurement, then, may make a difference. "Thus, official delinquency and self-reported delinquent behavior need not be related to family structure in the same way" (R. E. Johnson, 1986, p. 66). Conceptual difficulties also plague research of this nature in that it is not always clear exactly what constitutes a single-parent home. Some studies, for example, merely differentiate between intact and nonintact homes whereas others take into account the nature of the separation, whether by death, divorce, or illegitimacy. Furthermore, the assumption that single-parent homes are unhappy ones is not necessarily true (Nye, 1958). Nor is the reverse necessarily true, that two-parent homes reflect a happy, nurturing family.

In his review of research focusing on the single-parent home, Hirschi (1983) concludes that all else being equal, one parent is probably sufficient. The problem, however, is that all else is rarely equal. As Hirschi (1983, p. 62) notes:

> The single parent (usually a woman) must devote a good deal to support and maintenance activities that are at least to some extent shared in the two parent family. Further, she must do so in the absence of psychological or social support. As a result, she is less able to

devote time to monitoring and punishment, and is more likely to be involved in negative, abusive contacts with her children.

It may well be the case therefore that factors often associated with nonintact homes such as working outside the home or the nature of discipline and supervision may be conducive to delinquency (Aldous, 1982; Rosen, 1985), as well as structural conditions such as poverty and racial discrimination (Chilman, 1988). (See also Volume 5, Chapter 1 of this series.) Some earlier research suggests that the children of women working outside the home are more likely to be delinquent (Glueck & Glueck, 1957; Hirschi, 1969). However, other research fails to show this connection. For instance, it has been noted that in those homes where there was an adequate degree of supervision, there was no relationship between delinquency and whether the mother worked outside the home (Riege, 1972).

Research also suggests that defective home discipline is more common among delinquents than nondelinquents (Glueck & Glueck, 1962). Welsh (1978), among others, noted that the use of severe punishments may lead to aggressive delinquent behavior in later life; on the other hand, unduly lenient discipline may also play a part in delinquent behavior. Thus, excessive parental control may lead to hostility, whereas excessive leniency may lead to isolation, feelings of neglect, and poor impulse control. Perhaps most important is the consistency of firm, mild discipline (McCord & McCord, 1959). (See also Chapter 5 on parent–child relationships in Volume 3 of this series.)

Research also suggests that the quality of interpersonal relationships within the family unit may have a strong influence on later delinquency (Hindelang, 1973; Hirschi, 1969; Poole & Regoli, 1979; Wiatrowski et al., 1981). In a cross-cultural comparison Rosenquist and Megargee (1969) found that delinquent youth were more likely to come from homes considered to be less cohesive and less stable.

Generally, research suggests that youths who are weakly attached to their parents are more likely to be delinquent (Hirschi, 1969). This is especially true for those youths who had poor relationships with their mothers (Glueck & Glueck, 1958; McCord & McCord, 1959). In addition, delinquent boys were found in one study to have overprotective, indifferent, hostile and rejecting mothers (Glueck & Glueck, 1958). It should be noted, however, that these studies were done over 30 years ago under different social conditions. At that point much research focused on male delinquents and mother–child relationships while virtually ignoring the role of the father.

Family size has also been related to future delinquency. Hirschi (1969) in his self-report study of delinquent behavior in northern California schools found that delinquents tended to come from larger families than nondelinquents. Only children reported delinquent acts 33% of the time compared to 49% for those youths coming from homes with four or more siblings. Other siblings may well be important in the socialization process (Wilkinson et al., 1982), and monitoring and punishment may be less effective in larger families (Hirschi, 1983). The impact of family size has also been found to be more important for those families with low socioeconomic status (West, 1982), as large families are more pronounced among the poor, especially among blacks and Hispanics. While these data are not conclusive, they do suggest that what transpires within the family setting has important implications for later delinquency and adult crime.

POVERTY, CRIME, AND THE FAMILY

It has frequently been suggested that there is a relationship between poverty and crime. In its simplest form, the argument is that poverty breeds crime. The logic of this argument is reflected in the fact that the vast majority of those processed through the criminal justice system are poor. While available research linking poverty to crime is not consistent (Wilson & Herrnstein, 1985), there is evidence that poor families (especially those that are nonintact) are at a greater risk of becoming enmeshed in the juvenile and adult criminal justice systems (Silberman, 1978). As a way of understanding the relationship between poverty, family life, and crime, it is useful to review the origin and maintenance of the black "underclass," a segment of society frequently characterized by extreme poverty and family disorganization.

In *The Declining Significance of Race,* Wilson (1978) examines the relationship of black Americans to the economic structure of society from both historical and contemporary perspectives. In doing so he identifies three stages of American race relations: The first encompasses the period of antebellum slavery and the early postbellum era; the second extends from the last quarter of the nineteenth century to the New Deal era; the third covers the post-

World War II modern industrial era. Essentially what Wilson argues is that during the first two eras blacks were systematically excluded from any meaningful participation in the economy because of their race. Up to the end of the New Deal era, labor markets were characterized by a system of institutionalized racism. However, the advent of World War II opened up expanded job opportunities for blacks, which ushered in a period of progressive transition from race inequalities to class inequalities. In sum, Wilson argues that class position has become as important as race, if not more so, in determining the life chances of black Americans. Unfortunately, opportunities for many blacks have become greatly diminished as their class position has excluded them from any meaningful economic participation.

What began to occur in the 1960s and culminated in the 1980s is the creation of a permanently entrenched black underclass (Wilson, 1978). The changing nature of the economy (e.g., the decline in industrial and manufacturing jobs and the erosion of many unskilled, entry-level positions) has created a separate class mostly composed of black Americans who have little chance of successfully competing in a largely advanced technological society. The major characteristics of this underclass are ". . . their poverty and the social decay in which they are forced to survive" (Pinkney, 1984, p. 170). Often unable to subsist within the legal economy, many of the underclass take refuge in the illegal subeconomy such as prostitution, gambling, drugs, and the like (Fagan et al., 1986; Miller, 1986). Frequently they express their frustration in acts of expressive and instrumental violence, as witnessed in the recent resurgence of youth gang activity (Hagedorn et al., 1987). As a result, members of the underclass comprise the bulk of juvenile and adult institutionalized populations and represent the most frequent clients of the criminal justice system.

Expanding on Wilson's thesis, Lehman (1986a, b) has examined the origin of the underclass by focusing on the city of Chicago. In doing so, Lehman identifies three major factors that characterize Chicago's black underclass. The first is a series of migratory patterns that began in the early 1900s. These migrations involved the movement of large numbers of blacks from rural southern plantations to the industrialized north. They came principally to improve their economic position by obtaining jobs in the industries of northern cities such as Chicago. The second migration occurring during the 1960s involved the departure of the black middle- and working-classes from the inner city. Seeking a better quality of life, these blacks often relocated in the suburbs, with their improved housing, schools, and other services. As Silberman (1978) notes, an indirect effect of this second migration was the removal of black leadership and economic power from the inner city. In one sense, then, inner-city areas were left to stagnate and perpetuate a vicious cycle of pathology, disorganization, poverty, and crime.

A second characteristic of Chicago's black underclass is its southern roots. According to Lehman (1986a) the mass migrations transferred the rural sharecropper mentality of the south to the northern cities. Rapid urbanization and residential isolation combined to produce a culture of failure that only the strong were able to escape.

A third characteristic, and most important in terms of this discussion, is the predominance of female-based households (Lehman, 1986a). Chicago's black underclass is characterized by high illegitimate birth rates and single-parent homes typically revolving around the mother. The single most important factor associated with those who were able to escape the ghetto was having been raised in a two-parent household.

As Lehman (1986a, b) suggests, what characterized those who were able to overcome their underclass position was typically a two-parent household that stressed values conducive to hard work and success. However, as other research has shown, one-parent households may be the result of poverty, unemployment, and other social factors rather than the cause of these conditions (see, for example, Volume 1, Chapter 5). Together Wilson (1978), Pinkney (1984), and Lehman (1986a, b) identify a black underclass that is unable to compete effectively in today's economic market, remains in a state of extreme poverty, and frequently has a family structure and value system that maintains and perpetuates their underclass position. Unfortunately, there is no indication that conditions will improve, at least in the near future. Recent data, for example, indicate that economic polarization between the earned income of two-parent black families and single female households is continuing to increase (Farley, 1984).

This discussion has focused on blacks and the underclass because they are its principal occupants. However, the underclass is larger in scope and includes other minority groups as well as poor whites. Many of the underclass characteristics associated with black, single-parent households, such as low earned income, are also associated with white, single-parent households (Farley, 1984). The point to be stressed is that family structure, poverty, and the poverty environ-

ment may combine in such a way that high rates of crime and
delinquency are the likely results. In their study of violent, delinquent inner-city youth, Fagan and colleagues (1986, p. 463) con-
clude:

> The association of weakened maternal authority with violent delin-
> quents points to the impact of poverty on the family. The absence of
> material resources in inner-city neighborhoods will naturally weaken
> the ability of single parents (predominantly mothers) to control and
> socialize adolescents. Family composition of the violent delinquents
> often includes an adult other than birth parent or stepparent. While the
> relationship between family composition and delinquency is still un-
> clear, these data suggest that family process and resources are attenu-
> ated by neighborhood resources.

THEORETICAL PERSPECTIVES ON CRIME AND THE FAMILY

To varying degrees, most theoretical explanations of crime and
delinquency can incorporate family variables. Although biological,
psychological, and sociological interpretations seek explanations in
different aspects of human behavior, the context of family life can
enhance our understanding of those processes leading to crime and
delinquency. In the few remaining pages, it would be an impossible
task to review all existing theory related to crime and delinquency.
Therefore, this discussion is limited to those perspectives that seem
to be the most relevant in linking family experiences to later acts of
crime and delinquency. Before beginning this discussion, it should be
emphasized that there is no one, all-encompassing theoretical explanation for the etiology of crime. Although some theories are more
elegant and sophisticated than are others and have been subject to
more empirical testing, none offers a complete explanation. Further,
all existing theory has been criticized on logical and empirical
grounds (Lincoln & Kirpatrick, 1985; Vold & Bernard, 1986). With
these caveats in mind, the following is an attempt to make some
sense out of the research findings discussed previously.

Writing at the turn of the century, Emile Durkheim (1964), the
eminent French sociologist, developed the concept of anomie, or
"normlessness" to explain pathological conditions existing in society. According to Durkheim, as society became more complex and
industrialized, people no longer knew what rules to follow and obey.
The customary ways of behaving in a more simple or communal
society were no longer applicable. The sense of anomie introduced

by a more complex division of labor led to increased rates of suicide, mental illness, crime, and delinquency. Hence, changing structural conditions within society led to increases in individual pathology. Taking Durkheim's lead, Robert K. Merton, a contemporary criminologist, revised the theory in an attempt to explain crime among the urban lower classes.

According to Merton (1968), modern society comprises a system of goals (ends) to which people aspire and different ways (means) of achieving them. In the United States the success goal is all pervasive and is usually defined in terms of monetary success. Legitimate opportunities for achieving success are differentially distributed so that not all people have equal access to them. Often those in the urban lower classes, while striving to achieve success, have limited legitimate opportunities and are then pushed toward illegitimate avenues to achieve their goals. Merton identified five modes of adaptation consisting of conformity, innovation, ritualism, retreatism, and rebellion. Of these, only the first two are important to this discussion. The conformist accepts society's goals and engages in legitimate means to achieve them—for example, university students who study and prepare themselves for future rewards. The innovator, on the other hand, also accepts the goals of society but rejects (or is unable to attain) legitimate means for achieving them. Hence, the innovator is likely to engage in delinquent and criminal acts to achieve success. This latter type is most commonly found among the urban poor.

Silberman (1978) uses Merton's theory to explain the relationship between poverty and crime. According to Silberman (1978), the factors that characterize lower-class life have their origin in the fact that American cultural goals (success) transcend class lines while the means of achieving them do not. Further, subcultural role models reinforce the fact that one can succeed through the illegal economy. As Silberman (1978, p. 121) notes:

> . . . the fabric and texture of life in urban slums and ghettos provide an environment in which opportunities for criminal activity are manifold, and in which the rewards for engaging in crime appear to be high— higher than the penalties for crime, and higher than the rewards for avoiding it.

Thus, Silberman (1978) combines Merton's (1968) opportunity structure theory linking poverty and crime to the emergence of a subculture that reinforces criminal and delinquent values.

Miller (1958) focuses on the emergence of the lower-class sub-culture and its relationship to the criminal justice system. According to Miller (1958), lower-class enclaves are characterized by a predominance of female-based households. Because there are few male role models present within the household, youths gain status and self-esteem from association with peers on the street. Miller (1958) further contends that there exists a lower-class way of life that is characterized by a distinct value system. These values, or "focal concerns," consist of trouble, toughness, smartness, excitement, fate, and autonomy. For example, according to Miller (1958) the lower-class person believes that life is trouble and what happens is in the hands of fate, for there is little that one can do to control one's circumstances. To survive, one has to be tough, smart, and able to take care of oneself. By conforming to these values, lower-class persons face a greater risk of breaking the law and becoming involved in the juvenile and adult criminal justice systems (Nettler, 1984). Thus, for Miller (1958), female-based households (most frequently found in poverty environments) are a major precipitating factor of a lower-class lifestyle that increases the risk of criminal involvement. It should be noted, however, that Miller's writings reflect the social conventions and conditions of the 1950s. More recent writings also emphasize the problem of father-absent households.

Although Miller (1958) and other subcultural theorists (Vold & Bernard, 1986) recognize the importance of family and peer influence, social control theorists begin to specify how that influence is transmitted. Central to control theory is the process of socialization. Children do not learn by instinct but rather must be socialized into acceptable patterns of behavior. Parental influence is central to the transmission of values (Rogers, 1977), especially in the early stages of life. As noted previously, many delinquents report unpleasant family experiences and have frequently rejected one or more of their parents or have been rejected by them (Medinnas, 1965). Control theory differs from most other theoretical perspectives in its starting premise. Rather than asking the question of why people commit criminal and delinquent acts, control theorists instead ask the question, "Why don't we all do it?" In other words, what bonds people to society, thus inhibiting such behavior?

Hirschi (1969) formulated the basic tenets of control theory from a sociological perspective and subsequently tested it on a sample of high school populations. Hirschi identified four components that bonded individuals to society, thus reducing delinquent and criminal behavior. These consisted of: (a) attachment, or the degree to which people are sensitive to the wishes and values of others; (b) commitment, or the degree to which people invest time and effort in conventional activity; (c) involvement, or the degree to which people are engrossed or emerged in conventional values and activities; and (d) belief, or the degree to which people accept the moral validity of conventional rules (Hirschi, 1969).

Using a self-report survey, Hirschi (1969) found that attachment to parents was strongly related to law-abiding and conventional behavior regardless of class position. Those youths who were sensitive to the wishes and values of their parents were less likely to be delinquent irrespective of whether the parents were upper-, middle-, or lower-class. As Hirschi (1969, p. 94) notes, "Consistent with much previous research, then, the present data indicate that the closer the child's relations with his parents, the more he is attached to and identifies with them, the lower his chances of delinquency."

Attachment to school and conventional friends were also found to be important inhibitors of delinquent activity. Academic ability, good school performance, and being sensitive to the opinions of one's teachers were strong predictors of lawful behavior as well as close personal associations with conventional friends. Thus, control theory stresses the importance of family relationships and views poor relations between parents and children as a major factor linked to future delinquency. However, as Merton (1968), among others, would emphasize, attachment to conventional, law-abiding behavior is undermined if the opportunity for adequate jobs, housing, and the like proves to be unavailable.

Finally, social learning theory has traditionally emphasized the importance of family in the process of socialization. Whereas control theory focuses on the bond of the child to his or her parents in the form of attachment, social learning theory focuses on the process by which children learn the "rules of the game." A primary place where this learning takes place is within the context of family life. If the messages given by the parents and other social groups are positive and if the child adequately receives them, then other influences being equal, the child is more apt to develop in socially-approved directions. Recent theories regarding family systems emphasize that children acquire much of their social learning from schools, neighborhoods, day care programs, mass media, and the like.

There is also a biogenic component to social learning theory that attempts to explain why some children are less adept than others in receiving messages. One approach is provided by Eysenck (1977) who argues that delinquents and adult criminals tend to be extroverted personalities who are generally stimulus seekers. According to Eysenck, extroverts condition more poorly than introverts in that they need more reinforcement to receive and learn the messages. The basis for extroversion can be found in an imbalance often associated with the autonomic nervous system. Thus, Eysenck's theory seeks to explain individual differences in the process of social learning. Other researchers emphasize other constitutional factors that may affect a child's temperament at birth, with some children being especially active and difficult to control from their early infancy. Interactions of parents and others with such children shape their behavioral tendencies. However, this is a large complex topic beyond the scope of this chapter.

All the theoretical perspectives briefly discussed above, in one way or another, touch on the role of the family in the genesis of crime and delinquency. Strain or opportunity theory (Merton, 1968) focuses on the relationship between lack of legitimate and presence of illegitimate opportunity structures in poverty environments and their relationship to crime. Crime and delinquency have also been linked to the role of subcultures (Silberman, 1978) in reinforcing and providing opportunities for illegal behavior. Subcultural theory (Miller, 1958) deals with the presence of father-absent, female-based households and a lower-class life-style that frequently leads to involvement with the criminal justice system. Control theory (Hirschi, 1969) focuses on conventional bonds that link people to society and specifies attachment to parents as a major inhibitor of delinquent behavior. Social learning theory builds on control theory (Conger, 1980) by examining the process by which messages (or norms of acceptable behavior) are transmitted within the family. When the lessons are poor or improperly taught, it is more likely that the child will be maladjusted. It may also be the case that some children are less receptive to the messages (Eysenck, 1977) even when they are positive. Thus, research and theory point to a link between family life and, in combination with other factors, the possibility of future maladaptive behaviors. As Fagan and colleagues (1986, p. 443) note in their study of delinquency in the inner city:

> . . . poor interaction with family members, schools, legal institutions, or employers presents opportunities and motivations to associate with

delinquent peers which in turn leads to serious delinquency. And these events appear to be the outcome of a developmental sequence beginning in the family and proceeding through school, peer and community influences.

SUMMARY

This chapter has reviewed trends, research, and theory that link family-life factors to the possibility of future involvement in crime and delinquency. It has also briefly reviewed the impact that criminal involvement may have on the family. Data from the Uniform Crime Reports and the National Crime Panel reveal that the problem of violence within the family is a continuing and serious issue, as shown in Chapter 7 of this volume. Homicides, for example, are most likely to occur among family members, friends, and other acquaintances. Spouse and child abuse is a relatively frequent occurrence, and there is evidence to suggest that those who were abused as children are more likely than others to become future abusers. Some research suggests that violence within the family is linked to nonfamily violence and crime (Straus, 1985).

Further, Farrington and colleagues (1985, p. 205) discovered that "If one or more other members of his family have a criminal conviction, an individual has a considerably increased risk of acquiring a criminal record himself." Although research on the family has not revealed consistent findings, there is evidence to suggest that factors associated with certain families may provide a push into delinquent and criminal behavior. Thus, divorce and single-parent homes, inappropriate parental discipline, poor supervision, lack of positive attachment to parents, large family size, and the like have been identified in one way or another as potential correlates of maladjusted behavior. Contextual conditions such as extreme poverty and unemployment were also seen to interact with family characteristics in correlation with criminal behavior.

Family Approaches to Treating Delinquents

7

JAMES F. ALEXANDER, HOLLY B. WALDRON,
ALICE M. NEWBERRY, AND NORMAN LIDDLE

To the consternation of many proponents of rehabilitation, during the last decade several major reviews of treatment programs for delinquents concluded that across the board "nothing works" (Berleman, 1980; Martinson, 1974; McCord, 1978). However, this conclusion has been effectively challenged in such recent major works as those by Garrett (1985), Gendreau and Ross (1980), and Greenwood and Zimring (1985). For example, using a metaanalysis approach, Garrett (1985) reviewed 111 studies (13,055 total subjects), all sufficiently well-controlled so that treatment effectiveness could be judged. This analysis demonstrated that across all studies there is evidence that intervention programs for delinquents do produce positive change.

Further, Garrett identified and evaluated 13 major intervention strategies in different treatment programs. The three strategies with the greatest magnitude of effect were family therapy, cognitive–behavioral techniques, and clear behavioral contingencies. In contrast, negligible effect sizes were obtained for such popular components as individual therapy, group therapy, and vocational approaches. Although sample sizes were too small to make confident assertions, Garrett also found that when the evaluation was restricted to the most rigorous studies, family therapy stood alone as the component with the highest effect size. Consistent with these findings, the purpose of this chapter is to discuss family therapy as a viable approach to treating delinquency, emphasizing two programs that have been demonstrated to be effective and replicable.

The two major family-based approaches that have been identified as having proven effective with delinquency are Behavioral Family Therapy and Functional Family Therapy (Gurman et al., 1986). Behavioral Family Therapy is identified primarily with Patterson and his associates at the Oregon Social Learning Center (OSLC). Patterson and Reid's (1970) classic paper on reciprocity and coercion, which emphasizes the interdependence of parent and child effects, shares with most family systems therapy models the assumption that families represent mutually causal networks (Speer, 1970). Nonetheless, Behavioral Family Therapy developed a parent-focused intervention program that emphasizes Garrett's third component of successful therapy, contingency management (Alexander et al., in press). The basic strategy of the model involves training parents to observe and appropriately reinforce the child's behaviors (Patterson, 1970; Patterson et al., 1973; Ross, 1979).

More recently the Behavioral Family Therapy model has come to see parental resistance or noncooperation as a major issue (Patterson, 1985). Consequently, the treatment process is currently conceptualized as being bidirectional between parents and therapist and having three primary components. The first is parent training in family management skills. These skills include monitoring, discipline, positive reinforcement, and family problem solving. Parents are trained to identify prosocial and antisocial behaviors, to design behavioral contracts, and to carefully monitor the child. The second component comprises what are loosely described as therapist clinical skills, necessary to minimize the resistance of parents. The third component is a support group for the therapist because the wearing effects of an obstinately resistant parent may reduce the efficiency of the therapist. The first two components have been shown to be useful, whereas the third has not been tested (Patterson, 1985).

The early work of the OSLC group was applied almost exclusively to preadolescent antisocial and aggressive children (Patterson et al., 1973; Viken et al., in press). More recently the OSLC has applied the same principles to adolescents identified as juvenile delinquents, particularly chronic or multiple-offending delinquents. This work with chronic delinquents clearly is successful (Marlowe et al., in press; Viken et al., in press). The two recent research efforts with chronic delinquents demonstrated significantly lowered numbers of offenses in all treatment groups with the exception of status offenses. In contrast, the control-group rates had actually increased during the same period. The reductions in offense rate still persisted in the third follow-up year.

Despite their successes the authors have a number of concerns with the meaning of their data. Because only about 18% of the treated subjects had no offenses in the 3 follow-up years, they believe that delinquency was not eradicated. The authors were also concerned about the generalizability of these results, both to other family behaviors and to other treatment contexts. No differences were found in the general family interaction patterns other than in the monitoring and control of targeted behaviors. In addition, staff members in their study had small caseloads, found the work theoretically interesting, and were given extensive support. Despite the optimum conditions of this study staff, burnout was still a problem. The researchers concluded that on a broad scale, over an unlimited period of time and under typical therapist working conditions, implementing a comparable delivery system would be difficult. Thus, the OSLC group views any work with chronic delinquents as unlikely to be cost effective and considers it more useful to work in a preventive program with preadolescent aggressive children who have been targeted as likely future juvenile delinquents (Viken et al., in press).

The second major family-based approach identified by Gurman and colleagues (1986) integrates behavioral, systems, and cognitive intervention strategies and is called the Functional Family Therapy (FFT) model. This model is reviewed in greater detail here. In an early demonstration of effectiveness using random assignment, this model produced reductions in recidivism of 21% to 47%, depending on the comparison group, at a 1-year follow-up interval (Alexander & Parsons, 1973). No treatment produced a 48% recidivism, two comparison treatments produced 46% and 73%, whereas FFT experienced only a 26% recidivism. A later evaluation at 3-year follow-up demonstrated a significant reduction in sibling referrals of 20% to 43%, (Klein et al., 1976).

While these early programs dealt with status delinquents, more recent evaluations involved multiple-offending "hard-core" delinquents who had averaged over 20 adjudicated offenses prior to program referral. These delinquents were imprisoned at the time of referral but were then released to the FFT program or alternative forms of treatment (e.g., group homes). Results demonstrated that compared to baseline (annual recidivism rate of 89%) and to alternative treatment (recidivism 93%), FFT demonstrated effectiveness with a 33% reduction in recidivism (recidivism 60%) at 16-month follow-up (Barton et al., 1985).

The effectiveness of FFT also has been demonstrated with probationers (repeat offenders of moderate severity) and with youth at high risk for foster placement (Barton et al., 1985). Moreover, the model has also been replicated at a different site with totally different treatment staff, producing recidivism rates of only 10% for the treated group and a 70% recidivism rate for controls (Gordon et al., 1985). Based on such outcomes, FFT often is cited as an important family-based program with demonstrated effectiveness for delinquents (e.g., Todd & Stanton, 1983).

The purpose of this chapter is to describe the elements and philosophy of this model, highlighting the model's particular strengths. These strengths include a strong research base; the inclusion of all three major components identified in Garrett's (1985) and Gendreau and Ross' (1980) reviews (a family focus, the use of cognitive techniques, and the use of specific behavior change techniques with consequences for behavior); a dialectical flavor of both generality and specificity that includes a multivariate and multilevel focus; and a careful specification of the different phases of intervention.

The outcome data reviewed above reflect the research base for the model. A considerable amount of additional research has focused on the process of family therapy, including the effects of therapist gender (Mas et al., 1985; Warburton et al., 1980), the effects of therapist characteristics (Alexander et al., 1976), and changes in family behavior (Parsons & Alexander, 1973). Recent research also has focused on some of the mechanisms of change in family therapy (Barton & Alexander, 1979; Mas, 1986; Morris et al., in press; Waldron, 1987). This research is described below as it applies to the therapy context.

The dialectical flavor of FFT derives from the inclusion of general principles that apply across most if not all families, coupled with goals and techniques that are individualized for each family. An effective model must have sufficient flexibility of techniques so as to be applicable across a variety of treatment contexts and populations. At the same time it must have sufficient conceptual integrity so that therapists and program developers can understand how general principles relate and can be uniquely tailored to each individual context. FFT postulates that all therapeutic contexts involve certain general features. At the same time FFT emphasizes the individualization of treatment goals and techniques for each case and the unique context in which it exists. This individualization requires a wide range of clinical maneuvers that can be applied differentially to individual contexts, a wider range of maneuvers than is generally described in other treatment programs.

These wide-range maneuvers contrast with juvenile delinquency treatment programs that have been developed with a relatively specific focus. Many approaches have assumed that delinquency results from one or more major deficiencies (e.g., parents are not in control; parents don't monitor and effectively consequate appropriate behaviors; parents and adolescents lack effective communication behaviors; the community fails to provide resources and extrinsic motivators). However, to be effective, an intervention program must be able to deal flexibly with not one or two but all these variables in various combinations.

Moreover, programs must be able to be adapted to the unique circumstances of each family. For example, many families of delinquents are economically deprived, but some are in fact wealthy. Many parents of delinquents have neglected their children, but others have been overprotective. And many delinquents appear to have learning problems, but others are clearly quick learners. FFT has the relatively broad multivariate and multilevel focus necessary for effectively working with the diverse delinquent population.

FFT also emphasizes that family therapy does not occur in a vacuum, nor can it by itself modify all the (at times seemingly myriad) factors that influence delinquent behavior. If family approaches fail to look outside the family, they fail to recognize that the "treatment unit" they are dealing with is part of a larger and very influential context. So while FFT treats the family as an interdependent unit, at the same time it formally considers extrafamilial factors in both assessment and treatment planning. For example, a learning-disabled adolescent's verbal aggression in school may in part result from the adolescent's frustration with an inappropriate classroom placement. The poor school placement may compound the conflict in the family when the adolescent's parents pressure him or her for better grades. Integrating a focus on schoolwork with family therapy may preclude school problems from "undoing" progress made in the therapy session. Similarly, collaborating with the adolescent's juvenile court probation officer may allow the therapist and the probation officer to develop a court treatment plan that is consistent with family therapy.

Finally, along with the family focus and the extrafamily focus, FFT integrates an individual focus. The values, needs, and behaviors of each individual family member are assessed in addition to more global family patterns. Further, as a therapeutic goal the needs of all family members must be respected and incorporated into family change. So-called family cure must not be accomplished at the expense of any single member.

In conceptually integrating individuals, intrafamily relationships, and extrafamily factors, FFT considers the bidirectional effects each of these levels has on one another (Alexander et al., in press). This consideration creates complexity for the therapist but at the same time provides the therapist with a wide range of possible avenues to change.

PHASES OF INTERVENTION: A SCHEMATIC FOR CHANGE

FFT and a more recently developed framework (AIM—Analysis of Intervention Model), which describes therapy process at a general level, have identified five phases in the process of family therapy. Each of these phases must be addressed if the intervention process is to work effectively (Alexander et al., 1983). Within each phase goals are described that often require unique therapist skills and techniques. The five phases of intervention articulated by the FFT and AIM Models are introduction/impression, assessment/understanding, induction/therapy, behavior change education, and generalization/termination. These phases are conceptually separate, but in practice therapists may switch between one phase and another on a frequent basis, to the point that some phases may appear to be occurring simultaneously. However, the tasks of some phases must be completed before the therapist can proceed to tasks of later stages. For example, a considerable amount of assessment must be accomplished to identify the targets of change before long-term change techniques can be initiated safely (Barton & Alexander, 1981).

The Introduction/Impression Phase

This phase concerns the clients' expectations that are created prior to therapeutic interaction, up to and including the clients' initial responses to the superficial stimulus qualities of the therapist as well as the service delivery system as a whole. For example, Mas and colleagues (1985) and Warburton and colleagues (1980) have demonstrated that therapist gender alone is a context for markedly different patterns of communication behavior among participants beginning early in the first session of family therapy. With younger female therapists (versus male therapists), fathers seem to be more defensive and less accepting of the therapist as "credible." Delinquents of both sexes also talk significantly less when the therapist is female versus male. These different patterns appear to demand different therapeutic strategies for male-versus-female family therapy trainees. For example, younger female therapists may need to move more quickly to the induction phase, which addresses resistance more directly. The application of therapeutic strategies is likely to be less effective if family therapy models ignore the differential impact of superficial therapist characteristics (e.g., attire) during the early moments of intervention (Alexander et al., 1983). Of course, therapist gender is but one of many variables that may influence client expectations.

The therapist's major goal in the introduction/impression phase of intervention is to create positive expectations for change in the family, taking into account the family's reactions to the therapist, agency, and referral process. Although the families' positive expectations must be maintained throughout the therapy process, this acquainting phase can be seen as relatively transitory because it ends at the point when therapists begin to engage in the processes of assessment, therapy, and education. Nevertheless, since this phase sets the stage for subsequent activities, it can either facilitate or inhibit the subsequent intervention process.

For family members' expectations to be productive, the therapist must present an image of one who can help move the family from its fixed, dysfunctional patterns of behavior to more positive patterns. More simply, family members must perceive the therapist as someone who can help them solve their problems and reduce their pain. To do so, the family therapist must appear credible as a helper to the family. Even the best therapist encounters resistance in moving a family toward its desired goals during subsequent phases of treatment if at the outset the family finds the therapist unconvincing as a change agent. For example, a 16-year-old minority gang member from a lower-class background may wonder how a middle-aged, well-to-do white therapist in a three-piece suit could empathize with or understand him. Similarly, the father of a delinquent youth might have trouble accepting an unmarried young female therapist in jeans as a credible change agent because "she couldn't possibly know what it's like to be the parent of an adolescent."

The Assessment Phase

Assessment occurs throughout the intervention process but receives greatest emphasis during and between the first few sessions. During these sessions one of the therapist's goals is to identify the affective, behavioral, and cognitive expectations of each family member. In addition, the therapist must understand what family processes must be changed and what family variables, including reactions to the therapist, will enhance and/or impede beneficial change. This helps the therapist to understand actual and potential sources of resistance and to plan the unique set of changes that must be accomplished in each family. The therapist's own reactions, the clients' behaviors, and formal assessment devices such as questionnaires can be sources of information that yield both subjective and objective information about the behavior, affect, and cognitions of clients.

From this information the therapist can devise a unique assessment picture for each family that takes into account the characteristics and needs of each individual as well as the fit between these individual characteristics at the relationship level. For example, the family therapist may observe a situation in which the daughter of a single-parent father is constantly getting into trouble with the law. This behavior pulls the father into contact with his daughter and away from his girlfriend. The FFT therapist would involve all three persons, finding ways for the daughter to maintain a relationship with the father that does not involve pathological behaviors while helping the father develop skills so that he can, if he chooses, keep his relationship with his girlfriend intact.

The therapist skills necessary during this phase to elicit and interpret relevant information and identify the targets for change are intelligence, perceptiveness, and the use of a clear conceptual model. This model can help the therapist distinguish between those aspects of delinquent families that must be changed (e.g., coercive family processes—see Patterson & Reid, 1970) and those aspects that can be allowed to remain unchanged without interfering with long-term beneficial outcomes. For example, FFT considers it unnecessary to change either the presence or absence of certain basic values (e.g., political and religious) and basic functions of interpersonal behavior (e.g., interpersonal distance–closeness needs). In fact, FFT argues that techniques that attempts to change interpersonal functions elicit considerable resistance and are inappropriate for use in a short-term intervention program (Barton & Alexander, 1981).

Assessing Functions

The FFT concept of a person's interpersonal function is unique to this model. People develop characteristic interpersonal ways to regulate their relationships, and the concept of function helps the therapist understand how each of the members of a particular family accomplishes this end. Stated simply, a function is the interpersonal interdependency one person attempts to create with another. Because people may have markedly different capacities, learned behaviors, and behavioral contexts, different people can have different ways to attain their desired interdependency. Regardless of how functions are achieved, relationships between any two individuals can be reduced to three basic interpersonal states: closeness (high interdependency), distance (low interdependency), or a mixture that is an in-between amount of each (midpointing).

Although the functional states of contact/closeness and distance/independence are often seen as opposite ends of a continuum, it is more accurate to consider each as a separate dimension. The magnitude of each dimension can vary from little to large amounts. For example, a teenager can create considerable distance (e.g., by running away to another state), can create considerable contact (e.g., by becoming depressed and overtly begging for nurturance), and can send strong messages of both (e.g., by alternating messages of anger with messages of dependency). When family therapists are observing a set of problematic interactions, the result of these interpersonal payoffs and interactions from a relational standpoint must be addressed; that is, what was their function in regulating relationships within this family? By asking this question, therapists can often achieve an insight into families' behaviors when the family members are unable to tell them. For example, a mother's arguments with her teenage daughter may pull the father out of his usual isolated behavior and into a disciplining role along with the mother. In such a situation, one function of the argument is to force the father into involvement. However, if in a different situation the same argument forces the father out of the house, then in this case one function of the argument is to create distance for the father.

Therefore, to understand families, therapists must look beyond the apparent problem and refocus on all relationships and the interpersonal impact of repetitive, problematic, behavioral sequences. In this process therapists often must go beyond the motives people verbalize and focus on the interpersonal results—the function of the behavior. Therapists must understand both the context and functions of problematic behavior to understand why family members contribute to interactions that on the surface seem to create misery for all of them (Barton & Alexander, 1981).

A problem that can arise for both therapists and family members is to think of these functions as good or bad. Our society typically stereotypes closeness or intimacy as desirable in relationships and distance as undesirable. However, "smothering" represents closeness but in the nonadaptive form of enmeshment. Furthermore, rather than being necessarily "bad," maintaining distance from other people may facilitate the development of independent thinking and a sense of autonomy and competence. Thus, both types of functions are legitimate. The ways people attain them may be problematic, however, and may need to be changed. For example, the adolescent who attains contact by constantly being "in trouble" should not be labeled "bad" because of the function of closeness that is created. The behavior used to create the contact is unacceptable, but not the function per se. Thus, in FFT the therapist modifies the family system so that some alternative behavior such as seeking advice in a friendly manner can serve to create contact/closeness.

Some members in family systems may behave in ways that produce neither closeness nor distance but contain elements of both functions. This "midpointing" function also can be expressed in either adaptive or maladaptive ways. For example, a drug-abusing adolescent may at times use his addiction as a way of escaping from his family and at other times use it as a way of bringing them closer ("You need to help me pay this fine"). There also can be nonpathological expressions of midpointing, such as the teenager who remains active in her family's affairs but also has a part-time job after school and a boyfriend with whom she spends time. Both of these contexts create a balance of contact and distance, albeit in very different ways.

An important factor to be considered is that functions are unique to each relationship. A teenage girl simultaneously may create the functions of distancing from her father, midpointing with her mother, and closeness with her boyfriend. In addition, while certain behaviors more commonly produce certain functions (e.g., running away produces distance), a particular behavior must never be assumed to create a specific function. For example, an adolescent's running away, which may create distance for the adolescent in some families, characteristically may produce an end result of contact/ closeness in other families. Thus, an entire behavioral sequence must be examined and the final result determined so that an accurate functional assessment can be inferred for each family member.

As a result, for each family a unique assessment picture must be drawn that takes into account the characteristics and needs of each individual. Then the picture must identify the configurations, that is, "fit" between these individual characteristics at the relationship level. For example, a total blended family picture may involve a mother's functions of closeness with her new husband while she is simultaneously midpointing with her daughter and young son. The daughter in turn may attempt to create closeness with her boyfriend, midpointing with her brother and stepfather, and distance from her mother. The stepfather may be developing closeness with his new wife and distancing with the children, and the son may attempt to achieve closeness with his parents and distance from his sister. All these functions must be ascertained and taken into consideration when long-term change is initiated.

The Induction/Therapy Phase

This phase specifically targets the motivational and attributional realities of disturbed families. Family members typically enter therapy with strong ideas about what the problems are and who is "to blame." In delinquent families these blaming attributions often center around the traits or dispositions of the referred adolescent. This adolescent is frequently seen as "the problem": "If only he (she) was not so 'lazy' (or 'irresponsible'), everything would be fine." The recipient of the negative attributions in turn tends to meet the expectations of the family by behaving defensively and being uncooperative (Alexander & Parsons, 1982). Upon referral for delinquent behavior, then, other family members tend to view therapy as a way to "fix" the member who is seen as causing the problem. Often, however, therapy is not expected to work, as the family has given up on finding a solution.

Explaining problems in terms of personality is quite common. Attribution theorists see people as having a need to explain and predict the events around them, particularly those involving other people (Heider, 1958). When problems begin to arise, a cause is searched for, usually in terms of a trait attributed to one or more family members (Jones & Davis, 1965). Once this label has been applied, it serves to explain and predict future behavior, which in turn reinforces the label. The family develops patterns of interaction that maintain the dysfunctional behaviors (Brehm & Smith, 1986; Minuchin, 1974; Snyder & Swann, 1978; Watzlawick et al., 1967).

The primary goal of the induction/therapy phase is to change this situation by creating a context or climate in which families are willing and motivated to change. During this phase, therapists set the stage for long-term change by changing the meaning of family members' behavior with particular emphasis on decreasing negative attributions. If family members can be helped to consider their behavior as being motivated and maintained by variables other than individual malevolence (i.e., "they don't know how to show their affection"; "expressing anger is really demonstrating concern"), they are much more motivated to change and more likely to see it as possible. This, along with focusing on relationships, are the therapist's two major strategies for effecting cognitive changes in families.

Surprisingly, to do this the therapist first must "confuse" the family by disrupting the negative attributions family members have about each other and requiring them to search for new explanations of family behavior (Morris et al., in press). There are many maneuvers that allow the therapist to accomplish these goals, but these strategies cannot be applied in a cookbook fashion (Alexander & Newberry, in press). Instead, the therapist must respond contingently to different members so that each member within a family feels that the therapist hears, cares for, and empathizes with her or him. Further, because the therapist is interacting with a specific family and, indeed, with a number of specific individuals, the therapist's behavior must fit the value system, learning history, and the intellectual abilities of each family member. Techniques must be plausible and appropriate for each individual as well as the family members taken together. Thus, while the therapist needs interpersonal skill and sensitivity in any phase of intervention, these characteristics are essential for success in the induction/therapy phase.

A number of cognitive techniques are used heavily in the induction phase (Alexander & Parsons, 1982). *Relabeling* changes the meaning and value of a negative behavior by describing positive antonym properties of the behavior, and/or by suggesting positive motives for the behavior, and/or by portraying family members as victims rather than perpetrators (Barton & Alexander, 1981). For example, a delinquent may be described as someone who is struggling to become independent and is confused about her identity (Morris et al., in press). A relabel gives family members new information about behaviors and is most effective if it ascribes benign or benevolent motives. *Nonblaming* lowers defensiveness and allows for the possibility of changing without being forced to admit fault for previous difficulties. If family members can see others in the family as victims, then the maladaptive patterns of hostility are diminished.

Another useful technique is *overtly discussing* what would happen if the symptom were removed. For example, to help family members consider other relationship issues, a therapist may ask what a marriage would be like if the adolescent was not a constant problem. The therapist may also attempt *changing the impact or context of the symptom* by exaggerating the symptom. If the parents of a young fire setter are instructed to monitor the child as he lights matches, the interactions around his fire setting are dramatically changed (Minuchin, 1974). The symptom has lost its meaning, and the typical sequence of parental behaviors after fire setting is changed (Alexander & Parsons, 1982). *Shifting the focus* from one problem or person to another is sometimes useful in demonstrating the relational impact of symptoms. The therapist can move to issues in the family by changing the emphasis from the identified patient.

Focusing on the relationship also "takes the heat off" the identified patient, which may allow him or her to be less defensive and willing to change with the rest of the family. In disturbed families, individuals don't usually see their behavior as contributing to their current difficulties in a contingent or interdependent fashion. Rather, they view their own behavior as a necessary reaction to the misbehavior of other members (Barton & Alexander, 1981). Part of the therapist's job is to point out the interactions between family members so that they become aware of how they affect each other and how the relationships affect their behavior. For example, Sam is a straight-A student who gets lots of praise from his mom, a single parent. Sam's little brother, George, age 13, recently started stealing and using drugs. Their therapist can shift the focus from George's "problem" by helping the family to understand George's need for attention and feelings of inadequacy when compared to Sam.

The therapist can begin to make this shift by using yet other techniques, those of *asking relational questions* and *identifying sequences*. The therapist can guide the family away from discussions of the adolescent's misbehavior by asking about relationships and about the roles people play in the family. This can help families to see how their behaviors are contingent on one another. When families tend to become involved in rapid chains of interaction, identifying these sequences helps to slow the interaction. If Mom is complaining about Debbie's misbehavior, for example, the therapist may ask how Grandma, who lives with the family, fits in. What was she doing during the last argument? In contrast, asking questions about the "problem person" may encourage blaming.

Two other techniques the therapist can use are *making nonblaming process comments* on the apparent impact various behaviors and feelings have on other family members and *showing how feelings, behaviors, and thoughts interrelate*. These comments help family members to see themselves as having unhappy relationships in which everyone is suffering instead of having a bad person in the family. For example, in Debbie's family Grandma may dread coming home from work because both Mom and Debbie will want her immediate support. The therapist can point out how one person's behavior is interpreted by another and how that person then feels. This technique diminishes the need to prove that someone else is the cause of the problem. For example, Mom may be thinking that Debbie does not need her anymore when Debbie tries to assert her independence. Further, Grandma interprets both their behavior as a demand for her to take sides.

Making interpretations goes beyond the obvious and makes inferences about long-term motivations and the impact of behaviors. The therapist uses knowledge about the family, inferences, and guesswork to make interpretations about behavior. These can be very powerful in changing people's understanding of their family's history. For example, Roger has been caught stealing several times. During court-referred therapy, the therapist learns that Roger's dad left home early in life after a family battle. His mom was 15 years old when she married Roger's dad. The therapist may suggest that neither parent had any experience in the normal exiting of a teenager from the home. Thus, Roger knows no other way to "grow up" and leave his family than to get in trouble.

Finally, *stopping and starting interactions* is also an option for the therapist. Stopping an interaction that is a customary pattern for the family helps them experience a change, albeit brief, in the usual outcome. Coupled with relabeling, the therapist may reduce the blaming that takes place between family members. As the family interacts in a less blaming fashion, they may in turn change their perspective on the behaviors being discussed. The therapist may also ask the family to try a new positive interaction, which again can foster positive attributions and an increased motivation for change. For example, Susan is an adolescent with cerebral palsy. She has been violating her curfew by coming home after dark, alone, in her wheelchair. By the time she enters the door, her mother is so distraught that a battle begins at once. The therapist may concentrate on Susan's need for independence and point out that the family can discuss safer ways to reach this goal. The therapist then can help Susan and her mother discuss a plan for Susan to go to a city museum alone during the daytime. They could negotiate on issues of safety and let Susan demonstrate her ability to cope more independently.

While engaging in these various techniques, the therapist must take care to avoid forming a coalition with one family member at the expense of another. For example, a parent often tries to enlist a therapist, particularly a therapist of the same sex, to be on his or her side. If not dealt with carefully, this process can alienate a teenager and/or the other parent in the family. The therapist can sometimes overtly comment on how he or she fits into the family system as a way of defusing these coalition attempts and reducing the defensiveness of the other family members.

The Behavior Change/Education Phase

The major goal of this phase is to produce long-term behavior change in the family. During the previously described induction/ therapy phase, techniques are used to change the meaning of behavior, the attributions family members have about one another, and family members' motivations. Although such changes are important prerequisites to long-term change, by themselves those changes may not be maintained unless interaction patterns are changed in a carefully planned way. Behavior change education is designed to implement these latter changes and involves the application of behavior-change techniques such as communication training, contracting, modeling, and the manipulation of environmental events. Which of the activities or techniques are used and how they are applied in changing interaction patterns depends on the configuration of individual characteristics and relationship patterns previously identified in assessment.

A successful induction/therapy phase can create positive motivation and even attempts at change on the part of the family. To avoid false starts and perhaps disillusionment, therapists must take control early in the behavior-change phase. During this time the goal is not so much to develop "final" positive interactions but to initiate new and positive interactions so the family can experience that such interactions are possible (Alexander & Parsons, 1982).

Interactions during this phase are highly structured and usually involve some degree of communication training and technical aids.

Sessions are also held as closely together as possible, again to minimize the family's opportunity to relapse into maladaptive interacting between sessions. By maximizing the success experience of families, the therapist can decrease resistance and continue the positive momentum established through increased family motivation in the induction phase. If initial behavior-change attempts are unsuccessful during this phase, the high degree of structure and short time frame make it easier to target exactly what went wrong. When change attempts do go awry, the problem may be therapy technology or may be therapist skill (Warburton & Alexander, 1985). That is, an inappropriate behavior-change strategy may have been presented or the therapist may not have been sufficiently clear, directive, and otherwise informative for family members to be able to carry out the behavior.

However, even technically correct and well-developed behavior-change strategies will fail, that is, meet resistance, if they are inconsistent with one or more of the family members' interpersonal functions. Therapists must match the correct intervention techniques in a way that protects each family member's functions. Resistance arises if the therapist begins to elicit changes from one family member without simultaneously making certain the changes allow others to maintain the functions they previously held. For example, consider a truant adolescent whose behavior provides a context for her father's contact/closeness function with her mother who otherwise is distant from him. That is, the daughter's acting out allows the father to call the mother and talk to her about the problem, whereas the mother stays very busy in her job when the "kids don't need me." While a contingency contract with the daughter may reduce the daughter's truancy, such an intervention alone, which decreases the delinquent behavior, may not allow for maintaining the father's interdependency (closeness function) with his wife. If this is the case, the father may resist or "undermine" change. Hence, the intervention must be tailored not only to address the target behavior but to do so while not interrupting other family members' functions (Barton & Alexander, 1981).

Thus, during the education phase, noncompliance (or resistance, in "traditional" terms) may occur if the tasks of earlier phases such as assessment have not been completely and effectively accomplished. When resistance occurs, therapists must change their conceptual "set" and "recycle" back to the assessment/understanding and induction/therapy phases to identify and modify the family parameters that are producing the resistance, before again proceeding with the treatment/education phase (Warburton & Alexander, 1985).

The Generalization/Termination Phase

The goals of the generalization/termination phase are to maintain the changes previously initiated while producing independence from the therapist. The therapist in this phase attempts to disengage from the family and provide temporal and setting generalizability. To accomplish this, the therapist must ensure that not only have the referral problems been terminated but also that family members have been able to develop adaptive interaction patterns and problem-solving styles. Additionally, these interaction processes and problem-solving styles must be spontaneous and operate independently of the therapist's constant monitoring and prompting.

If this spontaneity and independence are not evident, specific educational techniques that ensure generalization must be applied. Such techniques begin with the therapist taking a less active role in intrafamily process. As family members experience short-term changes, they are helped to consider alternative ways to continue positive change. However, rather than dictating highly structured interactions that are designed to last only a few days, the therapist asks family members if they can develop techniques that might work for them on their own and at the same time extends the interval between sessions.

During this time, therapists also consider and sometimes deal directly with relevant extrafamily influences such as school personnel, employees, and so on. In doing so, FFT specifically can help families interact more effectively with extrafamilial influences not only by enhancing adaptive intrafamilial processes but also by anticipating extrafamilial stresses and helping family members develop more effective interactive styles to deal with them. On occasion FFT therapists even deal directly with extrafamilial influences such as legal and educational systems on behalf of the family, particularly during the later stages of therapy when a family is about to complete therapy (Alexander et al., 1983). During sessions family members are helped by exploring, and often role playing, solutions to future difficulties with other family members and extrafamily influences. For example, the therapist may role play the principal while the delinquent practices positive assertive behaviors in order to be allowed back into school. Parents in turn are helped to learn how to facilitate such behaviors.

CONCLUDING REMARKS

At this point it is important to restate that the skills and techniques presented here cannot be discussed in strict behavioral terms independent of the family members' reactions. Each phase of family therapy represents a context for therapist–family interaction, and the meaning and impact of the therapist's behavior in each phase is a function of all participants. That is, therapist goals and behaviors cannot be defined in terms of their intent and form alone because their meaning and impact depend on family members. For example, a female therapist's behavior that might be perceived as "warm" when directed at a teenage daughter may be perceived quite differently (e.g., seductive) if the very same behavior is directed at the father. And to add further complexity, that behavior that the daughter perceives as warm may be seen by Mom as "coddling" or "siding with" the daughter.

This contextual and interactive nature of family therapy requires that therapists (and family therapy researchers) must consider two different kinds of "reality." One reality is that perceived by the therapist based on his or her theory, experience, intuition, and various sources of information. The other reality (actually, set of realities) represents how each family member perceives events. The therapist's and family members' realities exist in a parallel fashion, and while they may overlap, these realities are not necessarily integrated at a given point. In the induction phase, the therapist must focus on reality as the family experiences it and may choose to withhold even accurate interpretations if these interpretations will be experienced as blaming by family members (Haley, 1963).

In the assessment phase the therapist's focus is on reality as the therapist experiences it and is based on the therapist's conceptual model. Then in behavior change education both realities must be considered: Change techniques must produce the changes identified by the therapist, but at the same time the changes must make sense to the family. Thus, during behavior change education a true partnership emerges where all participants work toward an overtly and consensually defined goal. This partnership continues throughout the rest of treatment as family members, using their own energy and motivation, become increasingly skilled at solving their own problems. Therapists and family members alike enjoy the fact that, in a sense, therapists become increasingly "useless" to the point of successful termination.

8

Neglect in Families

ALFRED KADUSHIN

"Child neglect" is a subset of the broader rubric "child maltreatment," which includes all kinds of harm to the child—physical abuse, sexual abuse, emotional abuse, and the various kinds of neglect. Other terms have been used to identify "child mistreatment" and the "endangered child." We use the term "child maltreatment" to designate the broader context of which neglect is a subset.

Public interest in child abuse and neglect has had an uneven history. "Discovered" as a social problem in the 1870s, there was a sudden and dramatic growth of public concern about the problem. Between 1874 when the first of the societies for prevention of cruelty to children was organized and 1900, some 150 such organizations were developed in one city after another. Cases of neglect were frequently included in the reports of work done. Thus, the 1881 report of the Boston Society includes such items as:

> Case 1349: Three children ages 3 to 13. Dirty, ragged, almost naked, no furniture, no food. Father interferate and indifferent. Mother dead. Rescued under the "neglect laws."
>
> Case 1375: Four children, ages 5 months to 9 years. Father interferate. Sickly. Mother negligent and dissolute absenting herself for weeks at a time, abandoning her nursing infant. (Bremmer, 1971, p. 204)

As a matter of fact, while the titles of early protective service agencies emphasized the prevention of cruelty, suggesting a focus on abuse, most of the cases were of neglect.

In examining the case records of the British National Society for the Protection of Cruelty to Children, Behlmer (1982, p. 181) notes that

> . . . By the opening years of the 20th century a great majority of its cases involved neglected rather than physically abused children. Whereas assaults on the young constituted roughly half of the societies' complaints in four of the first five years, by 1900 these cases made up only an eighth of its total work. And after a quarter century of experience the National Society for the Prevention of Cruelty to Children found that a mere 7% of its complaints could be attributed to "violence."

Following World War I, however, interest in the problem of child maltreatment dropped from public concern. The number of protective agencies declined, and funding and activities were curtailed.

Child maltreatment was "rediscovered" in the 1960s, this time, however, under different auspices. The "rediscovery" was given primary impetus by radiologists and pediatricians. Child maltreatment was "medicalized" and was almost totally identified with physical abuse, the kinds of maltreatment situations most likely to come to the attention of doctors.

The picture of "rediscovered" child maltreatment that was and is communicated to the public, thus shaping public perception of and response to child maltreatment, was and is focused primarily on child abuse.

The relative secondary consideration given to neglect is only partly a result of the increased medical interest in child maltreatment. Although neglect has always been a matter of concern to protective service agencies, it has also been the kind of child maltreatment that has had low priority, limited interest, and muted visibility. Neglect was neglected in the past and is neglected in the present, despite the greater prevalence and incidence of neglect reports as compared to reports of other kinds of child maltreatment.

Even though neglect was more frequent than abuse in the early turn of the century, reports to the British National Society for the Prevention of Cruelty to Children "continued to dwell on acts of parental violence long after they had ceased to form a large proportion of the society's case load, a preoccupation that seems to have stemmed in part from the shock value of such behavior" (Behlmer, 1982, p. 181).

The tendency to perceive child maltreatment almost exclusively in terms of physical abuse persisted for some time following the rediscovery of the problem in the 1960s for a number of other reasons. As compared to physical abuse, neglect is more diffuse, more insidious, more chronic, more problematic. It is less dramatic, less easily identified, and less easily corrected.

The *Selected Annotated Bibliography on Child Neglect* published by the National Center on Child Abuse and Neglect (National Center on Child Abuse and Neglect, 1985, p. 1) starts by noting that "of all forms of child maltreatment, child neglect may be the most difficult to define, identify and document and to address through designing an effective approach to intervention and prevention." As a consequence, when efforts were being made after the rediscovery of child maltreatment in the 1960s to get the problem on the public agenda for federal legislation and funding, the focus of concern and policy pronouncements primarily emphasized physical abuse.

Analyzing the details of the process that culminated in the passage of the Child Abuse Prevention and Treatment Act of 1974, Hoffman (1980, p. 169) says,

> The legislative history, testimony, committee reports and floor statements reflect the clear intent of Congress that priority be given to helping victims of child abuse. Over and over again supporters of the bill made reference to children who are "beaten," "tortured," and "stabbed" and so on. Awareness of lack of resources available also gave Congress the luxury of not plunging into a controversial area of definition of "child neglect" or making a definite statement on how the program should relate to it.

Reviewing the congressional hearings that preceded the passage of the bill, Patti (1976, p. 3) notes that "There were no more than two to three pages in the Senate hearings that addressed child neglect as opposed to abuse." Patti concludes that it is clear that the intention was to restrict the definition of the problem to instances of severe physical abuse. The title of the act which was finally passed—The Child Abuse Prevention and Treatment Act (PL 93–247, 1974)—reflects the intended priority given to abuse, to the neglect of neglect.

The Child Abuse Prevention and Treatment Act tended to set state standards for protective service programs, providing some $3.7 million per year in support of state programs. However, eligibility for such funds was based on a state's compliance with federal regulations regarding how such programs should be administered and the kinds of maltreatment that were addressed. Initially only state reporting of physical abuse was required; however, reporting of neglect was subsequently added but only over some considerable opposition.

According to Senator Walter Mondale, author of The Child Abuse Prevention and Treatment Act, it was not intended that reporting of neglect be made mandatory by states. In a letter to the Secretary of the Department of Health and Welfare dated October 27, 1975, Senator Mondale objected to extending mandatory reporting to cover neglect situations. In the letter he noted that "the intention of The Child Abuse Prevention and Treatment Act was to address the problem of the most severely threatened and abused children in our country. It was clear from the time the Senate first considered this legislation that the resources it could provide would not be adequate to deal effectively with the much more complicated and difficult problem of child neglect" (pp. 4–5).

Physical and sexual abuse are much more frequently the subjects of books and periodical literature, both lay and professional. The lower priority given to the problem of neglect contradicts the fact that neglect affects more children than abuse and it affects children more seriously. Every study of the comparative prevalence of neglect and abuse shows neglect to be more prevalent by ratios ranging from 3 to 1 (Nagi, 1977) to 10 to 1 (Polansky et al., 1975).

Reviewing the national reporting statistics over time, Schene (1986, p. 1) notes that "although fatalities are seriously under-reported, there are at least 1500 documented cases of children who have died related to neglect since 1976." Children who die as a result of neglect tend to be very young, with an average age of three. (See also Anderson et al., 1983.) Neglect more frequently has serious consequences for family stability than does abuse. More neglected children than abused children are placed in foster care and once placed tend to remain in care longer (Jackson, 1984).

In short, while throughout the history of protective service, from discovery to receding interest to rediscovery of child maltreatment, abuse rather than neglect has been given priority for attention and concern, despite the fact that neglect is, in fact, the more serious child maltreatment problem.

DEFINITION AND RELATED PROBLEMS

Polansky, the most persistent and consistent researcher of child neglect in the United States, defines neglect as a "condition in which a caretaker responsible for the child either deliberately or by extraordinary inattentiveness permits the child to experience avoidable present suffering and/or fails to provide one or more ingredients generally deemed essential for developing a person's physical, intellectual and emotional capacities" (Polansky et al., 1985a).

The parent who abuses or cruelly mistreats the child is guilty of an act of commission; neglect is more frequently a problem of omission.

Physical abuse incidents are episodic, discrete, and time limited; neglect is chronic and continual. The behaviors associated with abuse are sporadic, often impulsive outbursts of anger, aggression, hostility, and feelings of frustration. Indifference, inattentiveness, and lack of concern and awareness of the child's condition are behaviors associated with neglect.

Neglect implies an absence of caring, a lack of concern for and disregard of the child's basic needs. It suggests inaction compounded by indifference and speaks of things undone, a failure to do that which needs doing. It is an abdication of parental responsibility, the ultimate point of which is child abandonment.

There is a problem with defining neglect clearly, resulting from considerations that are matters of dispute. Among these considerations is the impreciseness of legislation that determines the sanction for community intervention. Noting that " 'neglect' is an uncertain concept both legally and in social application," Katz and colleagues (1985) indicate the repetition of ambiguous, vague terms and phrases such as "lack of proper parental care," "unfit home, "exposure to an immoral environment," "failure to exercise minimal degree of care," "home injurious to child's welfare," "failure to provide necessary substances for well-being," "failure to provide adequate care," and "failure to exercise sufficient control." Terms such as "proper," "unfit," "sufficient," "minimum care," "adequate care," "necessary subsistance," and "immoral environment" all require precise definition if one is to avoid subjectivity in designating neglect. Many statutes lack a definition of neglect, perhaps in recognition of the difficulties associated with defining the term.

Thus, human service professionals are not only required to define in practice what legislatures were unable to define precisely in statutes, they are also required to make predictions of the possible harmful consequences of neglect based on limited information and tenuously validated theories of child development. Inevitable errors in definition and prediction subject workers to possible public criticism, administrative reprimand, and, increasingly, the possibility of legal action against them.

Is a definition of neglect applicable to those situations in which both poverty-stricken parents and their children are victims of deprivation, when child neglect is secondary to the self-deprivation experienced by parents?

Most of the sources of ambiguity regarding a definition of neglect are not subject to empirical resolution. However, differences in the perception of neglect that derive from subcultural reference-group affiliation have been researched. The results indicate that there is more of a consensus about what constitutes neglect than had been supposed.

Polansky and colleagues (1978, 1981) have done a considerable amount of work in developing and validating a Childhood Level of Living Scale in quantifying and objectifying neglect. The scale, applicable to school-age children, includes items on the mother's care and concern for the child, the quality of health and grooming, emotional care and discipline, state of repair of the house, and so on.

Polansky and colleagues (1983) used the Childhood Level of Living Scale to test cultural bias related to neglect on populations of white, black, working-class, and middle-class rural and urban women. These varied groups agreed substantially about their perceptions of what constituted neglectful behavior; differences were minor and in terms of emphasis. Middle-class respondents were more concerned with psychological care, working-class mothers with physical care. In these studies Polansky and colleagues followed a tradition of considering maternal attitudes only, a tradition now viewed by many as sexist. Paternal as well as maternal attitudes and behaviors are now seen as equally important.

A study of neighbors' reactions to a neglectful family using a social distance scale (asking the respondents to identify the people whose home they would allow their children to visit, the people whose children they would want as friends for their own children, and the like) confirmed once again the fact that there are consensual norms regarding child care that transcend class differences (Polansky & Gaudin, 1983, p. 198).

A study of judicial code provisions of 51 Indian tribes having a tribal court system indicate that the Native American definition of neglect parallels that of the one used in American society generally. All tribal laws include abandonment and "failure to provide necessary and proper care—necessary and proper care generally means the provision in adequate amounts of medical attention, clothing, hygiene, living quarters and in many cases education" (National Center on Child Abuse and Neglect, 1981, p. 11).

The general conclusion of these studies is that despite some differences in emphasis, there is considerable consensus among different racial, ethnic, social class, and occupational subcultures in our society about what constitutes acceptable parental behavior and minimal child care.

VARIETIES OF NEGLECT

The general term "neglect" includes a variety of different types. These include deprivation of necessities, inadequate supervision, medical neglect, educational neglect, emotional neglect, failure to protect from injurious circumstances, and community and institutional neglect.

Deprivation of Necessities

With this type of neglect, parents fail to provide at some minimally adequate level the food, clothing, and habitation that the child needs and without which he or she will not thrive and may not survive. Deprivation of necessities is the most frequent type of neglect reported by protective service agencies.

Inadequate Supervision

Inadequate supervision means that a caretaker is not available to protect the child from possible harm. Danger may derive from the child's ignorance—touching a hot stove, playing with a sharp knife, or walking out into traffic. It may relate to a child's physical limitations such as the inability to cope with a sudden fire or negotiate a steep stairwell.

Adequate supervision involves reasonable parental care in safeguarding young children from dangerous objects such as broken glass, knives, guns, matches, poisons, dangerous pharmaceuticals, spoiled food, and peeling paint. It also involves action to correct such hazards as gas and steam leaks, unprotected windows, and unguarded crumbling staircases.

Abandonment is the ultimate inadequate supervision. The child is left by parents to fend for him- or herself, unpossessed, unclaimed, and unattended, without prearranged provision for care and supervision by adults.

Inadequate supervision reports constitute the second most frequent type of neglect reports received by protective agencies.

Medical Neglect

Parents may be ignorant about and fail to recognize symptoms that suggest serious illness in the child. Even if recognized, the parents' attitudes about obtaining medical help may be so casual or confidence in doctors may be so limited that parents fail to provide such help. Then, too, parents may lack the finances to obtain medical care.

Medical neglect includes failure to obtain or allow diagnosis of a clearly manifested medical difficulty, failure to obtain or allow treatment of such a condition, or imposition on the child of treatment that according to accepted medical opinion is likely to be harmful.

Perhaps because of the difficulty of obtaining medical care, poor families may be more likely to overlook physical problems that may seem minor to them. A persistent cough, chronic backaches, loss of appetite, general fatigue, a low-grade fever, or a continuing infection do not typically result in medical attention for many children in low-income families.

The question of medical neglect has always been complicated because of the beliefs of certain religious groups regarding some medical procedures. These include Christian Scientists and Jehovah's Witnesses. Regulations formulated by the U.S. Department of Health and Human Services indicate that failure to provide medical care is not neglect if such failure is in response to a person's religious beliefs, and most states grant exemptions from immunizations that run counter to these beliefs.

However, the regulations go on to note that "nothing shall prohibit court intervention to protect the child." Freedom of religion and conscience is secondary to the right to life. In cases of medical neglect courts have generally acted to supercede parental autonomy with regard to medical treatment decisions if there is imminent danger of death to the child or probable serious impairment of the child's health.

An even more controversial problem regarding medical neglect gained widespread publicity and debate in 1983–1984. In several cases, known as Baby Doe cases, action was taken by right-to-life activists to petition the court to require parents to consent to medical treatment that they had rejected. Failure to provide consent was seen as a manifestation of medical neglect. After months of debate, both in and out of Congress, legislation was passed in 1984 defining as neglect the denial of care to newborn infants who have life-threatening handicaps. Child Abuse Prevention and Treatment Act funds were withheld from states that did not set up procedures to investigate and report the withholding of treatment and nutrition from infants "with life-threatening congenital impairments." In redefining maltreatment this legislation expanded the kinds of medical neglect cases for which the protective services have some responsibility.

Educational Neglect

This involves the failure of a parent to enroll a child in school or indifference to chronic truanting on the part of a child who is enrolled. Children might be kept out of school for the purpose of caring for younger siblings or may be kept home to work. A child may not be enrolled in school, but if carefully planned alternative provisions for the child's education are being implemented, this is not regarded as educational neglect. Some school absence may be acceptable, but truancy is defined as absence for 5 days a month after parents have been notified of the situation.

The refusal of parents to enroll a child in special educational programs if a clear need for this has been assessed might be regarded as educational neglect. For the preschool child the failure to meet needs for sensory stimulation by keeping the child isolated might also be classified as neglect.

Emotional Neglect

Parents may fail to provide children with the kinds of responses that make for healthy emotional development. Parents who withhold affection, who never praise or commend their children, who avoid contact with and rarely spontaneously talk with their youngsters, and who fail to exercise guidance or control over the child's activities are manifesting emotional neglect. Very permissive disciplinary approaches and overindulgence by parents can also be interpreted as neglect because they deny the child important controls.

Failure to Protect from Injurious Circumstances

The failure to protect a child from potentially injurious situations, both moral and behavioral, is regarded as neglectful. This involves failure to protect the child from exposure to criminal and/or immoral influences that endanger the child's socialization to the consensually accepted values of society.

Community and Institutional Neglect

Community neglect might be defined as persistent failure on the part of the community to take action to provide adequate child care resources despite the clearly established deprivation suffered by a significant group of children in the community.

Early in the history of child protective services, agencies were concerned with community neglect. Carstens, an early child welfare advocate, noted in 1912 that community neglect was manifested by a city that does not remove corrupting influences within its borders, enforce laws dealing with school attendance and child labor, or provide adequate playgrounds and sunny and sanitary dwellings.

The community is guilty of neglect when it fails to provide adequate housing, public assistance, schooling, health services, and recreational resources or makes no effort to control an open display of vice, narcotics traffic, and other illegal activities. Malnutrition in children that results from inadequate welfare grants can also be regarded as an example of community neglect.

DEMOGRAPHY OF NEGLECT

The true prevalence of neglect in the general community is unknown and probably unknowable. There are no community studies of a representative cross section of the American population providing information on the numbers of neglected children separate from those who are abused. What we do have is information on a residual group of children and families who have come to the attention of agencies because a report has been made that there is some reason to believe that a child is neglected.

The American Humane Association has been designated by the National Center for Child Abuse and Neglect as a clearinghouse for aggregating all state reports and for publishing national statistics on abuse and neglect. The material on the demography of neglect that follows is derived from such reports.

As has been true for every year since 1973 when the first national report was made available, the largest number of children reported as maltreated in 1984 were reported for neglect rather than abuse. In that year a little over 1 million reports of neglect were received.

There is a difference between the number of reports received and the actual number of substantiated cases of neglect, as some percentage of cases prove to be invalid upon investigation. In 1983 only 63.2% of the reports received were actually opened for protective services (American Humane Association, 1985, Table 12, p. 20). Some nonprofessional reports are made up out of spite and/or made anonymously.

In 1984 the average age of the child reported as neglected was 6.4 years, so in general neglected children tended to be younger than the overall group of maltreated children, who averaged 7.2 years old in 1984. Minority children were disproportionately overrepresented in the neglect statistics. While in 1984 15% of all children in the population were black, 22.5% of reported neglected children were black; 9.7% of all children in the population were Hispanic in contrast to 12.9% of reported neglected children.

A disproportionately high percentage of neglectful families were single-parent, female-headed families, many of whom were black, and a disproportionately high percentage of such families depended on public assistance as their main source of support.

Almost all of the perpetrators of neglect were the parents of the children neglected. While male adults were more frequently implicated in physical abuse cases and considerably more frequently in cases of sexual abuse, female adults were more frequently the designated perpetrator in cases of neglect. This is partly a reflection of the disproportionate percentage of female-headed families in the neglect category.

Although still the most frequently reported situation, the percentage contributed by neglect to the total maltreatment statistic has been declining. This is partly the result of the increased demands for service in a period of declining budgetary supports; thus, agencies are giving neglect lower priority than abuse. The decline is also a factor of the sharp increase in the percentage contributed by sexual abuse to the overall maltreatment statistic—an increase from 8.5% of all reports in 1983 to 13.3% of all reports in 1984. This increase may be primarily a result of a greater tendency to report such cases than was true in the past.

DIAGNOSIS AND ASSESSMENT

The general cultural patterns of the larger society help to explain neglect. Neglectful parents may have learned neglect from their own parents, but in addition many have experienced the neglect of their needs by the larger society. A high percentage of neglectful parents live in social and economic deprivation, their situation largely ignored by a society indifferent to their needs. They are not strangers to neglect. As a consequence, they are less likely to be responsive to the norms of a society that permits neglectful behavior toward them.

Despite recent emphases on the rights of children, as a group they are given secondary priority in the allocation of community resources. While the number of the aged in poverty has been steadily decreasing, the number of children in poverty has been increasing as a result, in part, of the differential allocation of resources (Moynihan, 1986). The present culture appears to dictate an acceptance and sanction of the neglect of children when their needs compete with those of adults. In part, then, parental neglect can be explained as a manifestation in the microsystem of the family of the neglect of children exhibited by the macrosystem.

Neglect may also be a consequence of the parent's mental or physical inability to care for the child. A psychotic parent, a parent with a serious physical disability, or a cognitively deficient parent may be unable to perform the skills required for adequate child care. Parents habitually incapacitated by substance abuse (Black & Mayer, 1980) are also at high risk for neglect. In a few instances the parents may strongly reject the child for a variety of reasons: an unwanted pregnancy, severe physical or mental problems of the child and/or the parents, a piling up of burdens carried by the parent, and so on.

Over the course of decades Polansky and colleagues (1972, 1975, 1981) have studied neglectful mothers at close range in such diverse settings as Appalachia and Philadelphia. These largely clinical studies have identified personality configurations that are characteristically typical of several different groups of neglectful mothers. (Fathers are frequently not present in the home, not available for study even when present, or overlooked by some of the investigations.) The external stress of a deprived environment of long-term chronic poverty is in each instance joined to inner personal chaos, a chaos which tends to have its major roots in the deprivations of the economically depressed environment. Thus, poverty in combination with a character-disordered personality and disturbed family system is the most likely equation for neglect, according to this research.

One group of mothers, characterized by an apathy–futility syndrome, are withdrawn and alienated. Passive resignation to a chronically deprived environment is manifested by a sense of futility that anything can be done to change the situation. There is no sense in trying. Such mothers show an emotional numbness and little intensity in their personal relationships. They appear to be lethargic and verbally inaccessible.

Lonely and apparently lacking in the capacity for experiencing pleasure, their clinically judged emotional indifference is thought to be associated with affect–inhibition resulting from developmental emotional deprivation. Apparently having limited intelligence, they seem to have little capacity for empathy with their children.

Another group of mothers is judged to be impulse ridden. They seem to be unable to tolerate stress and frustration and feel a sense of chronic restlessness. They find it difficult to plan their lives and more often than not act impulsively. The so-called normal control system for handling impulses appears to be deficient, and they show poor judgment about the probable consequences of the actions they take. The personal relationships of such mothers appear to be shallow and unstable. A third, smaller group of mothers shows symptoms of reactive depression, manifesting persistent moods of hopelessness and despair.

Many of the mothers studied appear to have low-level cognitive functioning, and they seem to be generally suspicious of the interviewers who study them. They have poor communication skills, seem difficult to engage in an affective relationship, and appear to be depressed and unable to assume heavy responsibilities. Given these attributes, they are a difficult group of clients with whom to work.

Less emphasized in these studies, but important to note, is that many mothers are in poor relationships with the fathers of their children. The fathers have often deserted or are incarcerated for delinquent or criminal behavior. When present the fathers tend to express their own lifetime deprivation in abusive, acting-out behavior or depressed withdrawal.

The major implication of this chiefly clinical research is that neglect is the consequence of damage that neglectful parents themselves suffered in their own childhood; that while poverty contributes to neglect and while the amelioration of poverty will reduce the stresses that are associated with neglect, some basic personality factors that determine neglectful behavior would still need to be addressed. Poverty is a basic contributing factor but not a sole explanation of neglect. (See also Volume 1, Chapters 1 to 4.)

Both Young (1964) and Meier (1964) in their studies of neglectful parents support Polansky's general orientation. Using mainly a psychological orientation, they see defects in ego development, distorted judgment, impulsive behavior, and the inability to implement caring responsibilities as implicated in neglect. However, it must be noted again that these psychological "deficits" are often correlated with long-term poverty, unemployment, rejection by the larger society, poor health, and the like.[1]

Investigating the differences between neglectful and non-neglectful mothers among low-income families, both Wolock and Horowitz (1979) and Giovannoni and Billingsley (1970) found that neglectful families were among the poorest of the poor, in the least adequate position to provide adequate care. Although Giovannoni and Billingsley (1970) did not find that developmental background variables significantly associated with later parental neglect, they did find stresses associated with low income and the deprivation of material resources that impaired the parents' capacity to care adequately for their children.

Extended interviews were conducted with agency-defined neglecting mothers and a matched group of nonneglecting mothers by Wolock and Horowitz (1979). (Note again the bias toward blaming *mothers.*) In contrast to the comparison group of nonneglecting mothers, neglecting mothers "have more children, encountered greater material, physical, and social deprivation when they were growing up, are currently living in even more difficult material circumstances and are more socially isolated than other welfare families. In short, these families are the poorest of the poor" (p. 186). In analyzing their findings, the researchers emphasize that "as one moves from intrapersonal to environmental and social factors—the ability to explain child maltreatment increases" (p. 190).

Nagi (1977, p. 51) asked respondents associated with hospitals, courts, schools, and social agencies to list the characteristics that in their experience were associated with abuse and neglect situations. Respondents gave economic factors greater importance in neglect situations than in abuse.

Interviews with neglectful parents, supplemented by detailed reviews of their agency records by the research staff of the Child Welfare League of America, indicated that "parents charged with neglect were more likely than others to be evaluated as being under exceptionally heavy stress" (Shapiro, 1979, p. 92). They were more likely to present problems regarding housing and alcohol abuse than other maltreating families in the study.

Reviewing the national study data on child abuse and neglect over the 1976–1979 reporting periods, Lapp (1983, p. 9) found that neglectful families registered an average of 2.2 stresses, the principal ones being "family interactional problems" (72.4%), economic problems (57.9%), and health problems (48%). It is difficult to know whether the level of felt stress was higher for this population than for the general nonneglectful population because no comparable statistics are available for this latter group.

Multiple-regression analysis of information from the case records of 489 cases of substantiated maltreatment, including 207 of neglect, obtained from county protective service units, indicated that overall there was a "positive relationship between neglect of children and circumstances within the family which indicate a poverty-induced low-living situation"; however, "The relatively high importance of parental intellectual inadequacies suggest that more than any other type of child maltreatment, neglect may be influenced by parental inadequacies" (Martin & Walters, 1982, p. 272).

Beyond poverty Jones and McNeely (1980) found significant differences in nurturing knowledge between a nonneglectful group of AFDC mothers and a matched group of low-income, neglectful mothers. They obtained self-report responses to an instrument focused on maternal nurturing knowledge, expectations, and support systems from neglecting mothers and a matched group of non-neglecting mothers. "The mothers of neglected children scored significantly lower than mothers of non-neglected children in their nurturing knowledge, giving substance to the position that child neglect may be due more to deficiencies in mothers' nurturing knowledge and behaviors than in their purposeful withholding of care" (p. 566). However, a host of studies have shown that knowledge lacks, as revealed by written tests, may be heavily influenced by cognitive and educational deficits that in turn are an outgrowth of long-term, extreme poverty (Chilman, 1973).

The same comment applies to the studies cited below. Using a development expectation questionnaire with a group of agency-identified neglectful parents and a matched comparison group of non-maltreating parents, Twentyman and Plotkin (1982, p. 502) also found that neglecting parents "are less knowledgeable about children's development processes than are matched controls" and that neglect may be partly a consequence of "an informational deficit." Confounding anticipated results, parental expectations of their children by neglectful parents were sometimes greater, sometimes lower than expectations of the comparison group.

Studying the circumstances surrounding the occurrence of some 800 incidents of neglect, Herrenkohl and colleagues (1983, p. 430) note evidence of knowledge and skills deficits. They note that "significant reasons" for neglect "include poor parenting skills and insufficient knowledge of children's needs."[2]

For example, neglectful families tend to be more socially isolated and alienated than a comparable group of families at the same socioeconomic level. They have fewer formal and informal social ties and supports. Comparing the reasons for the social isolation of neglectful families, Polansky and colleagues (1985a) found that such families had the same opportunities for social ties as a similarly situated comparison group of nonneglectful families; however, they were not able to effectively use the opportunities available. They were perceived by neighbors as deviant, and others distanced themselves from them. Nor were they able to reach out and involve themselves in informal helping networks as effectively as others.

Another study was carried out to ascertain the relative ecological impoverishment of their neighborhood as perceived by neglectful mothers, matched controls, and their immediate nonmaltreating neighbors. The findings indicated that while matched controls and neighbors tended to see their environment as friendly and helpful, maltreating mothers tended to see the same neighborhood as lacking in friendliness and support, one in which they live isolated and lonely lives. Both black and white, rural and urban mothers were included in the population of some 300 respondents studied (Polansky et al., 1985b).

Further study confirms the fact that neighbors of neglectful families seek to distance themselves socially from such families and show reluctance to develop close relationships with them. Not only is rejection of contact a response to a perception that neglectful families are violating child care standards of the neighborhood, it is also based on the perception that such families are less capable of reciprocating support (Gaudin & Polansky, 1986).

Attenuated social control provides another explanation. Social network information was obtained by Salzinger and colleagues (1983) through detailed interviews with 32 substantiated abuse and neglect families as compared to information from 24 nonmaltreating controls. Maltreating parents had fewer people in their networks but perhaps more significant was the fact that their networks, as compared to nonmaltreating parents, contained fewer nonfamily peer connections. "Because the limited social contact they have is confined primarily to their own immediate families who share many of their same values, their current patterns of behavior are" (p. 75) less likely to be subject to the norm-enforcing pressures of nonmaltreating peers. Rather than being subjected to critical negative feedback from nonmaltreating, nonfamily peers for neglectful behavior, their more insular, exclusive contact with similarly behaving immediate family contacts may reinforce neglectful behavior. These kinds of family systems appear to have overly rigid, tight boundaries that hold the outside world at bay and prevent sufficient individuation and socialization of their members.

A somewhat different approach to identifying the unique characteristics that differentiate neglectful parents from nonneglectful parents has been taken by some child psychologists. Their studies

involve detailed examination of small samples of microscopic interactional behaviors of neglectful mother–child pairs. (Editor's note:
Mothers again!) Generally, these studies involve small groups of
mothers, selected so that categorization of subjects into neglectful
and nonneglectful groups is defensible; detailed observations in the
clinic or during visits to the home; videotaping of interactions; and
coding by carefully trained observers using instruments such as
standardized observational scoring systems, which have been specifically designed or adapted for the studies.

Employing this general methodological approach, Disbrow and
colleagues (1977, p. 290) found neglectful parents low in "parental
facilitating behavior" and "communication between themselves and
their children."

Burgess and Conger (1977) found that neglectful parents directed
fewer positive contacts and more negative interactions to each other
than did matched control families. This pattern was mirrored in the
interactional pattern displayed by children in the neglect families
(p. 274). (See also Aragona and Eyberg, 1981.)

The researchers note that of all the mothers in the study those in
the neglect group stand out as the most negative and the least
positive in their relationship with other family members. Further,
"The fathers in the neglect sample are less compliant and less
positive with their children than controls" (Burgess & Conger, 1978,
p. 1171).

Crittenden (1981, p. 210) found that "neglecting mothers offered
so little stimulation and responded to so few infant signals that they
left their infants socially powerless and largely responsible for their
own stimulation. Their infants showed correspondingly depressed
levels of activity which reduced both the stimulation and feed-back
available to the already unresponsive mother. Mutual passivity was
easily maintained."

Twentyman, in a series of studies with others, has similarly examined these neglectful parent patterns of behavior through use of
direct observation in the home. Small groups of agency-substantiated
abusive parents and agency-substantiated neglectful parents were
compared with matched nonmaltreating controls (10 to 12 in each
group). Neglectful mothers showed the fewest social interactions,
had the lowest rate of verbal and nonverbal instructional behaviors,
and exhibited fewer positive affectionate interactions with their children. "The low rates of maternal interaction give some support to the
hypothesis that neglectful mothers are withdrawn from their en-

vironment. If both the maternal and the child neglect data are considered together, these families live in a social system that is characterized as one in which little information is exchanged, affection is infrequently provided and social isolation occurs within the home" (Bousha & Twentyman, 1984, p. 112). Somewhat similar results have been obtained in a number of other studies, too numerous to detail here (Azar et al., 1984; Crittenden, 1985; Friedrich et al., 1985).

In various studies neglected children were found to be different from other maltreated children in that they tended to engage in very few interactions with other youngsters (Hoffman-Plotken & Twentyman, 1984). Neglected children were observed to avoid their mothers and to be angry, noncompliant, and highly dependent. They had the most difficulty (compared to abused children and nonmaltreated controls) pulling themselves together to deal with various tasks (Egeland et al., 1983).

The detailed research around mother–infant dyadic interaction tends to be redundant. It shows neglectful mothers being unresponsive, passive, and nonfacilitative in initiating and encouraging interaction. In turn, these mothers elicit passivity and low responsiveness in their children. The research supports a picture of the characteralogical atypicality of neglectful mothers. Again, it should be noted that almost all of the available research focuses on the mother. The father is noticeable only by his absence: many more studies are needed that include both parents.

Summarizing the research, three principal clusters of variables tend to be identified: personality–characteralogical factors, family system variables, and social and economic ones. Personality–characteralogical deficits are exacerbated by low levels of cognitive functioning, and social and economic stress factors are exacerbated by social isolation and the lack of a mitigating social support system. The same may be said for family system difficulties.

The three sets of factors are in dynamic interaction. For example, the multiple sources of aggregate environmental stresses—limited income, dilapidated housing, unemployment, social isolation, single-parent responsibility for care of dependent children and/or a dysfunctional total family system—are the grounds that provide the potential for neglect. Such a highly stressful configuration, impacting on parents with limited capabilities for coping, actualizes the potential for neglect. Neither stressful conditions nor sociopsychological and familial characteristics are in themselves separately likely to create neglect. The three sets of factors in interaction help to account for the phenomenon. It is likely that physical health factors also play an important part, but they were not included by the social researchers in this field.

The more comprehensive "explanation" (suggested above) points to the interaction between parents, children, families, and the situations in which they live. Stress is a vector, a force with direction, that results from the interaction of these variables. Some parents with high coping capacity seem to be able to handle stress even in a highly depriving environment; some parents with inadequate coping capacity seem to feel stressed and behave inappropriately in a relatively benign one. However, the central issue is not so much the family's environment of the moment as it is the effects of their environment during the many years of their total lifetime experiences.

But while there is increasing recognition of the explanatory potential of the-person-and-family-in-interaction-with-the-situation approach to understanding, there is less discussion in the literature of another relevant interactional focus. This is the interaction between the principal participants in the neglect configuration—parent(s) and child. For example, some children are more independent, easier to accept and love, and more responsive to parent teaching, expectations, and demands than others. A bright, capable, independent 6-year-old may not be in danger of coming to harm if left alone at home for part of a day. Some children are more active and adventurous, so that "more" adequate supervision may be required. Some children are emotionally passive and unresponsive, making the parents' orientation toward emotional neglect easier to enact. Some children are more resistive to schooling and require greater efforts on the part of parents if they are to avoid charges of educational neglect.

Then, too, as shown by some of the research summarized above, the total family system may be dysfunctional. For example, some families may have such distant relationships among the members that there is little sense of parent–child or child–parent bonding. Some parents may neglect a particular child who serves as a scapegoat for other family problems. Some families have tightly fused, suffocating relationships that prevent reciprocal interactions of individuals. Some may be "stuck" in total family development, so that parents fail to move into the maturity required for nurturing their children. Others may have such rigid family boundaries that they become ingrown and isolated from the larger society. (See the Introduction to this volume for references regarding various family systems theories as well as Chapters 1 through 6 in Volume 3.)

SUMMARY

Neglect is the most prevalent form of child maltreatment. It is also a form of maltreatment that has serious harmful consequences for many children. Despite this, neglect has been neglected, in part a result of difficulties in defining and identifying neglect. Definitional ambiguity follows from controversies regarding boundaries as well as nationality and cultural diversity in childrearing practices. The neglectful family is disproportionately a low-income, female-headed, single-parent household of minority group affiliation.

There are a number of different specific types of neglect: deprivation of necessities, inadequate supervision, medical neglect, educational neglect, emotional neglect, failure to protect from injurious circumstances, and community and institutional neglect. Deprivation of necessities and inadequate supervision are the most frequent forms of neglect. Characteralogical and personality factors have been identified as "explaining" neglect, but these factors are most likely to be potentiated in a highly stressful deprived environment that is bereft of a social support system.

This chapter provides some basic background information regarding neglect that leads to the more important, more consequential question—what can be done to prevent or treat situations of neglect and what is being done. This is the focus of Chapter 9.

NOTES

1. Editor's note: In the whole field of child neglect, there is a tendency to hold only mothers responsible for problems in child care. This reflects the frequent difficulty in working with fathers as well as a sexist bias of the larger society.

2. Editor's note: It appears that these researchers may have exceeded their data in reaching the conclusions cited. A number of investigations regarding the interaction between parental knowledge and child development outcomes shows that this association is tenuous indeed. For example, child development is a product of the complex interaction of a host of factors, including the child's inborn temperamental tendencies, the structure and nature of the total family system, the impact of the many environments on the child and family, along with the parent's total *behaviors*—behaviors that may be quite different from their tested knowledge and skills.

9

Treatment of Families Who Neglect Their Children

JAMES M. GAUDIN, Jr.

The "neglect of neglect," to which Wolock and Horowitz (1984) called attention and which Kadushin recognized in Chapter 8, is reflected in the paucity of published studies on the treatment of child neglect. Perhaps it is the strong combination of economic as well as social and psychological deprivation that discourages efforts by researchers and practitioners to chronicle interventive initiatives to remedy child neglect.

The picture of neglectful parents painted by Polansky and colleagues (1981, p. 109) is not a promising one for the professional helper who seeks to remedy child neglect. They define neglectful parents as

> . . . a group of people with a modal personality: less able to love, less capable of working productively, less open about feelings, more prone to living painlessly and impulsively, but also susceptible to psychological symptoms and to phases of passive inactivity and numb fatalism."

DIRECTIONS FROM PUBLISHED RESEARCH

Most treatment programs for families who maltreat their children are aimed at physical abuse or a combined population of abuse and neglect. Few studies report separate results of interventions with neglectful families. A review of published studies of treatment programs with neglectful families reveals only a few well-documented studies. A lack of control groups and limited samples weakens the conclusions that may be drawn about effective treatment methods and programs.

Unpublished reports of special demonstration projects offer the most substantial information about what seems to work best with neglectful families. The Berkeley Planning Associates (Daro, 1985) evaluation report of 19 research and demonstration projects reported the results of interventions with specific subpopulations of child maltreatment that included neglect. The results suggest that there are significant differences in the kinds of interventions that are effective with neglectful, physically abused, and sexually abused families.

Neglectful families proved to be the most resistant to change. Only 40% of the neglectful families served by the demonstration projects were judged to be unlikely to further maltreat their children at termination. The prediction for the sexually abusive families served, however, was 70%.

The review did suggest some guidelines for the successful treatment of maltreating families and specifically for neglectful families. First, family and group interventions are more successful than individual counseling. The latter was inversely associated with successful outcomes for both abusive and neglectful families. For neglecting families, family counseling made a significant contribution to successful outcome. Second, multiservice models were associated with improvements in parenting. Finally, treatment for at least 6 to 18 months was required for successful outcome. Few families who received service for less than 6 months were significantly changed. Families served 13 to 18 months made the most significant gains. The indication was that service beyond 18 months did not significantly improve the quality of child care (Daro, 1985).

An examination of reports from seven of the demonstration projects for neglectful families as reviewed by Daro and published results from other interventive programs with neglectful families suggests the following directions for treatment of neglectful families.

First, most of the programs that were at least moderately successful in improving the parenting of the neglectful parents were multiservice projects. One of the earlier and best known was the Bowen Center Project (Sullivan et al., 1977). The project served 35 impoverished, severely neglectful families in a low-income area of Chicago. Initially the project offered intensive supportive casework services with the neglectful parents and therapeutic day care for their preschool-aged children. Gradually eight more services were added to meet the identified needs of the families. The program was built around a neighborhood center facility where services were provided by skilled staff. The treatment philosophy was basically psychodynamic, but the center was designed to serve as a substitute support network for the socially isolated and psychologically impoverished families. Although no systematic evaluation of the project was made, observable improvements were reported in the parents' personal care and modest improvements in the child care of all but 6 of the 35 families served.

Project Twelve Ways (Lutzker et al., 1984) and the Dallas Children and Youth Project (Edgington & Hall, 1982) are two more recent multiservice projects that provided a variety of in-home services to neglectful families. Both have data to support moderate success in improving the parental functioning of economically disadvantaged neglectful mothers and preventing recurrence of maltreatment. However, follow-up evaluations indicated a decline in parental functioning once services were terminated.

Project Time for Parents (Rozansky & Chambers, 1982), A Better Way (Conner et al., 1980), Project R & R, and Project Begin Again (Barrett, 1982) were other examples of multiservice programs that reported moderate success with neglectful parents.

Parenting education programs were one of the primary treatment methods in most of the child neglect demonstration programs. Group and individual in-home instruction were most often used to teach parenting skills. Homemakers (Edgington & Hall, 1982) and parent aides (Barrett, 1982) were also used to teach parenting skills. Behavioral skills training approaches were judged to be successful in three of the projects: Project R & R (Felt, 1983), Project Twelve Ways (Lutzker et al., 1984) and Project Time for Parents (Rozansky & Chambers, 1982).

Skilled casework services were a part of most of the intervention efforts but were especially emphasized in the Bowen Center Project (Sullivan et al., 1977) and Project Time for Parents (Rozansky & Chambers, 1982). The establishment of a trusting, supportive, nurturing professional helping relationship with the neglectful parent was viewed as essential preparation for progressively more responsible parental functioning (Austin, 1983; Polansky et al., 1981).

Therapeutic child day-care services were the major component of four of the 19 programs reviewed by Berkeley planning Associates (Daro, 1985). The majority of the children served in each of the four programs were victims of neglectful parenting. Project R & R (Felt, 1983) is one example of a program that combined therapeutic child care and intensive parenting skills training to bring about improvements in the functioning of parents and their children. Weekly parenting skills training classes and weekly in-home skills training with parents and children using a behavioral approach were the main features of the intervention, which lasted an average of 8 months per family. The neglected children made significant gains in cognitive, language, and verbal skills, and the neglectful parents increased positive interactions with their children, but the neglectful parents improved less and at a slower rate than the abusive parents. Similar intervention projects using therapeutic child care and parenting education as the core treatment strategies with abused and neglected children and their parents were judged to be useful in three other urban centers (Barrett, 1982).

The use of lay home helpers or parent aides is another treatment strategy that has been used with neglectful and abusive families with mixed results. An earlier evaluation by Berkeley Planning Associates of 11 specially funded National Center on Child Abuse and Neglect (NCCAN) demonstration projects (Cohn, 1979) during the period 1974–1978 concluded that service designs that included group counseling and services provided by lay helpers had higher success rates with the abusive and neglectful families than those that did not.

Swanson (1980) reported positive changes in parenting behavior and in social relationships with formal and informal resource systems by 24 neglectful families after interventions by assigned parent aides over a 12-month period. The social isolation of the families was significantly reduced as relationships became stronger, less stressful, and more reciprocal. Mothers over 30 years of age improved significantly more than younger mothers.

On the other hand, 20 failure-to-thrive infants who received lay home visiting in addition to medical treatment and other community services showed no significant improvement over other FTT children who did not receive this additional service. The lay home visitation intervention had no apparent effect on the children's weight, development, or improved mother–child interaction (Haynes et al., 1984).

Lay home helpers were used as an alternative to a standard professional multidisciplinary team approach[1] with neglectful and abusive families in Ontario, Canada (Hornick et al., 1983). The functions of the home helpers were to provide homemaker services and to serve as a nurturing parent figure for the abusive parent. The formal evaluation after 12 months of intervention revealed that the home helper approach resulted in significant improvements on measures of the mothers' nurturant practices and attitudes but not significantly greater improvement than for mothers who received the standard treatment team intervention. Effectiveness with neglectful families was not reported separately.

This review of reports from intervention programs, judged to be at least partially successful, suggests that modest improvements in the parenting behavior of neglectful parents can be achieved through interventive efforts characterized by the following:

1. In-home, outreach rather than in-office services
2. Strong, supportive professional helping relationships with the neglectful parent

3. A comprehensive, multiservice approach, including mobilization of resources such as income, housing, and health assistance
4. Parent groups for socialization, support, and social and parent skills training using behavioral approaches
5. Extended, long-term services of at least a year's duration
6. The use of lay parent aides to provide supplemental nurturing and support for the parents and the children

AN ECOLOGICAL PERSPECTIVE FOR INTERVENTION

The limited success of these multiservice demonstration programs (Daro, 1985) and the hypothesis of multiple-factor causality for child neglect outlined in Chapter 8 point to the need for interventions that target the family system and those ecological systems that surround the neglectful family and influence the neglectful pattern of parenting. Bronfenbrenner (1979), Belsky (1980), Garbarino (1977) and Polansky and colleagues (1985b) have stressed the critical importance of an ecological perspective on child development and child maltreatment. Kadushin has echoed this interdependent systems view in Chapter 8. This perspective includes an emphasis on the important part played by such environmental factors as income, employment, housing, health, schools, and the like.

Neglectful family systems tend to develop stable but dysfunctional balances in response to forces within and outside the family that are highly resistant to change. Achieving a new, more functional balance with improved child caring required modifying the external as well as the internal influences on the family in order to destabilize the current dysfunctional balance and create a new, improved level of functioning (Hally et al., 1980; Polansky et al., 1981). Interventions that focus exclusively on the neglectful parent and ignore the potent influence of extended family, social networks, and community systems on the neglectful parent were found to be ineffective (Daro, 1985). A multiservice, ecosystems model is required to bring about the desired improvement in parental functioning. The model outlined here reflects that perspective.

Theoretical Premises

This ecological understanding of child neglect calls for a model of intervention that brings influence to bear on the individual, the family unit, and the potentially supportive systems that surround the family unit. The model for intervention is based on the following theoretical premises, which are supported by the existing research on child neglect:

1. Neglectful parents tend to be characterized by very immature, egocentric, impulse-ridden, personalities; an apathetic, futile, fatalistic outlook on life; very poorly developed social and communication skills; extreme lack of awareness, sensitivity, and responsiveness to the needs of their children (Polansky et al., 1981); and poverty and other highly stressful life circumstances (Polansky et al., 1981; Polansky et al., 1985b; Wolock & Horowitz, 1979).
2. Neglectful parents tend to be socially isolated from formal and informal support systems (Polansky et al., 1985b).
3. Even when they live in communities that contain the requisite supportive resources, neglectful parents are usually not effectively connected to these potential supports for parenting (Polansky et al., 1985b). Neglectful parents are often rejected and socially isolated by their similarly situated but nonneglectful neighbors (Polansky & Gaudin, 1983).
4. If they do not receive supplemental parenting, children of neglectful parents are apt to suffer serious and continuing developmental deficits and social adjustment problems (Egeland et al., 1983; Polansky et al., 1981).

The ecological intervention model is further predicated on these theoretical assumptions:

1. Informal social networks provide critical resources for normal coping with child rearing tasks. Many parents are able to cope with parenting with help from these informal sources of support.
2. Even parents with limited personal and psychological resources can provide minimally adequate child care in an environment that provides emotional and tangible supports for parenting.

ECOLOGICAL MODEL FOR INTERVENTION

Assessment

Effective intervention must be based on a thorough psychosocial-ecological assessment of the child-rearing situation. This assessment must include psychological–ontogenic, microsystem, and ecosystems factors which in combination determine the adequacy of child rearing (Belsky, 1980).

Psychological–ontogenic factors include the personal psychological resources of the neglectful parent, flowing from his or her own developmental experience in his or her family of origin. Polansky and colleagues (1981) have posited several personality profiles of neglectful parents; as Kadushin has pointed out in Chapter 8, there are major differences in the intellectual and psychological profiles of neglectful parents, which have major implications for intervention. Certainly psychotic or severely retarded parents require different interventions from those required for infantile, impulsive, or apathetic neglectful parents or those with low normal intelligence, parental types that emerge from Polansky and colleagues' (1981) research.

A thorough assessment must be made of the neglectful parents' psychological and personality resources as a guide for intervention. The evaluation should include the apparent intellectual capacity and mental status of the parents, physical health, use of drugs and alcohol, their communication and social skills, and their sensitivity to and knowledge of their children's needs and realistic abilities. The assessment should consider the parents' strengths as well as deficits.

Microsystem factors include the marital system and relationships with other adult members of the household. Nonexistent, stressful, or nonsupportive relationships indicate the need for interventions to add, strengthen, modify, or neutralize dysfunctional relationships in support of improved parental functioning. Children with special mental or physical disabilities create increased stress on parents and require specialized treatment and supportive services. The research indicates that the interactions between neglectful family members tend to be infrequent and predominantly negative ones (Burgess & Conger, 1978). Interventions to alter family structure, roles, and dynamics are usually indicated, with due attention given to cultural factors of norms, values, beliefs, and goals.

Ecosystem factors are those environmental systems that directly impinge on the parent-child relationship in such a way as to facilitate and support effective parenting or to create a stressful, nonsupportive ecology for parenting. Here the availability of formal institutional services such as day care, adequate housing, health services, financial assistance, educational and recreational resources, and homemaker services must be assessed. The informal help and support from neighbors, friends, and relatives must be assessed and strengthened if needed. The availability of help from informal social networks and the availability of formally organized social, educational, medical, and recreational services in the immediate community have a critical impact on the adequacy of child care provided by marginally adequate parents. Informal networks offer role models for parents and provide necessary feedback and information to parents on accepted community standards of child care (Caplan, 1974; Garbarino, 1977).

Based on this ecological understanding, an effective intervention model with neglectful families should include the following components:

1. Supportive individual, professional counseling/therapy with parents, supplemented by a nurturing relationship with a trained parent aide.
2. Family therapy/counseling with the nuclear family unit to modify family roles, communication, and structure to improve the supports for and quality of parenting.
3. Parenting education using a social learning approach to teach specific child care skills and to increase parents' knowledge of childrens' developmental needs and capabilities.
4. Parent support groups to decrease social isolation, increase self-esteem, provide opportunities for learning social skills, and learn new parenting skills.
5. Social network assessment and interventions to maintain, strengthen, modify, or create supportive informal network linkages.
6. Provision of services by linking families with formally organized health and social welfare services that provide tangible assistance for pressing needs and reduce stressful life circumstances.
7. Supplemental parenting services for the neglected children, provided through therapeutic child care centers, informal networks, or trained parent aides.

The goal of these interventions is to link the neglectful parents with the existing formal and informal community support systems that most families use to cope with life tasks. If the linkages with these ongoing normative systems can be accomplished, the family is apt to be enhanced and supported by stable helping systems that can favorably alter the ecology of child rearing and can endure long after the professional helper has terminated contact with the family.

Problem Definition and Goals

Before the process of helping a neglectful family can begin, the determination must be made that the parenting provided is indeed neglectful or less than minimally adequate. This is difficult, because as pointed out in Chapter 8, there is disagreement not only on what is best for children, but more importantly here, on what is really a "minimally adequate level of care." The "quality of parenting" is in reality a continuum that stretches from abandonment and infanticide to highly competent, nurturant parenting. Neglectful parenting is an arbitrary line drawn somewhere on that continuum that reflects the current level of knowledge and opinion in a community about what children need to develop and thrive within normal limits. The human services professional must make a judgment about whether the child is receiving "minimally adequate care" according to generally accepted community standards, with due consideration to subcultural differences in less severe situations of neglect.

The goal of treatment with neglectful families must be minimally adequate care (Washburne, 1981). Beyond this the sanction for intervention depends on the parents' motivation for improving this or other aspects of their personal and family lives. Neglectful parents typically have many deficits, and improvements over an extended period of treatment are small. Professional helpers must guard against a natural tendency to establish goals for levels of child care that are beyond the capabilities of most neglectful parents and thus doom the treatment effort to failure from the start.

Interventions

Work with Neglectful Parents

Having made the decision that the parenting is neglectful, the next step is to enlist the parents' involvement in efforts to improve the level of care. There must be some agreement on the parents' part that improvement is needed and is possible, and this commitment is often difficult to obtain. The neglectful parents' definitions of the problem are typically quite different from the professionals' definitions. Understandably, neglectful parents are frequently more concerned about finances, housing, employment, and poor treatment from agencies than learning about the needs of children. After all, these are family survival issues. A parent whose $300 AFDC check has run out 2 weeks into the month and who is about to be evicted may have little energy or interest in listening to the children or to a social worker's talk about the children's needs.

Effective intervention with neglectful families must begin with what the parents feel are their most critical, pressing concerns, whatever these may be. Having established that the reason for intervention is concern about the care of the children along with concern for the well-being of the parents on whom this care depends, the worker should listen to the parents' definition of the problem and respond with empathy and with tangible, effective helping. This demonstration of respect and responsible helping is a necessary first step in establishing a relationship with the parents and initiating change in the system.

The experience of the demonstration projects cited above indicates that a strong, supportive helping relationship between a professional social worker or helper and neglectful parents is a critical component of the intervention (Conner et al., 1980; Rozansky & Chambers, 1982; Sullivan et al., 1977; Washburne, 1981). The professional helper must develop relationships with parents that are characterized by trust, nurturance, dependability, acceptance of the person (though not the deficient parenting behavior), and effective help with critical life problems. For neglectful parents who have typically never experienced this kind of nurturing relationship, the formation of this bond of trust is a necessity before work toward more responsible performance of adult parenting tasks can occur (Austin, 1983). Parent aides may also be used to supply or supplement this supportive, nurturing relationship (Barrett, 1982; Hornick et al., 1983; Swanson, 1980), but the careful selection, preparation, and training of parent aides is critical to success.

The profile of the immature personality characteristic of many neglectful parents (Polansky et al., 1981) speaks convincingly to the necessity of "reparenting" many neglectful parents. Professional helpers must be able to accept the dependency of immature parents and provide emotional support and tangible aid until these parents are able to assume progressively more responsible, independent parental functioning. This relationship becomes the vital bridge to responsible parenting.

But the research clearly indicates that one-to-one professional counseling or casework is not sufficient by itself to bring about the desired improvement in parenting (Cohn, 1979; Daro, 1985). Successful intervention must also target surrounding environmental systems that so powerfully influence parenting behavior.

Family Systems Interventions

Numerous studies of informal helping networks indicate that marital and kinship relationships are primary sources of support that family members rely on in times of need (Cochran & Brassard, 1979; Dean & Lin, 1977; Fischer, 1982; Litwak & Szelenyi, 1969; Wellman, 1979). Married parents rely heavily on their spouses for support and assistance (Abernathy, 1973; Hetherington et al., 1976). Single parents lack this vital source of support but rely heavily on friends and kin for support in carrying out parenting and other life tasks (Coughey, 1981).

The predominance of single parents among those parents who neglect has been documented in Chapter 8 and in other studies (Polansky et al., 1981, 1985b; Schene, 1986). In two-parent, neglectful families interactions between spouses and other family members have been found to be generally less frequent and more negative than among nonneglectful family members (Burgess & Conger, 1978).

This picture of the dysfunctional, neglectful family unit points to the need for skilled professional intervention to increase supportive interactions, mediate conflicts, improve communications, and possibly restructure family roles. Family counseling and family therapy approaches have been found to be important components of successful intervention programs with neglectful families (Barrett, 1982; Daro, 1985; Rozansky & Chambers, 1982). For single, neglectful parents, interventions to maintain, rehabilitate, strengthen, or develop supportive social network linkages with extended family, friends, and neighbors are all the more critical for providing the necessary supportive relationships.

Social Network Interventions

Over the past 10 years there has been increasing evidence for the effectiveness of mobilizing informal support networks to supplement professional interventions to improve the social functioning of individuals and families in a variety of problem areas. Pancoast and Collins (1976) and Watson (1972) reported on the usefulness of social networks and natural helpers for developing day care for children. Garbarino and Stocking (1980) have urged the use of informal helping networks for treatment and prevention of child abuse and neglect. Speck and Attneave (1973) and Ruevini (1979) have assembled large groups of social networks for use as a therapeutic tool in psychotherapeutic work with families.

Froland and colleagues (1981) reviewed programs in 30 different human service agencies that combined the mobilization of informal helping through "helping networks" and formal professional clinical interventions. They identified five distinct forms of informal helping strategies:

1. Personal networking includes mobilizing existing or potential relationships with family, friends, neighbors, work associates, fellow parishioners, and the like to provide assistance.
2. Volunteer linking involves recruiting, training, and matching lay volunteers with clients.

3. Mutual aid networks are developed from existing or potential relationships among a set of individuals who are brought together because they share common problems, tasks, interest, or abilities.
4. Neighborhood helping networks are developed by identifying informal helpers and helping networks within a defined geographical area.
5. Community empowerment networks are formed by identifying and working with key figures in a specific community to define problems and develop solutions.

All these network interventions may be used to strengthen the informal support systems of neglectful parents.

Network Assessment

Interventions to sustain, enhance, or develop social network supports are based on assessments of existing social network linkages of individual neglecting parents and existing informal neighborhood or community helping networks. Network assessments reveal the strengths and weaknesses of existing informal support systems and the barriers that inhibit strong, supportive network linkages. This information gives direction for the required interventions to enhance the social networks of socially isolated, neglectful families.

Assessment of community networks is made through observations of informal neighborhood interactions, interviews with key community figures, and interviews with nonneglectful families residing in the community. Barbers, beauticians, storekeepers, clergy, pharmacists, trailer or apartment resident managers, mail carriers, and school teachers are key informants who can provide valuable information about existing informal support networks operating in the community. Service clubs, church groups, neighborhood organizations, sororities, and fraternal groups in the community often offer critical parent support services such as "mother's day out," low-cost day care, or emergency financial assistance. These organizations and groups can be identified and assessed in terms of both the helping resources they offer and their accessibility to neglectful families (Bertsch, et al., 1982).

Interviews with nonneglectful families using structured social network assessment instruments have revealed informal support systems that most families use to assist with and supplement their parenting. Analyses of these networks reveal frequently mentioned central helping figures who are generally known to others as natural neighborhood helpers, to whom others go for informal help and advice regarding child rearing, securing social services, getting a job, or finding a babysitter or other supportive services (Collins & Pancoast, 1976; Garbarino & Stocking, 1980). These individuals are valuable informal helping resources who can be linked with neglectful parents to enhance weak, informal support systems.

Assessments of the existing social networks of the neglectful parents are best made through informal interviews with the parents and the use of any of a number of structured network assessment instruments. Some examples are The Index of Social Network Strength (Gaudin, 1979), The Pattison Psychosocial Inventory (Hurd, et al., 1981), and the Social Network Form (Wolf, 1983). Hartman's Eco-map is also a useful instrument for quickly mapping the family's linkages with formal and informal systems in the community (Hartman & Laird, 1983).

The significant network dimensions include size, diversity of membership, frequency and intensity of interaction, the kinds of support inherent in the linkages, the stability of linkages, interconnectedness between network members, accessibility of members, mutuality of exchanges, and structure of communication linkages. An examination of these factors gives a picture of the strengths and weaknesses of the social network as an informal support system for the family.

A graphic approach to mapping social networks is illustrated in Figure 9.1, Social Network Map. This procedure is adapted from the network mapping approach of Gottlieb (1985) and Todd (as adapted in Biegel et al., 1984).

First, parents are asked to identify the adults that are most important in their lives, people to whom the parents feel they can turn for emotional support or tangible aid in times of need. Parents are encouraged to think of relatives, friends, neighbors, fellow church members, pastors, or work associates whom they view as someone to turn to for support.

Parents are then asked to locate the network member by a dot and identifying initials or number in the appropriate quadrant of the diagram for relative, friend, neighbor, or others. This gives a picture of the composition of the network. Some networks, for example, are totally dominated by kinship relationships, with little or no representation by friends, neighbors, or others.

The intensity of the relationship is indicated by the distance from the center of the circle. Strong, intense, very supportive relationships are indicated by placing the dot close to the center of the circle. Less intense, distant, nonsupportive linkages are indicated by placing the dot on one of the outer rings.

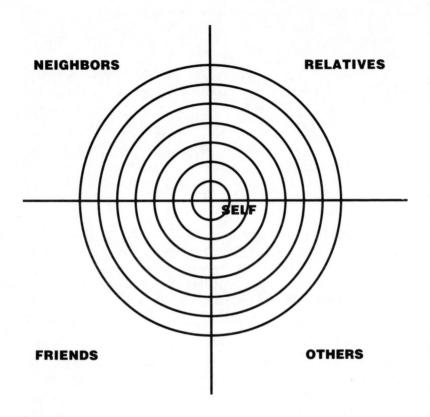

NEIGHBORS

RELATIVES

SELF

FRIENDS

OTHERS

Figure 9.1. Social network map.

The interconnectedness of the network is indicated by drawing a line between network members who know and have contact with one another independent of the neglecting parents. Highly dense or interconnected networks may provide strong support and tend to have highly consistent norms that may support adequate parenting. Normally, social networks tend to be composed of two or three highly connected clusters of persons (Wellman, 1981). Highly connected, kin-dominated networks of neglectful parents may be dysfunctional, for example, if they do not provide opportunities for learning new, more effective approaches to parenting.

The supportiveness of the network may be indicated on the network map by the color of the line connecting the neglectful parent and the network member. For instance, a red line could indicate the availability of emotional support, that is, someone who listens to problems and concerns about children, family, or marriage empathically. A blue line could represent the availability of tangible aid, that is, babysitting, loan of money or food, or provision of transportation. A black line could mean information and advice about child care, how to apply for food stamps, or where to go for financial assistance. A green line could indicate relationships that are purely social or recreational. Multiple colored lines connecting network members with the parent could indicate strong supportive linkages. Some linkages may not be supportive at all but may, on the contrary, be sources of stress.

The resulting visual map of the parents' existing social networks clarifies for parents and workers the strengths and weaknesses of the parents' existing social networks. It is a useful assessment tool that suggests goals and directions for intervention to strengthen vital informal network supports for child rearing.

The barriers to effective network support become evident as the professional helper discusses the social network with a neglectful parent. Through these assessment interviews the helper experiences the parent's communication and social skills and gains insights into the social distance between the parent and surrounding community support systems. The barriers may include (a) long-standing interpersonal conflicts with relatives, neighbors, or other potentially supportive social network members; (b) deficits in verbal or writing skills, nonassertiveness, or other social skills deficits; (c) distorted beliefs and stereotyping; (e) geographical isolation, absence of transportation, or telephone; or (f) concerns about reciprocal helping obligations. These barriers suggest specific treatment goals and interventions.

Assessment of the family's social network may reveal one of three situations:

1. An existing network that is adequate in size with an adequate number of supportive linkages.
2. An existing network that is inadequate in size, diversity of membership, intensity of interaction, stability, or supportiveness.
3. A very weak, nonexistent or nonsupportive network.

Table 9.1

Differential Network Assessments and Interventions

Assessed Strength, Existing Personal Social Network	*Interventions*	*Social Worker Roles/Tasks*
Moderately strong, supportive network	Encouragement and support Sustaining Encourage reciprocal exchanges Social skills training	Consultant Counselor Teacher
Small, weak nonsupportive network	Conflict resolution Communication and social skills training Mobilize natural helpers Cognitive restructuring Organize mutual support groups	Mediator/liaison Teacher Advocate/broker Consultant Behavior changer Group leader
Nonexistent or disfunctional network	Social skills training Cognitive restructuring Organize mutual support groups Mobilize natural helpers Broker entry into mainstream groups Community education	Teacher Behavior changer Group leader Community organizer Consultant Advocate/broker Educator

As illustrated in Table 9.1, Differential Network Assessments and Interventions, the three situations call for different interventions by professional helpers and correspondingly different helping roles and tasks.

Network Interventions

In the first case where a neglectful parent's social network is found to be adequate in size, diversity of composition, and supportiveness of linkages, the goal is to support and assist the parent in maintaining the supportive linkages. The professional helper may need to encourage the parent to reciprocate helping, to respond in a reinforcing manner to help received in order to prevent breakdowns in what are understood to be reciprocal helping linkages. Neglectful families often lack material resources to offer but can be helped to identify and offer personal resources that they do have to offer, that is, empathy, encouragement, information, or shared life experiences. Social skills training may be needed to enhance the neglectful parent's relationship-building abilities, which are necessary to maintain effective network linkages.

When the network assessment reveals an existing network with weak, distant, or nonsupportive linkages, the professional helper must intervene as a mediator/liaison/facilitator to strengthen or supplement the existing linkages. The helper first identifies the barriers that interfere with the critical exchange of support. Often the barriers are old or recent conflicts or distorted communications that can be removed or reduced through interventions to facilitate and clarify communication, correct distortions, and mediate conflicts. The professional helper serves as a bridge between two alienated network members to restore communication and the exchange of mutual support. In some cases the skilled professional helper may, with the parents' approval, convene all or part of the parents' social network as practiced by Ruevini (1979) or Garrison (1974) to clarify communications, mediate conflicts, remove obstacles to helping, or solicit active involvement in a joint problem-solving process.

When lack of social skills is a cause of a parent's deficient support network, teaching appropriate, culturally relevant communication, assertiveness, and other necessary social skills may be a useful component of the intervention. Social skills are best taught in a group setting where the parents are provided a safe environment to learn and practice social skills and receive encouragement and constructive feedback from peers. Lange and Jakubowski's assertiveness training (1976) or Goldstein and colleagues' (1986) structured social learning approach to teaching basic social skills to abusive parents can be used with neglectful parents. Neglectful parents can also learn social skills by observing the social behavior of the professional helper or a trained volunteer parent aide.

Where the assessment of a neglectful parent's social network indicates a very limited or nonexistent support system, the worker intervenes to help the parent develop an effective support network. First, the worker engages the parent in brainstorming to identify any potentially supportive network members. The parent is encouraged to evaluate neighbors, friends, relatives, work associates, a pastor, or fellow church members as potential supports and to identify and critically assess any barriers to actualizing these potentially supportive linkages. Plans are then developed for overcoming the barriers and forming the supportive social network linkages. The parent is prepared through coaching, rehearsal, and role play to initiate the necessary social interaction. One may also need to intervene with the potential network members to facilitate communication, mediate conflict, or reduce other barriers.

The identification and mobilization of neighborhood "natural helpers" can also be an effective approach to developing a support network for the neglectful parent. These natural helpers, who are identified through the assessment of existing networks in the area, can become key members of the support network for neglectful parents with professional support and consultation (Pancoast, 1980; Pancoast & Collins, 1976; Watson, 1972).

The formation of support groups composed of neglectful parents who share the same problems, social skills deficits, and social status has been found to be an effective approach to strengthening the social networks and improving the coping abilities of neglectful parents (Cole & Taylor, 1984; Conner et al., 1980; Felt, 1983), for example, the experience of Parents Anonymous groups over the past 15 years (Collins, 1978; Lieber & Baker, 1977). From their evaluative studies Cohn (1979) and Daro (1985) have concluded that group approaches with neglectful and abusive families are associated with positive outcomes. The mutually supportive ties with group members frequently continue long after the termination of the group and thus provide more permanent enrichment of the parents' informal support network.

Groups should begin with minimal structure and offer opportunity for sharing concerns, issues, and problems so as to build cohesion and establish agendas and goals for the group. The initial focus, in response to neglectful parents' powerful needs for nurturance and attention, is on personal concerns and self-development. Successful support groups with neglectful parents have used simple arts-and-crafts activities, shopping and other field trips, cosmetologists as guest speakers on makeup and beauty care, "pot luck" meals, and recipe pooling as cohesion-building activities. Providing refreshments is a tangible way of nurturing and an important feature of the meetings. Groups may then move on to more structured activities for learning specific problem-solving, parenting, social, and communication skills (Treating chronic neglect, 1984).

The recruitment, training, and linking of volunteer parent aides is another approach that has been used successfully to strengthen the informal helping network of neglectful parents (Swanson, 1980). Lay volunteers can teach child care in the home through modeling, instruction, coaching, and advice. The careful selection and training of lay volunteers is critical, as is professional supervision and backup (Gifford et al., 1979).

Parenting Education

Research indicates that traditional parenting education is not effective as a primary method of intervention with socially isolated, disadvantaged parents (Dumas & Wahler, 1983) or with abusive parents (Gaudin & Kurtz, 1985). However, most of the demonstration projects cited above used some type of parenting education as a component of the intervention with neglectful parents, and most judged this component as important to successful results (Conner et al., 1980; Felt, 1983; Rozansky & Chambers, 1982). Behavioral approaches to teaching specific parenting skills were the preferred and apparently most successful approaches. Parenting training efforts with abusive or neglectful parents appear from the research more likely to be effective when a skills training approach is used that combines group instruction, modeling and observation, guided practice, and in-home, one-to-one coaching (Gaudin & Kurtz, 1985).

Parent training should teach empathic listening and nurturing responses to the emotional and physical nurturance needs of children. It should teach age-appropriate expectations and nonabusive forms of discipline using positive reinforcement, time out, and logical consequences. Parenting education programs like Bavolek and Comstock's Nurturing Program (1983) or Yang and colleagues' Parent Training Program (1981), which have been developed specifically for teaching parenting skills to abusive parents, offer structure and useful teaching aids. However, structured programs should be introduced only after there has been some airing of concerns by the parents, some work on pressing issues, and some provision of nurturing activities in response to the parents' personal needs.

Programs judged to be successful have included home visits or opportunities in child care centers for neglectful parents to observe professionals or skilled parent aides model the appropriate skills and then to practice the skills with coaching and encouragement from the expert (Barrett, 1982; Felt, 1983; Rozansky & Chambers, 1982). It is important, however, to bear in mind that to be effective this intervention must be combined with others, including helping to meet the family's physical survival needs.

Interventions with the Children

The experience of the demonstration projects clearly indicates that changes in parental behavior come slowly, and continuing support is needed (Daro, 1985; Edgington & Hall, 1982; Felt, 1983).

Meanwhile, the child victims of neglect still suffer from inadequate child care. Without supplemental nurturing, the children of neglectful parents tend to suffer serious and continuing developmental deficits and social adjustment problems (Egeland et al., 1983; Polansky et al., 1981).

Intervention with neglectful families is incomplete without direct services to neglected children to provide the supplemental stimulation, nurturing, and care that their parents are unable to provide. The necessary nurturing experiences can be provided, at least in part, through therapeutic child care center programs (Barrett, 1982; Felt, 1983) or through the use of homemakers and volunteer parent aides who visit in the child's home on a regular, frequent schedule and supplement the neglectful parents' child care efforts. Concerned neighbors, relatives, or friends who are already members of the neglectful parents' social network may be mobilized to provide supplemental nurturing and care. Natural helpers in the community may also be enabled to initiate a nurturing relationship with the children to supplement the parents' efforts.

Nonorganic failure-to-thrive children are a special group of neglected children who frequently require hospitalization and intensive medical follow-up care to remedy the serious developmental delays and deficits they have suffered. Even with intensive medical and follow-up services, the efforts are often not very successful in correcting the deficits (Haynes et al., 1984).

Advocacy and Linking with Formal Community Systems

Neglectful parents are often isolated from formally organized community helping resources (Giovannoni, 1971). They often lack information about the availability of resources or are reluctant to seek help because of negative experiences with seeking help in the past. The parents must be linked effectively to agencies and programs offering child care, homemaker services, financial assistance, food, housing assistance, job placement, and counseling. These concrete services are often needed to reduce the highly stressful life conditions of neglectful parents. These services frequently make the difference between adequate care and neglectful care.

The barriers to effective helping linkages between neglectful families and community service organizations must be identified and assessed and appropriate interventions made to neutralize the barriers and strengthen the vital linkages. These may be distorted communication, previous negative experiences with seeking help, geographical or social distance, or negative stereotyping on the part of the neglectful families or the helping organization. The professional must facilitate communication, correct distorted perceptions and stereotypes, allay fears, serve as mediator/liaison, and advocate and educate to build bridges between social agencies, churches, schools, civic organizations, and the isolated neglectful parents and their children.

CONCLUSIONS

The modest results of intervention programs with neglectful families indicate the size of the treatment challenge. Even with well-designed and well-financed multiservice efforts, intervention has been successful in bringing the level of parenting up to a minimally sufficient level in less than half of the families studied. Many neglectful families are doubly handicapped by impoverished personal psychological resources and highly stressful, nonsupportive environmental systems.

Elements found in the more successful treatment programs offer some guidelines for effective intervention with neglectful families:

1. Multiservice programs are required to meet the multiple needs of neglectful families. Reliance on a single treatment approach is not sufficient to bring about the desired improvements in child-rearing practices.
2. Intervention of at least 6 months' duration is necessary for achieving even moderately successful outcomes. Most significant changes occur as a result of interventions within the first 18 months.
3. Outreach, in-home services are required.
4. The ecological supports for at least minimally adequate parenting must be improved by interventions to improve functioning of the family system, sustain, enhance, or develop informal support networks, and improve linkages with formally organized community service systems. These supports must include assistance as indicated, with income supplements, housing, health services, child care centers, job training and placement, and the like.
5. Parenting and social skills training, using behavioral approaches, may be helpful as part of a multiservice effort in remedying knowledge and skills deficits. Parent groups can serve as supportive environments for developing these skills.
6. Intervention programs should include therapeutic child care to supplement the efforts of neglectful parents and to remedy the developmental deficits suffered by the children.

7. A strong, supportive, nurturing relationship with a skilled professional helper is an important component of intervention with neglectful parents but must be supplemented by an array of supportive services.

The model for intervention with neglectful families developed in this chapter is an ecosystems, multiservice approach that incorporates the interventions found to be useful in previous efforts and adds specific interventions to strengthen supportive social network linkages. Empirical validation of this network intervention approach by the author is under way at this writing with the support of the National Center on Child Abuse and Neglect (Grant No. 90 CA1189/01).

NOTE

1. The "standard team approach" used a bilevel structure composed of a treatment team and an organizational team. The treatment team was an interdisciplinary group of professionals that included a primary therapist who coordinated all treatment activities. The organizational team, composed of social workers/prime therapists, assisted the individual prime therapist in the treatment of target families by giving guidance and help with decision making about interventions, involvement of community agencies, removal of children, court actions, and so on. The direct interventions by the prime therapist involved providing nurturance and support to the parent, teaching problem-solving and parenting skills, and coordinating community resources in the interest of the parent (Hornick et al., 1983).

10

Public Policies and Families

CATHERINE S. CHILMAN

This chapter briefly discusses some of the salient aspects of public policies and families. It is a prelude to Chapter 11, which addresses legislation and policies concerning families troubled with mental illnesses and addictions, and is very like one with a similar title in other volumes in this series.

DEFINITIONS OF FAMILY WELL-BEING

It can be argued that the chief goal of public policies concerning families is the promotion of family well-being. There are a number of conflicting definitions of this term, a term that often includes the words "strong families." To traditionalists, strong families are apt to mean patriarchal ones in which members marry as young adults "until death do us part," have a number of children, refrain from the use of artificial contraceptives and abortion, and follow traditional sex roles with husbands as the only (and adequate) wage earners and wives as full-time homemakers and mothers. Such families are often conceptualized as "stable and strong." They present a united front to the outside world, regardless of the divisions and conflicts that may occur within them.

A more modernist view is that strong families are ones that function in such a way as to promote the physical, social, psychological, and economic well-being of each person, both as members of the family and as autonomous individuals. This well-being is viewed in process terms, that is, each family member, young *and* old, is capable (in fact, needful) of growth and development throughout the life span. The processes of this kind of family system support individual growth through respect for the autonomy of each family member and through the nurturance of each member as an integral part of a caring, interdependent, intimate family group. Following such a definition, family stability is not necessarily seen as desirable if stability means that marriages should be permanent regardless of their quality and that parenthood should be perpetually selfless regardless of the problems that offspring may present in their adult years as well as their younger ones (Terkelson, 1980).

PUBLIC POLICY PROCESSES

As in the case of "family well-being," the term "policy" has numerous definitions and interpretations. A full discussion of this topic alone could fill many volumes. For the present purposes, however, the term means public (i.e., government) policy and is conceptualized as a series of processes. Moreover, the primary emphasis is on *federal* public policies as constituting the most general approach. Public policy by itself might be thought of as a guiding principle of government, such as "every child in the United States shall receive a high quality of education," a familiar and enticing principle! However, the principle does not move beyond the enticement (and probably vote-getting) stage unless it is developed into legislative proposals that must be passed by Congress and signed by the President.

The outcome of these processes is affected by highly political forces. Typically, numerous lobbying groups and individual citizens become involved. Action by Congress and the President is strongly influenced by these groups and individuals, most especially by strong, well-financed, national lobbies.

The process is far from finished, however, even if legislation is approved and signed. Appropriations that provide *adequate funding* must be made by Congress, and this funding is strongly influenced by the nature of political support for and opposition to the legislation. Then, too, relevant federal departments must be provided with administrative personnel, processes that are also affected by political considerations. Following these steps, administrative guidelines must be developed.

The legislation then moves for its further financing and implementation to state levels. In turn, state governments must develop programs that are to be carried out by local units of government. These units, then, must further develop and administer programs so that they actually reach the individuals and families for whom the legislation was intended. The degree to which this legislation is funded and implemented at state and local levels also depends on political considerations within the various units of government and, ultimately, on the views that individual local staff members may have about the matter. Even more ultimately the ways in which these programs are used or not used by individuals and families is strongly affected by *their* particular attitudes, values, and behaviors in relation to the services offered. (Consider government-supported family-planning programs, for instance.)

Furthermore, if it happens that some person or persons question the constitutionality of the law and this challenge reaches the Supreme Court who, in turn, finds the legislation in violation of the Constitution, the entire process will be moved back to square one. In short, there is a long series of processes that must occur for a policy to have real effect: a study in the many trials and triumphs of a democracy in a federal (national–state–local) system![1]

Although ideally public policy development and implementation is a rational process based on the best scientific knowledge, rational process is only one piece of the much larger policy puzzle. For instance, findings from scientific research are often brought into the policy process to provide a patina of rational respectability to a piece of legislation that more fundamentally has pragmatic political purposes.

The complex, lengthy, political processes described above may well be discouraging to those who wish to affect public policies. To be effective, it is often useful for individuals to select a few policy issues that seem to them to be crucial, to affiliate with groups (often representative of one or more of the human services professions) who share their concerns, and to keep informed and politically active with that group or groups and follow the legislation through its many processes: congressional and presidential legislative actions, budget appropriations, development of administrative guidelines, state and local implementation, and court challenges. It also helps to know one's elected local, state, and federal representatives and to join and contribute to the political party of choice as well as campaign organizations for candidates supporting desired public policies.

In general, it is unproductive to complain, as many do, that public policies are "just a mess of politics." Within the American system of government, "politics" is a process of democracy in action. As discussed above the many processes involved are heavily affected by pressures from politically active individuals and groups. Thus, the way for human service professionals to affect policies is to become politically active themselves, especially through knowledgeable, well-organized groups. To simply criticize and stay outside of the processes is to pass the power to others who *are* actively involved and often involved with pushing agendas that are not in the best interests of families in trouble, especially poor and minority families who have relatively little power themselves.

A major point to the policy chapters in this series is to provide both a knowledge background and stimulus to readers to involve themselves, to one extent or another, in political activities to affect public policies that play such a large part in the lives of troubled families. An ecological approach to services for families clearly implies that concerned human service professionals should involve themselves, to one degree or another, in policy- and planning-oriented political activities as well as in the provision of direct services, the major focus of most practitioners serving families today (1987).[2]

FAMILY-RELATED POLICIES

This leads to another definition: family policies or family-related policies. Again, policies referred to here are public, that is, government policies. Again, the term "family policy" has numerous meanings and involves numerous controversies. As of the mid-1980s the term was attracting increased attention, sparking heated debates covering the entire political spectrum from the extreme conservative political right to the extreme liberal left. Virtually everybody appeared to be "pro-family" and in favor of supports for family well-being, including supports for their economic and occupational well-being. But as we have seen, definitions of family and family well-being have many interpretations. To some the term "public family policy" may mean that certain kinds of families and family-related behaviors, as determined by government action, should be promoted and other kinds officially opposed.

On the other hand, many others hold that "family public policies" should be defined as including all government policies and programs that have an impact on families; they also tend to believe that government should not impose a particular standard of family roles and functions on its citizens. The concept that family policies consist of all policies affecting families has lead in a number of directions, including that of family-impact analysis, a term that became popular during the Carter–Mondale administration of the late 1970s (Zimmerman, 1982).

Family-impact analysis takes a rational planning approach to family policy. It seeks to gather large bodies of data concerning numerous public programs that affect families and to assess their effects through complex statistical analyses of relevant data. Impact is measured by demonstrated or probable effects on birth, marriage, divorce, separation, illegitimacy, employment, and income. These statistics are primarily provided by the U.S. Bureau of the Census, the National Center of Vital Statistics, and the U.S. Department of Labor. Moreover, numerous studies of various aspects of family well-being and of program effectiveness of family life, broadly defined, have been carried out by numerous government agencies and universities as well as by human service public and private organizations. Findings from these investigations are also used to supplement the above data. Many of these studies are also discussed in the relevant chapters of this series.

Senator Patrick Moynihan, who has had a long-time interest in family policy, writes that in essence family policy focuses on the outcomes of other policies. He sees family welfare as being the business of numerous social and economic programs at national, state, and local levels and holds that their impact on families can be assessed, at least in part, by analyses of family data, as discussed above (Moynihan, 1986).

Kamerman and Kahn (1978), who have conducted extensive surveys of family policies and programs in this and other countries, define family policies in ways that are close to Moynihan's conceptions. They hold that family policy consists of activities funded and sponsored by government that affect families directly or indirectly, intentionally or unintentionally, whether or not these policies have specific family objectives. They write that family policy is both a perspective and a set of activities. As an activity it includes such family-specific programs as family-planning services, food stamps, income maintenance, foster care, adoption, homemaker services, day care, child development programs, family counseling and therapy, and employment services.

All of the above views include, or can include, the concept of family impact analysis. As I see it, this analysis has considerable merit primarily because it recognizes the huge network of government programs that impinge on families. This analysis also calls for the application of survey data and many kinds of research, both basic and applied, to the formation and analysis of public family-related programs and policies. However, family-impact analysis by itself cannot be expected to change public policy. Those who apply its methods will have major problems if they fail to recognize and deal with the many political processes that are also necessary to actualize policies as discussed above.

Also, family-impact analysis is deficient if it merely takes the passive approach of simply analyzing what effects government programs and policies will have or are having on families. An active approach is also needed in which the needs of families are the primary consideration and planning activities are then directed to formulating what programs and policies, both existing and not yet existing, are needed.

Another and far more conservative view of family policy was presented by President Reagan's Working Group on the Family in 1986 (Washington Cofo Memo, 1986). Their report called for less government infringement on the rights and responsibilities of families. State-funded day care, income assistance through public family allowances for children, school feeding programs, and national health care systems were all seen as socialistic evils that undermine American families and the larger society. The report called for local, volunteer assistance to families in lieu of federal/state government programs. On the other hand, government should take an active stand to affect cultural patterns perceived by the working group as being hostile to families; these patterns included drug use, pornography, and "bigoted" stands against religions.

The report also saw economic expansion as essentially a pro-family program. Such expansion could be brought about, the group stated, through such measures as low taxes, control of inflation, and the end of "social spending schemes." The report further stated that old principles that prevent erosion of family rights and responsibilities through court actions, dominance by public education, and control by social programs must be reaffirmed. Senator Moynihan called this report not so much an analysis of public policies and families as a "conservative tantrum." Indeed, it seemed to reflect some of the main aspects of the extreme conservative position. Furthermore, the report illustrates the principle that *all* aspects of the functioning of society can be viewed as relevant to family policies. It also shows that the field of family policy is highly sensitive and readily politicized.

Family issues deeply engage the heart as well as the mind. They touch upon the most intimate, significant aspects of our lives, the central identity each of us derives through our total development from infancy onward. Family issues include our most private and personal attachments, values, and beliefs. For many, probably the majority of Americans, family issues are closely intertwined with religious ones. And a basic principle of the American credo is a separation of church and state. Probably all religions see the guidance and succor of families as being central to their function and sharply different from those of government.

Furthermore, individual and hence family freedom from government interference is also basic to the American tradition. Millions of immigrants from the early 1600s to the present have come to this country in search of this freedom. Thus, the very words "family policy" can serve as a red flag to many of our citizens of all political persuasions.

Schorr (1986) writes that it is preferable to plan for wide-range public policies and programs that families need rather than advocating for family policies per se because the former term is less sensitive and controversial than the latter. Moreover, many such programs can be offered as services that may be chosen or not, depending on the values and beliefs of individual families and their members, thus safeguarding principles of freedom.

FAMILIES VERSUS SOCIETAL RESPONSIBILITY

The concept of "family responsibility" is another controversial and complicated one that usually arises in debates about families and policies. It lies at the heart of many issues. Although our traditional cultural patterns hold that it is desirable for families to be self-reliant and self-supporting, responsible toward each of their members, and independent of any public aid, virtually *no* family in today's highly urbanized, technological society is totally independent of the services provided by large networks of external systems, both private and governmental. Government-aided and/or regulated systems within the country that are crucial to the well-being of virtually all families include transportation in its many aspects, water supplies, waste disposal, fire and police protection, dependable money supplies and insured savings bank deposits, public education systems, public health services, social security provisions, the court systems, and so on. And international programs aimed at implementation of foreign policy and national defense as well as improved international trade, theoretically at least, provide important assistance for every individual and family in the country.

Although many of these forms of assistance are more or less taken for granted, sharp arguments quickly arise over such issues as special income, health, employment, housing, child care, and education assistance targeted to the poor and near poor. Such programs are highly visible, are incorrectly seen as inordinately expensive, and are often viewed as replacing family responsibilities—with many of these responsibilities fundamentally being the traditional functions of women, including child care, nursing care of the ill and disabled, and stretching the food, housing, and clothing dollar through home production. Some traditionalists claim that keeping these kinds of responsibilities within the family actually enhances the well-being of families. However, if we return to our earlier definition of family well-being, we can see that this well-being is eroded, rather than supported, if the basic survival and developmental needs of families and all their members, including wives and mothers, are not met. An overload of economic adversities or severe illnesses or handicaps may make it impossible for some families to handle problems such as these without the supplementary assistance of public programs. Although conservatives often argue that private, voluntary efforts should provide the assistance needed, our society has become too urbanized, costly, and complex for these activities by themselves to make much of a dent on the host of problems that many families encounter today. These voluntary efforts can be helpful as a supplement to, but not a substitute for, necessary family assistance programs.

As shown in the foregoing chapters, families in our complex, technologically advanced society have only limited control over their own physical health and over mobilizing the frequently costly resources for treatment of the physical illnesses and disabilities that may afflict family members.

A careful analysis of the points listed above can lead to the recognition that many of the problems faced by families today are not solely a result of irresponsible actions on their part; rather, to a large extent they are a result of a combination of factors external to families. These include the many stressors in our complex, impersonal society, problematic characteristics of our mental health programs, cutbacks in public housing programs, and the like. Thus, a number of public policies and programs are needed to promote and support the well-being of troubled families and their members, as is discussed in more detail in Chapter 11.

NOTES

1. Other legal challenges regarding legislation and its administration may be raised through the courts at various local, state, and regional levels, but a discussion of details concerning this and other issues affecting public policies transcends the space constraints of this chapter.

2. Although the foregoing paragraphs may seem like a high school lesson in civics, it is my experience that the majority of citizens, including graduate students, many academicians, and human service professionals, fail to understand any number of the principles sketched here. These principles grow out of my experience and study as a university professor, as a former staff member of the (then) U.S. Department of Health, Education and Welfare during the 1960s, and as a former staff member of various state governments and private social agencies.

It was my common government experience during the 1960s that both academicians and human service professionals outside the federal government sought to impress me with their views of what policies and programs were needed because they assumed I was an "influential policy-maker." In actuality, the executive branch of government (i.e., the President, his Cabinet, and the staff of the various federal departments) cannot create public domestic policies (with "domestic" referring to policies *internal* to this country) without supportive legislation and appropriations as provided by congressional action. Also, any staff actions must be within guidelines provided by the relevant legislation. Furthermore, federal staff members must be sensitive to the reactions of citizens, as groups and as individuals, at local levels because these citizens may protest to their Congresspeople if they object to any part of federal programs and the way they are administered.

Thus, it seems to me that the term "federal domestic policy makers" tends to be a fallacy if it refers to federal staff personnel because their options are limited by many factors. In fact, given the constraints, it is something of a miracle that federal "bureaucrats" can act at all. Similar comments apply to local and state governments, but our focus here is on the federal government.

11

Federal Mental Health Policy:

ITS UNHAPPY PAST AND UNCERTAIN FUTURE

BRIAN L. WILCOX AND MARY UYEDA

This chapter provides a brief, general overview of the federal government's role in mental health programs and policies. Chapter 12 emphasizes federal policy and program trends in deinstitutionalization of mentally disordered people and the effects of these trends on patients and their families.

Federal mental health policy has changed quite dramatically over the past two decades. The federal government has radically scaled back its direct involvement in the delivery of mental health services to the degree that it is probably fair to characterize current federal efforts in mental health, with a few exceptions, as a set of health care financing strategies.

This chapter offers a brief history of federal policy regarding the care of mentally disordered individuals, followed by a more detailed description of current federal policy. We will not attempt to describe in detail the variety of state policy activities in the mental health area, as these vastly outnumber the more limited federal efforts.

It is perhaps appropriate to begin by noting that we view mental health from a broad ecological or contextual perspective (Holahan et al., 1979). This ecological perspective considers psychological adjustment in transactional terms: "Behavior is not viewed as sick or well but is defined as transactional—an outcome of reciprocal interaction between specific social situations and the individual" (Kelly, 1966, p. 538). Or, as Smith and Hobbs (1966, p. 500) note, mental disorder is not the "private misery of an individual but is tied to the entire fabric of the individual's life: It is not just an individual who has faltered; the social systems in which he is embedded through family, school, or job, through religious affiliation, or through friendship, have failed to sustain him as an effective participant." Also, as discussed in Chapter 1, mental disorders are a multidetermined syndrome with heterogenous forms and causes that include interactive biological, psychological, social, and economic factors.

Having noted this conceptual orientation, we must point out that public policy is an extremely blunt instrument of social change. Broad social policies of the nature we describe are inherently rather crude and hence usually insensitive to the programmatic implications of such conceptual models. As a result, federal mental health policies generally do not reflect an appreciation of the complexities associated with mental health problems. For example, policy provisions rarely include the role of families, schools, employers, or other contexts central to the individual in the treatment of mental health problems.

FEDERAL MENTAL HEALTH POLICY UNTIL 1965

Federal mental health policy in the United States is, relatively speaking, a fairly recent phenomenon. Historically, responsibility for the care of the mentally disabled has resided with the family, the community, or the state. Before the federal government became involved with the care of the mentally disturbed, states had gradually taken at least partial responsibility for this population. The movement by governments toward institutionalization started in Europe during the seventeenth and eighteenth centuries as the power of churches waned along with the view that disturbed behavior was a manifestation of the devil to be "cured" by exorcism or execution. This concept was replaced by the idea that mental disorders were caused by immorality, to be dealt with by punishment and segregation from the community. Institutionalization replaced witch hunting, but the basic goal was to protect society rather than help the individual. However, along with other social reforms of the early nineteenth century went the idea that the mentally disturbed required understanding and treatment rather than punishment.

These reforms began in western Europe and gradually spread to the United States where seriously deranged people had been chiefly segregated in such settings as jails and almshouses. During the second half of the nineteenth century, social, economic, and medical reformers, lead by Dorothea Dix, stimulated the development of, first, county mental hospitals and, later, as a move toward greater efficiency, state hospitals. By 1900 more than 100 new state institutions had been built.

These hospitals, started as a humanitarian effort, soon became overcrowded with a wide range of chronically deranged and socially troublesome individuals, including many of the poor and socially deviant. "By early in this century the network of state mental hospitals, once a proud tribute to an era of reform, had largely turned into a bureaucratic morass within which patients were interned, often neglected and sometimes abused" (Bassuk & Gerson, 1985, p. 129).

Between 1920 and 1940 there was a growing tendency to place older people who were diagnosed as senile or suffering from cerebral arteriosclerosis in mental hospitals. During periods of economic depression the numbers of these commitments increased dramatically, especially among those without economic or social resources and among those immigrants who had difficulty adjusting to a society that was alien to them (Mechanic, 1980).

Federal involvement in the mental health arena has occurred in fits and starts and is largely a post–World War II development. The earlier rationale for federal resistance to involvement in mental health is exemplified by the statement offered by President Pierce in 1854 upon his veto of a bill that would have allowed states to use federal lands to finance the construction of state mental hospitals. President Pierce argued that mental problems were at their root individual concerns and, therefore, of no concern to the federal government (Pierce, 1854). Others similarly opposed federal involvement in the mental health arena on the grounds that the Constitution alloted most such domestic concerns to the states unless a compelling federal concern could be shown to outweigh the interest of the states.

World War I provided the first clear case in which the national interest intervened to foster a federal involvement in mental health. In the aftermath of the war a large number of soldiers returned who experienced significant mental distress. Concern for these "shell-shocked" veterans led to the federal government's first foray into the delivery of mental health services, through the Veterans Administration.

From these beginnings federal involvement in mental health services expanded slowly. For example, in 1929 Congress passed legislation creating a Division of Mental Hygiene within the Public Health Service to oversee the operation of two new federal narcotic treatment centers. In the mid-1930s the Public Health Service was given responsibility for the provision of mental health services in federal prisons. Each of these changes, although relatively small in scope, established precedent for an expanded federal role.

In response to the problems noted above, Congress first passed the National Mental Health Act in 1946, which recognized mental disturbances as a national public health problem and provided the authority for the eventual creation of the National Institute of Mental Health in 1949. This act provided funding for research, training of professional personnel, and assistance to the states for the creation of pilot demonstration studies and projects. The leaders of NIMH were interested in the prevention aspects of mental health as well as direct treatment services, that is, in both primary prevention (efforts to foster positive mental health) and secondary prevention (early treatment in the community). The concept of community-based care, rather than hospitalization, appealed to state mental health authorities who were overwhelmed by the enormous, rising expenses of mental hospitals. Moreover, the advent of mood-altering drugs made community-based care increasingly practical (Lieby, 1978).

In 1955 Congress passed the Mental Health Study Act, which established a private nonprofit corporation, the Joint Commission on Mental Illness and Health, to report on the mental health needs of the nation and offer recommendations on how policy makers might address these needs. This commission emphasized the importance of deinstitutionalization and recommended increased recruitment of professional personnel, establishment of full-time community mental health clinics and general hospital psychiatric units, and investment in long-term, basic mental health research.

The final report of this commission, *Action for Mental Health* (Joint Commission on Mental Illness and Health, 1961), was delivered to Congress on December 31, 1960, just days before John F. Kennedy took office. Roughly 2 years later President Kennedy delivered his famous Message to Congress on Mental Illness and Mental Retardation, the first time a president specifically addressed these issues in a major policy statement. Kennedy called for a "bold new approach" to the problems of mental illness and mental retardation, emphasizing the need for prevention efforts focusing on the alteration of social conditions associated with these problems. The emphasis of the Joint Commission and the resulting message from President Kennedy to the effect that new community mental health centers were to be independent of the old mental hospital system was tremendously important. It endorsed the concept that mental illness is not inherently different from a large range of psychological difficulties common in the community (Mechanic, 1980).

The policy outgrowth of Kennedy's message was the Community Mental Health Centers Act of 1963, signed into law shortly after Kennedy's death. This act initially provided funds for the construction of community-based mental health treatment facilities designed to serve delimited geographic regions known as catchment areas. Not until 1965 was the act amended to provide grants to support the staffing of the centers. Over the following 5 years

Congress amended the act several times to expand the mandate of the centers to include services for substance abusers and to enhance services for children, the latter change growing out of the recommendations of the Joint Commission on the Mental Health of Children (1969).

This report emphasized that the mental health system was seriously neglecting the needs of children, youth, and their families. Taking a broad ecological—preventive as well as treatment—approach, it called for a national child development council in the office of the President. This council was to serve as an advocate for public programs at local, state, and federal levels to foster the total physical, social, and psychological well-being of children and youth. This report called for both an expansion and coordination of a wide range of human services as well as concerted federal–state–local efforts to reduce poverty and racism and their deleterious effects on families and their children. The report had little direct impact on public policies and programs, possibly because the recommendations were overly general, broad, and costly and partly because of the change in federal domestic policies with the election of President Nixon, along with the nation's increasing involvement in the war in Vietnam.

Over the years since 1969 the federal share of the funding of community mental health centers has been scaled back considerably, and state and local government sources, along with third-party payees through public and private insurance plans, have become the most significant source of funding for community mental health services.

In 1980 Congress passed and President Carter signed into law the Mental Health Systems Act (PL 96–398). This legislation, which replaced the Community Mental Health Centers Act, would have expanded the community mental health centers program and funded a vast array of new mental health service programs. Included among the priority areas were new programs for the chronically mentally ill, children and adolescents, and the elderly (President's Commission on Mental Health, 1979). Funds were also authorized for mental health promotion projects and mental health advocacy, along with programs for the prevention of mental disturbance. (Note the similarities to the 1969 Joint Commission report discussed above.)

This act represented the first major expansion of the federal role in the provision of service dollars (outside of the Medicare and Medicaid programs) since the passage of the Community Health Centers Act in 1963. Unfortunately, the Mental Health Systems Act, a product of the Democratic Carter Administration, was never put into place. With the election of President Reagan in 1980 Congress quickly moved forward with the new president's legislative agenda: the Reagan Revolution. A significant component of that revolution involved the dismantling of large, federal, categorical grant programs. The Mental Health Systems Act was one of the early casualties. In 1981 federal funding of the community mental health centers shifted from categorical grants, which featured federal guidelines to the states for standards of service, to block grants. The result was that state programs became highly variable, depending on public attitudes, political conditions, and economic resources within each state.

We now describe the more recent developments in federal mental health policy, beginning with the major health care programs that today represent the largest federal contribution to mental health services. In describing these programs, we return to their historical origins.

CONTEMPORARY MENTAL HEALTH POLICIES

If mental conditions or behavioral problems are seen primarily as the consequences of social and economic conditions, it means that the federal role in addressing them takes the form of attempting to alter the social and economic contexts in which people live. If, on the other hand, mental disorders are seen as a health problem, the federal role is expressed through health care policies, which in turn are shaped by notions of disease and cure. The federal role in both these areas has undergone profound changes over the past two decades. Federal involvement in social and economic issues reached its zenith during the late 1960s, stimulated by the consciousness of social injustice, racism, and economic disparities addressed by the New Frontier programs of that period.

As we have seen, until 1965 the federal role in health care in general was focused on activities in the Veterans Administration and the Department of Defense for enlisted military personnel. Public health activities were focused chiefly on basic public health problems such as sanitation and disease control.

By 1965, however, the federal debate that had begun in earnest during the 1930s depression resulted in the adoption of two programs for groups whose health care needs were not being addressed adequately by the private sector. Medicare (Title XVIII of the Social

Security Act), the federal insurance program to assist in payment for health care services for the elderly, and Medicaid (Title XIX), the medical services program for low-income persons, were enacted. In 1974 Medicare programs were expanded to include the formerly employed disabled and their dependents.

Medicare operates on the insurance principle. Federally administered, it pays for a considerable portion of hospital and physician services for those physically ill elderly and their spouses who are covered by the Social Security Act by virtue of their having worked in covered employment for a total of 10 years or more. Medicaid pays for the medical care of the physical problems of the poor including those low-income disabled or elderly who do not qualify for Medicare. The costs of this program are far less than those of Medicare partly because it serves many fewer people and partly because its payments are far less generous. Moreover, Medicaid is administered by the states, rather than the federal government, although it receives some help from federal funds. Thus, the quantity and quality of services covered by Medicaid vary considerably from state to state.

Both of these programs have represented a compromise between the professional medical community, which had resisted government "interference" with medical care, and the federal government, which was concerned with the provision of adequate health care for the aged and the needy. The result of this legislation was twofold. First, the programs were modeled on existing service delivery models: Fee-for-service, private-practice physicians were not only left with their autonomy but also were accorded decision-making authority over all the treatment services the programs supported. Second, the programs were based on an acute-care model, which emphasized intense, hospital-based episodes, and, most unfortunately, paid minimal attention to the need for both early intervention and prevention services as well as follow-up aftercare. Acute-care models are frequently not suitable for the treatment of mental disorders over the long run. Of necessity, effective management of the problem is often the aim rather than cure. This is because the etiology and treatment of mental health disorders fit rather more readily into a chronic-care model requiring a flexible variety of treatment settings and modalities.

Neither Medicare nor Medicaid devotes sufficient attention to coverage for mental health services. The Medicare program added benefits for mental health services almost as an afterthought, and its notoriously limited coverage has remained unchanged since the program's enactment. Medicare provides limited inpatient coverage in state hospitals and more extensive coverage in general hospitals. It allows no more than $250.00 a year for outpatient services, a figure that has remained unchanged since 1965 despite marked inflation since then. Medicaid legislation stipulated that the program cover "medically necessary" services and left the determination of the exact scope and nature of services up to the individual states. Inpatient benefits are largely for either general hospitals or nursing homes rather than for psychiatric hospitals or day-care programs (Bassuk & Gerson, 1985).

The provisions of both Medicaid and Medicare have promoted a constrained view of mental conditions within only a medical model of care rather than a more appropriate broadened concept that considers the parts also played by social, psychological, and economic factors.

Unfortunately, as noted above, both Medicaid and Medicare provide very limited coverage for *outpatient* services, with the result that continuing care by mental health professionals in the community is seriously limited. This is particularly true since government funding of community mental health centers has suffered from numerous budget cuts. Medicaid coverage for mental health services is exceptionally inadequate. No specialty services under this program are mandated by the federal government for adults. On the other hand, outpatient diagnosis and treatment for children under the age of 21 is required, and physician services are covered. Inpatient psychiatric care for children under age 21 is an optional benefit, allowed if a state so chooses. However, as we have seen, states have wide latitude to limit the scope and nature of services, both mandatory and optional.

The Medicaid program covers only half of all poor households with children. This factor plus meager benefit provisions means that many children do not receive either the physical or mental health services they need. Furthermore, the concept that health care should be delivered with a sensitivity to family dynamics or membership has not even been considered in most of these public programs. (See also Chapter 12.)

A significant change in eligibility for Medicaid was enacted in 1986 when the link between the receipt of cash benefits through AFDC and Medicaid eligibility was severed. Prior to this change the dependence on AFDC eligibility for Medicaid assistance meant that only families well below the federal poverty level could receive Medicaid benefits. By making Medicaid participation criteria directly related to the *federal* poverty level rather than to state AFDC assistance criteria, states now do not have to raise their AFDC program thresholds to allow low-income families to receive Medicaid services. This change allows for improved Medicaid coverage for all persons with incomes below the official federal poverty line. On the other hand, this new provision fails to aid the so-called medically indigent, those people with incomes above the poverty line but still so limited that they are unable to pay bills for hospital and professional health services. This is a particularly difficult problem for that portion of the marginally employed population that has the misfortune to lack health insurance coverage at the workplace.

Some of these people, among others, obtain mental health services through a variety of smaller programs that also comprise a portion of the federal contribution to mental health. For instance, the never-implemented Mental Health Systems Act of 1980 was replaced in 1981 by the Alcohol, Drug Abuse, and Mental Health (ADM) block grant. This program funnels funds to states for use in supporting state and local mental health programs, primarily through existing community mental health centers. A complex formula determines the level of funding for each state. Total funding for fiscal year (FY) 1987 is set at $495 million, with a portion of these funds designated for mental health services. As with most block grants the ADM block grant places few restrictions on the state recipients as to how they should spend their federal aid. Because of a lack of reporting requirements from the states, little information is available concerning the uses to which the ADM block grant funds have been put.

In late 1987, however, both the Senate and the House of Representatives were considering, but had not passed, major changes for this program, including new evaluation and reporting requirements, a mental health prevention demonstration program, a requirement that most of the funds be directed to innovative programs serving chronically mentally disturbed individuals, and a 10% set-aside of funds to be used for services to severely disturbed children and youth. Nevertheless, the overall proposed funding for this program remained significantly below the pre-1981 level for mental health services provided through the Community Mental Health Centers Act.

Two additional programs, the Community Support Program (CSP) and the Child Adolescent Service System Program (CASSP), were developed and provided small amounts of funds to assist states in improving their mental health service delivery systems. CSP, initiated in 1977, was developed as a means to promote community integration of deinstitutionalized and inappropriately institutionalized persons with chronic mental disorders. The major component of CSP has been a grants program. From 1977 through 1984 CSP funded demonstration grants in all 50 states, the District of Columbia, and two territories. These grants, used in a variety of ways, had as their central goal encouraging states to place greater emphasis on the needs of the deinstitutionalized chronically mentally disturbed population. Attention was directed particularly toward the need for states to make the necessary legislative, administrative, and budgetary changes to allow for a greater degree of "services integration." CSP is predicated on the notion that the needs of the mentally disturbed extend well beyond traditional mental health services. It is recognized that as long as mental health services are delivered in isolation from other necessary social and economic aids, the mentally disturbed person is at considerable risk for reinstitutionalization.

The more recent Child and Adolescent Service System Program (CASSP) is an outgrowth of CSP. In 1986 Congress earmarked $4.7 million to extend the CSP philosophy to the needs of emotionally disturbed children and youth. CASSP supports grants to states and localities to assist them in improving the availability of integrated mental health and social service care systems for children and youth much in the way that the older CSP program targeted chronically disturbed adults. Grant recipients are required to bring together a variety of public and private agencies as part of a coalition dedicated to assuring that child mental health service gaps and barriers are identified and overcome through changed legislation, regulations, agency policy, and/or funding patterns. State-level recipients are to coordinate state agencies such as mental health, juvenile justice, education, child welfare, and physical health. After a focal point for child and adolescent mental health services has been developed at the state level, states are then urged to replicate the process at the community level.

The CASSP program also includes a substantial investment in technical assistance to state and local personnel. Given the limited size of the CASSP budget, the technical assistance component of the program attempts to facilitate dissemination and adoption of this services integration model by developing publications for distribution to government officials and service providers and by working directly with federal, state, and local officials concerned with the improvement of mental health services for the CASSP target population.

Note that the $1.5 million voted by Congress for this program amounts to very little when it is divided among the 50 states. This is especially true when, simultaneously, federal funding of related state programs such as public assistance, education, Medicaid, and housing programs has been drastically cut by the Reagan administration. (See Volume 1 of this series.)

One problem area that has recently led to renewed interest in mental health services by policy makers is the plight of the mentally disturbed homeless, a problem that has been exacerbated since 1981 because of federal cuts in public assistance and subsidies of low-income housing. Congress recently (1987) passed the Stewart B. McKinney Homeless Assistance Act (PL 100–7). Title VI, Health Care for the Homeless, authorizes several new programs to address, in part, the needs of those homeless persons with mental health problems. The major initiative is a new block grant for community health services to these persons. Eligible services include outreach, community mental health treatment, case management, staff training, and referrals to substance abuse and health service providers. States are required to provide a 25% match for the federal funding. The initial appropriation for FY 1987 is $32.2 million.

A second initiative expands the already existing CSP (Community Support Program) Demonstration Projects for Homeless Chronically Mentally Ill individuals by allotting $7.7 million to fund new demonstration programs testing the effectiveness of comprehensive community-based mental health and social services for chronically disturbed homeless adults. An additional $1 million will fund similar innovative programs designed to service severely disturbed children and youth. (Note the contrast between $32.2 million for adults and $1 million for children and youth.) Note, too, that the above legislation provides for increased mental health services but appears not to relieve the fundamental problems: lack of an adequate supply of low-cost housing and sufficient financial assistance to mentally disturbed, low-income people.

BARRIERS TO THE REFORM OF MENTAL HEALTH POLICY

This review of federal involvement in mental health services gives a glimpse of the disjointed nature of U.S. mental health policy. The reasons for the lack of comprehensiveness and coordination are several. Federal policy generally develops in a manner described by Baybrooke and Lindbloom (1963, p. 71) as "disjoined incrementalism." "It is decision making through small or incremental moves on particular programs rather than through a comprehensive reform program. . . . It is also better described as moving *away* from known social ills rather than as moving *toward* a known and relatively stable social goal." This policy process is rooted in the structure of the federal policy-making apparatus: bicameralism (the House of Representatives and the Senate); separation of powers between federal, state, and local levels of government; and the system of checks and balances between the legislative, executive, and judicial branches of government. (See also Chapter 12 in this volume.) Given that mental health policy development has not proceeded apace with health policy development in general, however, we must look for other reasons for the chaotic state of mental health policy.

Mechanic (1985, p. 78) argues that persons with emotional disorders are "significantly disadvantaged in the political process" that determines the course of mental health policy development. These persons often lack the capacity to represent themselves effectively in the political arena. Moreover, the various groups representing the subsets of individuals included in the broad category of "emotionally disordered" frequently find themselves at odds with one another due to differences in philosophy and problem definition. The resulting fragmentation undermines these groups' abilities to successfully mobilize support for their constituents. Further exacerbating this situation is the fact that the mental health professions do not have a particularly high standing among the health professions nor do they always agree among themselves and make a coordinated political effort for improved mental health policies and programs.

A formidable barrier to the development of a comprehensive mental health policy is concern with costs. As the federal budget deficits have grown through the 1980s, the fastest-growing segment of the budget has become the interest payments on the national debt, which currently (late 1987) stands at $2.37 trillion. Policy discussions invariably center on costs, and proposals with high price tags fare poorly in the current budgetary climate. Even programs that might offer long-term cost savings but have high initial costs are likely to be carefully scrutinized. In a context where "cost savings" and "cost containment" are the watchwords, policy proposals that call for an expansion of the federal role in mental health services financing and delivery are severely disadvantaged.

A final barrier to the development of sound mental health policy is the paucity of data available on the distribution, effectiveness, and cost effectiveness of mental health care. Kiesler (1987) has argued persuasively for significant expansion of investment in the development of a national data base on outcomes of various approaches to mental health treatment. In the absence of such information, policy makers are hesitant to put additional scarce resources into programs they view as unproven. *Systems* of service delivery also must be more thoroughly studied, particularly in light of the fact that responsibility for mental health services will continue to be shared by federal, state, and local government entitlements and third-party payments for mental health services primarily rendered through private insurance programs.

Somewhat the same might be said for programs that allegedly will *prevent* the development of mental disorders. Although persuasive pleas have been made for the supposed preventative benefits of such programs as mental health education, early treatment of children with emotional disturbances, social and economic reforms, and the like, unfortunately solid evidence is not available as to the actual effectiveness of such programs. Here, again, rigorous evaluative research is needed to test the outcomes of a range of hypothetically useful strategies.

The possibilities for reform of the mental health service delivery system are not quite so bleak as the foregoing analysis might suggest. In general, health care policy in the United States is undergoing intense scrutiny and will continue to take a leading place in the domestic social policy agenda for a number of years. Significant reform seems likely. What remains unclear is the particular direction reform efforts will take and to what extent mental health services will be included in this process. Among other things, human service professionals who are proponents of reforms in mental health policies and programs must take a part in carrying out the research that will allow them to be effective participants in this process.

12
Public Policy and Noninstitutional Care of People with Mental Disorders

CATHERINE S. CHILMAN

This chapter presents a brief overview of trends in government policies regarding noninstitutional care of people with mental disorders; the effects of these policies on individuals, families, and communities; critical policy issues regarding noninstitutional care; and recommended directions for the future. Family issues are emphasized for two major reasons: (a) The focus of the series to which this volume belongs is on families faced with serious problems, and (b) the needs of families with mentally disturbed members tend to be either underrecognized or discussed in now-outdated and pejorative terms that mistakenly view families as being the cause of a member's disorders.

As discussed in Chapter 11, there was a push in the 1950s for the care of mentally disturbed people outside of mental hospitals. Following the recommendations of the President's Joint Commission on Mental Illness and Health, the Community Mental Health Centers and Construction Act of 1963 called for the establishment of a new kind of community-based mental health center with federal funding for five essential services: inpatient care, outpatient care, emergency treatment, partial hospitalization, and consultation and education (Bassuk & Gerson, 1985). These recommendations included the recognition that mental disorders have interacting biological, social, psychological, and economic aspects.

The impetus for the shift from institutional to community care came from five major sources:

1. Concerns among the states over the high and rising costs of their mental hospitals.
2. The development of federal policies in the early 1960s, which provided federal matching grants to state public assistance programs for aid to people released from mental hospitals into communities, *plus* the 1965 legislation, which paid at least part of the costs of health care for the elderly, through Medicare, and for the poor, through Medicaid.
3. The development and further refinement of psychoactive drug therapy.
4. The civil liberties movement, which pushed for the rights of mentally disturbed individuals to make their own decisions about whether they

would be hospitalized or live in the community. This movement argued effectively for court decisions that opposed involuntary commitment to mental hospitals unless it could be proven that the mentally disturbed person was dangerous either to the self or to others. Court decisions put an end to long-term institutionalization through indefinite term commitments and limited involuntary commitments to restricted periods of time.

5. Research findings regarding the adverse effects of institutionalization on people, with major effects including increased dependency, depression, loss of initiative and social skills, and the like (Mechanic, 1980).

As a result of the Community Mental Health Centers and Construction Act of 1963 plus court decisions along the lines sketched above, many thousands of women and men were released from mental hospitals into their communities. This process of deinstitutionalization was supplemented by increased trends in noninstitutionalization, that is, refraining from committing to institutional care people with newly developed (or newly diagnosed) mental disorders. The end result of these related trends was a marked increase in nonhospitalized mentally disturbed people within the various communities throughout the nation.

These trends caused a number of problems for many of the afflicted individuals as well as for their families and communities. These problems might well have been fewer and less severe, however, if more services of better quality had been developed to meet the wide range of needs of mentally disturbed people.

MAJOR ADVERSE EFFECTS OF DEINSTITUTIONALIZATION AND NONINSTITUTIONALIZATION

Effects on the Mentally Disturbed

Recommendations for the deinstitutionalization of mentally disturbed people and the resulting federal legislation in 1963 was predicated on allied plans for a wide range of community support systems, as shown above. Yet few communities developed these resources during the 1960s, and by and large there was a further retrenchment during the 1970s and on into the 1980s.

The result was and still is (1987) that many mentally disordered people have been "dumped" into communities without adequate health, psychological, or social services. Many of these people also lack sufficient income as well as adequate housing, employment, food, or clothing. Some specialists in the field note that a number of mentally disordered people are living in situations that are as bad or worse than the state mental hospitals where some had formerly lived (Bassuk & Gerson, 1985).

The reasons for the unfortunate plight of many mentally disordered people include the following: Mental disorders tend to be chronic; onset often (but not always) occurs during late adolescence and tends to persist throughout the life span. Like other chronic conditions, the situation is apt to become depressing, debilitating, and expensive both for the patients and their families as well as for the community and its human service professionals.

Although antipsychotic medication has been of important assistance in helping patients control the extreme manifestations of their disorders, the various medications often have serious side effects, especially over a long period of time. People who use these medications need continuing supervision and encouragement by a trained professional who not only checks on the physical condition of the person but is able to provide (or help the person acquire) the social, psychological, or economic services that are frequently needed (Parloff, 1979). There has been an unfortunate tendency to focus only on the medication aspects of the person's treatment rather than including the more complex and expensive cluster of services that are so often indicated.

Mentally disordered people with chronic conditions are apt to need a complex of services because even when psychotic symptoms are controlled, patients are likely to suffer from continuing cognitive, perceptual, social, emotional, and personality difficulties that make it hard for them to make and maintain positive social relationships; obtain and hold employment; negotiate the complexities of bureaucratic community service systems (such as health, welfare, recreation, housing, and education facilities); and handle many of the details of daily living. Difficulties of these kinds are apt to become more severe during acute episodes. These difficulties are not only a serious handicap for the disturbed person but also tend to alienate the people around them.

Bassuk and Gerson (1985) discuss further deficits in community care, including the lack of communication between state hospitals and community facilities. Partly owing to the separation of the two systems by law, hospitals often discharge patients without checking whether community and family resources exist. There is a lack of research regarding how patients get along after they leave mental hospitals. The authors cite their own experiences with patients who were maintained well in hospitals with adequate medication but when released to the community led lives of poverty and social isolation and had to be readmitted.

Bassuk and Gerson (1985) also point out the poverty problems of many mentally disturbed people. A large proportion of this population is unemployed and dependent on the federal Social Security program, known as SSI (Supplemental Security Income). This is a federal program for the low-income elderly and for the disabled who have not been employed for a sufficient length of time to be eligible for benefits under other sections of the Social Security Act. SSI benefits tend to be meager ($325.00 a month for an individual living alone). Some states increase this grant from their own revenues, but many do not. SSI programs usually do not give benefits to people who live in group homes and halfway houses with the result that many of the disturbed live in a welfare hotel so that they can draw SSI benefits.

Unfortunately, the recognition that state hospitals can sometimes do more harm than good got translated to "they never do any good." An assumption that all patients would benefit from being released from mental hospitals has overlooked the fact that many chronic patients need some kind of institutional care throughout their lives or during acute episodes when they cannot adjust to the community (Morrissey et al., 1985). These authors hold that state hospitals have been prematurely dismantled and their "back wards" have moved to nursing homes and other residential care facilities. "Thus segregation of the mentally ill persists in a new ecological arrangement" (Morrissey et al., 1985, p. 91).

Mechanic (1980) also writes that conditions of the mentally disturbed in nursing homes are often as bad as in poor mental hospitals. He comments further that the civil rights movement, which has emphasized the individual rights of patients, has brought important assistance to many but has also caused considerable confusion in the field. For instance, court orders that prescribe high-quality hospital care have sometimes been unrealistic and far beyond the budget capabilities of hospitals. This has sometimes led to the premature discharge of patients into communities with highly inadequate provisions for patient care. Then, too, the strong emphasis on the individual rights of patients to determine their own commitment has tended to assume, often mistakenly, that mentally disordered people are able to make sound judgments about their own needs. This individualistic emphasis has also tended to overlook the rights of family members and the community to needed protections against the extremely disturbed behavior of some patients. Moreover, the usual provision that disturbed people should not be committed involuntarily unless it can be proven that they are a danger to themselves or others has highly variable interpretations of "danger" and is predicated in the ill-founded assumption that psychiatrists and courts can make accurate predictions about these matters.

Of course, not all mentally disordered people have serious problems. Some are able to gain control over many of their symptoms of disturbance and lead fairly normal lives in a far better condition than if they were institutionalized. Little is known about these people because they do not present serious, easily diagnosed problems, and thus their life situations are relatively unrecognized. As discussed in a later section, research is needed to learn more about people who have suffered from mental disorders and appear to be virtually problem-free as compared to those mentally disturbed who continue to have numerous difficulties.

One difference between two groups is surely economic. Affluent people can obtain needed private services for which they can pay, but the less fortunate depend on public or private charitable programs. As shown in Chapter 11, government-supported mental health services are chiefly available through Medicare (for the insured elderly and disabled) or Medicaid (for the poor). Neither of these programs was developed with mentally disordered people in mind. Rather, the focus was on physical illness. Thus, both programs provide payments primarily for services performed by physicians or by professionals under the direct supervision of physicians. Payments for services for problems of *mental* health are extremely limited, far more so than in the case of physical health problems. This is particularly true of payments for *outpatient* services. Both Medicare and Medicaid tend to favor payments for general hospital-based services (Medicare) or nursing homes (Medicaid). (See also Chapter 10 for its discussion of Medicaid and Medicare.)

The end result of these Medicare–Medicaid provisions is apt to be that mentally disturbed people who lack ample economic resources tend to receive much less outpatient care than they usually need and often poor-quality hospital or nursing home care. Medicaid recipients, all of whom are poor, are far too apt to be placed in general-purpose nursing homes where they usually do not receive specialized attention and where they often lead heavily sedated, miserable lives that are a burden to themselves and to their families. Lack of services other than medication is also a usual result of Medicare–Medicaid provisions. Because the emphasis is on physician services, treatment generally is focused on a biologically oriented approach (medication). To a large extent the social, psychological, employment, economic, and related needs of patients tend to go unmet, partly because Medicaid and Medicare programs generally do not provide payment for these services. Although it might seem wise to increase the training of physicians so that they could provide comprehensive services of these kinds, this would seem to place too many responsibilities on physicians who tend to be overburdened anyway. It would also rapidly escalate the costs of these services because physician fees tend to be very high.

A more sound approach would probably be that of coordinated treatment by a team of human service professionals such as general physicians, psychiatrists, psychologists, social workers, and nurses. This team concept has been used in many mental health centers, but the funding for these centers has been sharply reduced in the past 20 years or so.

Medicare and Medicaid programs do not cover all people in need. Medicare, a federal program, provides payments for the hospital costs of elderly or disabled people and their dependents. Outpatient physician services are reimbursed only if the person has elected to join and pay a fee for part B of the Medicare program; not all elderly or disabled choose this option.

Nor is it simple for younger people with disabilities to become and remain eligible for Medicare. They must be found by a physician to be severely disabled, and medical proof must be given that their disability rules out employment. Also, they must have worked for 20 out of 40 quarters of 10 years in Social Security–covered employment (6 out of 12 quarters for people under age 31). Some of the resulting, serious problems are that mentally disordered people with disability insurance benefits are fearful of attempting to gain employment because even partial success could result in losing these disability benefits, including Medicare (Levitan, 1985).

Medicaid is a federal–state program that makes limited payments for medical services for those poor under age 65 whom the state declares to be eligible (with differing eligibility rules in various states). It is estimated that at present over half of the people in this country with poverty-level incomes do not receive Medicaid. Then, too, there have been numerous cutbacks in both federal and state aid to the Medicaid program over the years. In general, fewer and fewer private physicians have been willing to work in this program with the result that services have tended to move to emergency rooms of hospitals, public clinics, and, as mentioned above, nursing homes. All in all, mental health services for poor people (with minority groups such as blacks, Hispanics, and Native Americans being overrepresented) have been inadequate for many years, both in institutions and the community, and community-based services have deteriorated markedly during the 1970s and 1980s. (Technical details regarding the operation and problems of both Medicare and Medicaid are exquisitely complex. For further reference see, for instance, Danziger & Weinberg, 1986; Levitan, 1985; Schorr, 1986.)

The marginally employed poor generally fail to receive assistance from Medicaid or Medicare programs or from private health insurance benefits at their place of employment. Many people in this group are employed only sporadically, part time, or in small operations that fail to provide fringe benefits that include health insurance.

Even those people who do have access to health insurance benefits through their employment tend to be limited in the number of psychotherapeutic sessions that their carrier will reimburse, with six sessions per year being a frequent arrangement. Moreover, most of these programs require that the service provider must be a physician or a certified professional (such as a psychologist or social worker) who is supervised by a physician. As noted above, these requirements tend to both limit the focus and range of services and to make the services extremely expensive.

In sum, there are serious deficits with respect to limited availability and restricted range of treatment services for mentally disturbed people with restricted incomes. The problems are particularly severe for persons with chronic disorders who probably constitute the majority of this group. The lack of adequate treatment services obviously exacerbates other employment, housing, financial, and social problems so often encountered by the mentally disturbed.

These difficulties are apt to have a sharply negative impact on the families of the mentally disturbed, an impact that is frequently overlooked or underestimated by clinicians and policy makers alike.

Effects on Families

In most localities no service system aids families in meeting the daily needs of patients or the crises that are apt to occur (Mechanic,

1980; also see Chapter 1 of this volume). Those patients who live with their families may be better off, but severe stress can result for family members, including the children in these families (Bassuk & Gerson, 1985; Hatfield & Lefley, 1987).

According to both Mechanic (1980) and McFarlane (Chapter 1), families with mentally disturbed members need a great deal of support and reassurance. It is imperative that a halt be put to past tendencies of psychiatrists and others to imply that parents are to blame for the mental disorders of their children. The problematic behaviors of family members sometimes observed by clinicians may well be more a *result* of living with a mentally disordered person than the precipitating cause of the disorder. However, family systems can develop a number of negative symptoms through the presence of a disturbed member. The entire family as well as the patient may develop increasingly serious difficulties if appropriate treatment services and community resources are not available.

As we have seen, many mentally disturbed people have *chronic* disorders. This is an important and discouraging fact for all concerned. The chronicity of the disturbance and frequently dysfunctional behavior of the afflicted person plus his or her many needs can put numerous, long-term stresses on families. These stresses can have adverse effects on the health, finances, employment, leisure time, social lives, and emotional balance of family members. These stresses can negatively affect all family relationships: marital, parent–child, and sibling–sibling (see also Chapters 1 to 4). According to Mechanic (1980), community-based programs without an adequate range of supportive services to both patients and families can have more severe effects on families than do the effects associated with institutionalization.

Families can be a potent force in a patient's rehabilitation, but "many family members feel excluded by professionals from the care process and rarely get the information they need" (Mechanic, 1980, p. 142). One reason for this unfortunate situation is that for the most part neither Medicaid, Medicare, nor private insurances provides reimbursement for provision of counseling and support to family members. This is a major flaw in the various insurance programs.

Since the 1970s there has been increased emphasis on families as "agents of rehabilitation as well as bearers of burdens" (Kreisman & Joy, 1974). Lack of information, dysfunctional attitudes, lack of links to community resources, and lack of the resources themselves are some of the major problems encountered by families with mentally disordered members (Goldstein, 1987).

Highly conflicted family situations in which numerous problems exist, including illness, poverty, unemployment and poor housing, tend to escalate the difficulties of mentally disturbed members. Moreover, the problems of these members then exacerbate the multi-problem nature of the entire family system (Test & Stein, 1978).

Mentally Disturbed Children and Adolescents

Space constraints prevent a full discussion of the mental health problems of children and adolescents; only a few salient points can be made here. It is estimated that there are 3 million children in this country who are seriously disturbed, and that two-thirds of them are not getting the services they need. As in the case of adults, this is particularly true for low-income and minority group children. Also, as in the case of adults, there is a severe shortage of prevention programs, services for families of the emotionally or mentally disturbed, and community resources for outpatient care; there is a corresponding overemphasis on inpatient services (residential treatment for the most part) and lack of services coordination (Children's Defense Fund, 1986). Then, too, recent studies have shown that residential treatment of children and adolescents does little good unless community services for them and their families are available following release from the institution (Whittaker, 1987). These points were also made by the National Commissions on Mental Health in both 1969 (Joint Commission on Mental Health of Children, 1969) and 1979 (President's Commission on Mental Health, 1979).

Again, as in the case of mentally disordered adults, recent federal cutbacks in social and economic programs have intensified the problems of young patients and their families. For example, in 1985 over one-fifth of the children in this country lived in families with incomes below the poverty line. As a result, there has been a marked increase in the homelessness of families, child abuse, family violence, family breakdown, and the like. (See also Volume 1 of this series.)

The emotional problems of children tend to persist into adolescence and adult life. It is thought, but not yet completely proven, that early treatment of these youngsters will prevent serious problems later. The federal grant program of 1984, Child and Adolescent Program (CASSP), provides modest federal supports to states ($4.7 million in 1986) to help improve their services. Child and adolescent mental health advocacy systems made up of both professionals and parents are becoming more active in a number of states and are using these grants to push for both services coordination and the provision of care programs outside of institutions. Such programs as outpatient counseling and therapy in the home are gaining support. However, the $4.7 million in federal grants is very small when distributed to programs in 50 states and, in actuality, only a few states seem to be developing significant allied programs to make effective use of this seed money.

Strong advocacy programs are needed in the states to develop federal–state–local programs and to both maintain and increase their funding. Parental involvement tends to be highly effective, but in the past the tendencies of professionals to blame the parents for the problems of their children has often erected a barrier against their participation in public advocacy programs. Many parents have found important help for themselves in support groups, and some move from these groups into advocacy activities (Children's Defense Fund, 1986). (See also later sections of this chapter on implications for policy research.)

IMPLICATIONS FOR PUBLIC POLICIES

Program and policy specialists in the field of mental health call for a large number of reforms. They write that while the deinstitutionalization movement has probably benefited many people, especially those who are affluent or who live in those rare communities with well-developed services, it has also resulted in a large number of severe problems for others.

A central difficulty has been the drive to save money through shifting mentally disordered people from state mental hospitals to communities. There is considerable disagreement as to whether community care is actually less expensive. This is particularly true when living costs (housing, food, clothing, transportation) are added to medical treatment and social and psychological services such as support groups, sheltered workshops, group homes, family counseling, intermediate-care facilities, and the like. Although some would argue that this range of services is unnecessary, others find that the lack of these services often leads to severe problems that frequently result in the need for the rehospitalization of patients (Bachrach, 1983; Goldstein, 1987; Group for the Advancement of Psychiatry, 1978; Levine, 1984; Mechanic, 1980; Morrissey et al., 1985; The President's Commission on Mental Health, 1979; Segal, 1987; Talbot, 1978).

Budget cuts during the 1970s and particularly the 1981 budget cuts of the Reagan administrations' Omnibus Budget Reconciliation Act (OBRA) made severe inroads into many crucial services for the mentally disturbed as well as for other people. These included cuts in public assistance; in Title XX of the Social Security Act, which, among other things, funded social services for troubled individuals and families; and in Medicaid, low-income housing, food stamps, and the like. Community mental health centers have also sustained crippling budget cuts. All of the above cuts *must* be restored. As shown above, basic support programs are essential for the well-being of low-income, mentally disordered people as well as for other individuals in economic trouble. (See Volume 1 of this series which analyzes issues of family poverty, employment, and unemployment in detail.)

Federal legislative and administrative changes during the Nixon and Reagan presidencies have also caused a deterioration in standards of service in many programs at the state level, including those of Medicaid and community mental health centers. By retreating from federal involvement in setting standards for state programs and turning most of the decision making over to state and local governments, there has been a politicizing and deterioration of professional standards in many communities. Mechanic (1980), among others, calls for a reexamination of problems that arise from this kind of decentralization. He also calls for an overhaul of the entire mental health system.

Morrissey and colleagues (1985), among others, strongly recommend the end of a two-class system of mental health services, a system that provides private care for the rich and inadequate, residual facilities for the poor. Mechanic (1980) also criticizes the fact that the rich are more apt than the poor to have generous health insurance programs, which emphasizes hospital care under the sole cated ways, and the ability to present themselves in an appealing fashion to psychiatrists.

More innovative forms of community treatment are needed that use a broad range of human services professionals working in a team approach. The exclusively medical model, supported by various insurance programs, which emphasize hospital care under the sole supervision of psychiatrists, is expensive and limited in terms of the community approaches indicated. Among other things, the exclusive medical model tends to rigidify and maintain traditional and ineffectual approaches to the treatment of the mentally disordered.

Mechanic (1980) advocates an adequate national health insurance program that provides for the development and stable maintenance of community programs for chronic patients who need care over long periods by a variety of personnel. He believes it is essential to provide financing for a range of services, such as those discussed above, especially for severely disordered, chronic patients.

The plight of the homeless has attracted a great deal of excited public attention in the past few years. It is estimated that about half of the homeless are people with mental disorders (Levine, 1984). Although their homelessness is, indeed, tragic, this condition is only one aspect of their total adverse situation. Levine (1984) writes that most of the homeless, mentally disordered people have chronic problems. Their homelessness is largely a product of deinstitutionalization and a concomitant lack of community resources to assist them. Moreover, the community services that exist tend to be highly fragmented and uncoordinated. She comments that deinstitutionalization has lead to an enormously complex system of community housing arrangements: nursing homes, board and care homes, single rooms, welfare hotels, apartments, residential treatment centers, living in homes with relatives, emergency shelters, and life on the streets.

While it is extremely important to provide for increased services coordination, as Levine (1984) and others (including recent legislation) recommend, this goal is exceptionally difficult to achieve. This is because of (a) the welter of differing federal, state, local, public, and private programs, each with its own vested interests and frequently tradition-bound, devoted constituencies and (b) the problems of the mentally disordered people themselves that may lead to their own resistance, confusion, and social behavior that can make adjustment to various forms of coordinated services difficult.

The prevalent public enthusiasm for constructing emergency shelters is seriously ill-advised, except as a temporary expedient. Such shelters could rapidly become places of misery and chaos. At its root homelessness is basically the result of high-cost housing (intensified by the retreat of federal and state governments from the subsidy of low-income housing) plus the inadequate incomes of unemployed and underemployed people, with their incomes having been drastically eroded by government cuts in health and welfare programs, despite inflationary trends. These factors are basic to the homelessness of the mentally disturbed, along with insufficient outreach and treatment services to help them with problems of daily living. Thus, the policy implications are for increased public subsidy of low-income housing, more adequate income assistance, and improved medical, social, and psychological services for mentally disturbed people *and* for those with whom they live, including their families.

SOME IMPLICATIONS FOR PUBLIC POLICY

Although Mechanic (1980) recommends a system of national health insurance to assure equity in payments for the care of people with all kinds of health problems—both physical and mental—this goal may not be politically or even practically feasible, at least in the near future. More intermediate steps may be indicated, steps that are clearly called for. Important general ones include:

1. Reduced emphasis on treating emotionally and mentally disturbed patients in hospitals (Medicare) or nursing homes (Medicaid) or residential treatment centers (Child Welfare Services) together with increased provisions for *outpatient* services provided by a broadened range of educational, medical, social, psychological, and rehabilitation professionals. These services should be available to the families of disturbed individuals as well as to the individuals themselves.
2. Provisions for "plugging the gap" in insurance benefits for the treatment of emotionally or mentally disturbed people who are not eligible for Medicare, Medicaid, or private insurance plans.

Beyond modification of insurance benefits for health care other programs are needed, such as provisions for a *continuum* of comprehensive services to meet the multiple needs of emotionally or mentally disturbed people and their families. These services include hospitals for severely disturbed people who need institutional protection, patient support groups, assistance for family or individual living, halfway houses, group homes, and so on. More general provisions are also indicated that are important to the effective functioning of many people in the community and are more appropriately offered to a broader group than the mentally disturbed alone. This recommendation is based on the concept of "mainstreaming" services for people in general rather than isolating particular groups who are then labeled as deviant and particularly problematic. Moreover, broad programs that provide assistance to many groups of people may attract more widespread public support because many people stand to benefit from them.

These services include such programs as income assistance for low-income families and individuals; job training and placement for the unemployed and underemployed; food stamps; day care for children; the subsidy of low-income housing; education at all levels; affirmative action to reduce racism, ethnocentrism, sexism, and "ageism"; and so on. As described earlier, the above programs have suffered severe budget cuts during the Reagan Administration. It is essential that, as a minimum, these cuts be restored and the programs improved. (See also Volume 1 of this series.)

Programs for mentally disturbed individuals and their families should take into account family systems theory, which views families as a group of individuals who interact in such a way that the behavior of one person affects the entire family system and its members in a multitude of ways. Each member of the family has his or her individual needs for both belonging to the family and for autonomous, continuing growth and development over the life cycle. Barriers within the family that prevent fulfillment of these needs tend to create family dysfunction.

Thus, treatment of mentally disordered people should include consideration of both the patient and of family members as parts of the family system and as individuals, each with his or her own goals and needs both within and outside the family. Contrary to traditional assumptions, this includes mothers as well as fathers, daughters as well as sons.

Treatment should go beyond training the family to help the patient; it should assist family members, as needed, in both patient care and self-care so as to maximize the patient's potential to remain in the family (if that is the best overall plan) and for all family members to cope effectively with the situation without sacrificing their own physical and mental health. This coping includes behaviors that promote "good-enough," rewarding, and responsible marital, parent–child, and sibling–sibling relationships as well as "good-enough" participation in the outside world of employment, community organizations, education, and social relationships.

In policy terms this means that a range of programs should be available to family members as these programs may be needed. (See also Chapter 10.) They may include support groups, home care assistance or respite care of patients away from home, emergency hospital care for patients with acute psychotic episodes, and opportunities for family members to enhance both their income and personal development through such means as further education and occupational training.

The foregoing recommendations that emphasize the needs and

rights of family members as individuals as well as being members of a complex family system is based on a number of principles. First, there is the basic practice- and policy-related concept stated above and in Chapter 9 to the effect that all people have needs to belong to their families and also to be autonomous. A secondary concept derives from the recognition that the nature of mental disorders is apt to be particularly stressful for both the patient and his or her kin. Because the condition tends to be chronic, stresses continue for many years. Because the condition is usually accompanied by a number of social, psychological, physical, and economic disabilities, it is apt to drain family resources and isolate family members from their social networks. Then, too, such patient feelings and behaviors as depression, disordered perceptions, confused thinking, high emotionality, and disturbed communication are apt to stimulate dysfunctional reactions in family members so that they, too, may become reactively disturbed. This is especially true if they are strongly bonded with the patient. Thus, family members may well need both corrective counseling and opportunities to differentiate themselves from constant, highly involved patient care. This is apt to be true even if the patient's psychosis is under control through medication because the medication is not a "cure all" and often has adverse side effects.

The emphasis here on *policies* that support and provide resources for both family care and self-care are not typically found in the literature on public policy and mental health. Rather, this emphasis is more an expression of the author's experiences, observations, research analyses, and philosophy along with the basic premises of this entire series, as presented in the preface to each volume.

Looking at another policy issue, it can be urged that the present trend for the federal government to provide general block grants to the states with few associated guidelines be reconsidered and that more federal standard setting for state programs be reinstituted. For example, Medicaid tends to vary enormously from state to state in terms of the quality and quantity of services supported and the persons declared eligible for Medicaid benefits. The current retreat of the federal government from responsibility for domestic programs is in opposition to the actual contemporary nature of the country. For example, a recent report of a group of outstanding scholars appointed by the Carnegie Corporation held that the federal role in promoting the social welfare of the nation should be reenergized and redirected in light of the great social problems the nation will be facing in the coming years. The report argues for renewed social activism toward a cooperative federal society because "so many of our problems are national in character and cannot be dealt with alone by state or local governments, the voluntary sector, or the business sector" (Carnegie Corporation of New York, 1987, p. 2). We need all the resources, knowledge, skill, and training available to develop and implement effective programs for the noninstitutionalized mentally disordered: Related needs do not start and stop at state lines but rather require a nationwide effort.

SOME IMPLICATIONS FOR RESEARCH

The foregoing recommendations need further research, both basic and applied. This is one aspect of a more general recommendation to the effect that there must be increased public funding of research concerning mental disorders: their epidemiology, causes, effects, and methods of treatment. It is essential that this research be administered and carried out in accordance with high scientific rather than political standards. Some of the major needed research areas are

1. Basic studies that seek to determine the origins of the various mental disorders, including attempts to tease out what roles, if any, parents and other family members may play in the causation and perpetuation of these disorders (Goldstein, 1985; Ledingham et al., 1984).
2. Basic research regarding the biological aspects of mental disorders and the effects and effectiveness of the medications used in treating them.
3. Well-designed, nationwide program evaluations of the effects of various forms of institutional and alternate types of community and family care of mentally disturbed people in an attempt to learn what kinds of programs are apt to be most effective and efficient for different kinds of people (Kiesler, 1985).
4. A series of practical evaluations to learn more about the effects and effectiveness of various kinds of direct treatment of individuals and families by different kinds of human services professionals.
5. Longitudinal studies of random samples of noninstitutionalized or deinstitutionalized mentally disturbed patients to learn more about how they get along in many aspects of their lives. As commented earlier, it seems likely that a number of mentally disturbed people actually do quite well in their communities. We probably know far more about those who have problems than those who do not. If some are relatively problem-free, how do they and their context differ from their problem-laden peers?

6. Studies of the outcomes of situations in which family or community members have sought involuntary commitment of mentally disordered people to institutions and the commitments were either denied or accepted by the courts. Much more information is needed regarding the difficult and sometimes conflicting issues of patient rights versus family versus community rights.

In all the evaluative studies suggested above, designs should include cost/benefit analyses of the various forms of patient care including, as appropriate, services to families. As emphasized in Chapter 10, recommendations for public programs must take into account their costs as well as their effectiveness.

SUMMARY

The noninstitutionalization or deinstitutionalization of mentally disordered people has both positive and negative aspects. While these principles support the civil libertarian view that mentally disabled people have a right to the least restrictive care possible, they may also create severe problems for both patients and families. Patient care outside of institutions cannot be effective unless a comprehensive array of free or low-cost community resources is readily available as needed to both disturbed individuals and their families in such areas as treatment, financial assistance, housing, job training and placement, and support groups. Few, if any, communities have an adequate coordinated array of these resources resulting, in many cases, in severe hardships for patients and their families.

Medicare, Medicaid, and private insurance systems that are meant to provide payments for needed services have numerous deficiencies such as a constricted range and number of services, overemphasis on biomedical care alone, and a too-heavy reliance on inpatient rather than outpatient services.

Policy recommendations call for closing the benefits gaps in services provision; development and implementation of a broader range of comprehensive biological, social, psychological, and economic services for patients and the members of their families; a stronger federal role in financing and guiding these services; restoration of recent federal cuts in such general programs as income assistance, housing, food stamps, job training, affirmative action, and employment; and increased support for high-quality basic, program, and practice research concerning the causes and treatment of mental disorders and the effects of comprehensive institutional and community care on people with those disorders. These studies need to take into account both costs and effectiveness of various kinds of approaches to services for mentally disturbed children, adolescents, and adults and their families. The political processes that are needed to implement recommendations such as the above are discussed in Chapter 10.

References

Abernathy, V. D. (1973). Social network and response to the maternal role. *International Journal of Marriage and the Family, 3,* 86–92.

Aldous, J. (Ed.) (1982). *Two paychecks: Life in the dual-earner families.* Beverly Hills, CA: Sage.

Alexander, J. F., Barton, C., Shiavo, R. S., & Parsons, B. V. (1976). Behavioral intervention with families of delinquents: Therapist characteristics and outcome. *Journal of Consulting and Clinical Psychology, 44*(4), 656–664.

Alexander, J. F., Barton, C., Waldron, H., & Mas, C. H. (1983). Beyond the technology of family therapy: The anatomy of intervention model. In K. D. Craig & R. J. McMahon (Eds.), *Advances in clinical behavior therapy* (pp. 48–73). New York: Brunner/Mazel.

Alexander, J. F., Mas, C. H., & Waldron, H. (in press). Behavioral and systems family therapies—or—Auld Lang Syne: Shall old perspectives be forgot? In R. DeV. Peters & R. S. McMahon (Eds.), *Marriages and families: Behavioral systems approaches.* New York: Brunner/Mazel.

Alexander, J. F., & Newberry, A. M. (in press). Interviewing in functional family therapy. In E. Lipchik (Ed.), *Interviewing in family therapy.* Rockville, MD: Aspen.

Alexander, J. F. & Parsons, B. V. (1973). Short term behavioral intervention with delinquent families: Impact on family process and recidivism. *Journal of Abnormal Psychology, 81*(3), 219–225.

Alexander, J. F. & Parsons, B. V. (1982). *Functional family therapy: Principles and procedures.* Monterey, CA: Brooks/Cole.

American Humane Association (1985). *Highlights of official child neglect and abuse reporting—1984.* Denver: Author.

American Psychiatric Association (1980). *Diagnostic and statistical manual of mental disorders* (3rd ed.). Washington, DC: Author.

Anderson, C. M. (1983). A psychoeducational program for families of patients with schizophrenia. In W. R. McFarlane (Ed.), *Family therapy in schizophrenia* (pp. 99–116). New York: Guilford.

Anderson, C. M., Hogarty, G. E., & Reiss, D. J. (1986). *Schizophrenia in the family.* New York: Guilford.

Anderson, C. M., Reiss, D. J., & Hogarty, G. E. (1980). Family treatment of adult schizophrenia: A psycho-educational approach. *Schizophrenia Bulletin, 6,* 490–505.

Anderson, R., Ambrosino, A., Valentine, D., & Lauderdale, M. (1983). Child death attributed to abuse and neglect: An empirical study. *Children and Youth Services Review, 5*(1), 75–89.

Anderson, S. (1987). Alcohol use and addiction. *Encyclopedia of social work* (pp. 133–140). Silver Spring, MD: National Association of Social Workers.

Appleton, W. S. (1974). Mistreatment of patients' families by psychiatrists. *American Journal of Psychiatry, 131,* 655–657.

Aragona, J., & Eyberg, S. (1981). Neglected children: Mother's report of child behavior problems and observed verbal behavior. *Child Development, 52,* 596–602.

Austin, D. J. (1983). Treating neglect: Learning how to see, feel, and touch it. In C. M. Trainor (Ed.), *The dilemma of child neglect: Identification and treatment* (pp. 29–33). Denver: American Humane Association.

Austin, R. L. (1978). Race, father-absence, and female delinquency. *Criminology, 15,* 487–504.

Azar, S. T, Robinson, D. R., Hekimian, E., & Twentyman, C. T. (1984). Unrealistic expectations and problem-solving ability in maltreating and comparison mothers. *Journal of Consulting and Clinical Psychology, 52*(4), 689–691.

Bachrach, L. (1983). *Hospital and community psychiatry, 34*(6), 560–562.

Barrett, L. (1982). *Therapeutic child care: Approaches to remediating the effects of child abuse and neglect.* Unpublished paper, Berkeley, CA, Berkeley Planning Associates.

Barton, C., & Alexander, J. F. (August 1979). *Delinquent and normal family interactions in competitive and cooperative conditions.* Paper presented at the annual convention of the American Psychological Association, New York.

Barton, C., & Alexander, J. F. (1981). Functional family therapy. In A. S. Gurman & D. P. Kniskern (Eds.), *Handbook of family therapy.* New York: Brunner/Mazel.

Barton, C., Alexander, J. F., Waldron, H., Turner, C. W., & Warburton, J. (1985). Generalizing treatment effects of functional family therapy: Three replications. *American Journal of Family Therapy, 13*(3), 16–26.

Bassuk, E., & Gerson, S. (1985). Deinstitutionalization and mental health services. In P. Brown (Ed.), *Mental health care and social policy* (pp. 129–144). Boston, London, Melbourne, Henley: Routledge and Kegan Paul.

Bateson, G. (1971). The cybernetics of "self": A theory of alcoholism. *Psychiatry, 34,* 1–18.

Bavolek, S. J., & Comstock, C. M. (1983). *Nurturing program for parents and children.* Schaumburg, IL: Family Development Associates.

Baybrooke, D., & Lindbloom, C. E. (1963). *A strategy of decision.* New York: Free Press.

Beels, C. C. (1981). Social support and schizophrenia. *Schizophrenia Bulletin, 7,* 58–72.

Beels, C. C., & McFarlane, W. R. (1983). Thoughts on family therapy and schizophrenia. In W. R. McFarlane (Ed.), *Family therapy in schizophrenia* (pp. 17–40). New York: Guilford.

Behlmer, K. (1982). *Child abuse and moral reform in England 1870–1908.* Stanford, CA: Stanford University Press.

Belsky, J. (1980). Child maltreatment: An ecological integration. *American Psychologist, 35*(4), 320–335.

Berleman, W. C. (1980). Juvenile delinquency prevention experiments: A review and analysis. *Reports of the National Juvenile Justice Assessment Centers.* U.S. Department of Justice.

Bertsch, J. W., Clark, F. W., & Iverson, M. J. (1982). *Using informal resources in child protective services.* University of Montana, Department of Social Work.

Biegel, D. E., Shore, B. K., & Gordon, E. (1984). *Building support networks for the elderly.* Beverly Hills, CA: Sage.

Black, R., & Mayer, J. (1980). Parents with special problems: Alcoholism and opiate addition. In C. Kempe, & R. Helfer (Eds.), *The battered child* (3rd ed., pp. 104–114). Chicago: University of Chicago Press.

Bousha, D., & Twentyman, C. T. (1984). Mother–child interactional style in abuse, neglect and control groups: Naturalistic observations in the home. *Journal of Abnormal Psychology, 93*(1), 106–114.

Bowen, M. (1974). A family systems approach to alcoholism. *Addictions, 21*(2), 3–11.

Breckinridge, A., & Abbott, E. (1912). *The delinquent child and the home.* New York: Russell Sage.

Brem, S. S., & Smith, T. W. (1986). Social psychological approaches to psychotherapy and behavior change. In S. L. Garfield & A. E. Bergin (Eds.), *Handbook of psychotherapy and behavior change* (3rd ed., pp. 69–115). New York: Wiley.

Bremmer, H. (Ed.) (1971). Specimen cases handled by Massachusetts S.P.C.C., 1981. In *Children and youth in America—A documentary history: Vol. II 1986–1932. Parts 1–6* (pp. 203–204). Cambridge, MA: Harvard University Press.

Bronfenbrenner, U. (1979). *The ecology of human development.* Cambridge, MA: Harvard University Press.

Brown, G. W., Birley, J. L. T., & Wing, J. K. (1972). Influence of family life on the course of schizophrenic disorders: A replication. *British Journal of Psychiatry, 121, 241–258.*

Brown, G. W., Monck, E. M., Carstairs, G. M., & Wing, J. K. (1962). Influence of family life on the course of schizophrenic illness. *British Journal of Psychiatry, 16,* 55–68.

Brundage, V. (1985). Gregory Bateson, Alcoholics Anonymous, and stoicism. *Psychiatry, 48,* 40–51.

Burgess, R. L., & Conger, R. D. (1977). Family interaction patterns related to child abuse and neglect: Some preliminary findings. *Child Abuse and Neglect, 1,* 269–277.

Burgess, R. L., & Conger, R. D. (1978). Family interaction in abusive, neglectful, and normal families. *Child Development, 49,* 1163–1173.

Callan, V. J., & Jackson, D. (1986). Children of alcoholic fathers and recovered alcoholic fathers: Personal and family functioning. *Journal of Studies on Alcohol, 47,* 180–182.

Callicutt, J. (1977). Comprehensive service systems or some unrandom thoughts on social policy and planning. In A. Nichols (Ed.), *Social work in the 1980's: Challenges and opportunities.* Arlington: University of Texas at Arlington, Graduate School of Social Work.

Campbell, E. J. M., Scadding, J. G., & Roberts, R. S. (1979). The concept of disease. *British Medical Journal, 2,* 757–762.

Canter, R. (1982). Family correlates of male and female delinquency. *Criminology, 28,* 149–167.

Caplan, G. (1974). *Support systems and community mental health.* New York: Behavioral Publications.

Carnegie Corporation of New York (1987). *Carnegie Quarterly, XXXII*(3), 1–5. New York: Author.

Cavan, R. S., & Ferdinand, T. N. (1975). *Juvenile delinquency.* New York: Lippincott.

Children's Defense Fund. (October 1986). *Children's defense fund reports* (pp. 1–5). Washington, DC: Author.

Chilman, C. (1973). Research on new trends in parent education and parent participation. In B. Caldwell & H. Recuitti (Eds.), *Review of child development research* (Vol. 3). Chicago: University of Chicago Press.

Chilman, C. (1988). Troubled relationships between parents and children. In E. Nunnally, C. Chilman, & F. Cox (Eds.), *Families in trouble* (Vol. 3). Beverly Hills, CA: Sage.

Chilton, R., & Markle, G. (1972). Family disruption, delinquent conduct and the effect of subclassification. *American Sociological Review, 37,* 93–99.

Christiansen, B. A., Golman, M. S., & Inn, A. (1982). Development of alcohol-related expectancies in adolescents: Separating pharmacological from social-learning influences. *Journal of Consulting and Clinical Psychology, 50,* 336–344.

Cochran, M. M., & Brassard, J. A. (1979). Child development and personal social networks. *Child Development, 50,* 601–616.

Cohn, A. (1979). Effective treatment of child abuse and neglect. *Social Work, 24*(6), 513–519.

Cole, G., & Taylor, K. (1984). Treating chronic neglect: Worker-led groups. In *Preventive services: A technical assistance memorandum for line supervisors.* Chapel Hill, NC: Group Child Care Consultant Services.

Collins, A. H., & Pancoast, D. L. (1976). *Natural helping networks: A strategy for prevention.* New York: National Association of Social Workers.

Collins, M. (1978). *Child abuser: A study of child abusers in self-help group therapy.* Littleton, MA: Publishing Sciences Group.

Conger, R. (1980). Juvenile delinquency: Behavior restraint or behavior facilitation? In T. Hirschi & M. Gottfredson (Eds.), *Understanding crime.* Beverly Hills, CA: Sage.

Conner, P., Branch, W., & Duryea, S. (1980). *A better way: Family intervention demonstration project, final report.* North Carolina: Edgecombe County Department of Social Services.

Coughey, K. (1981). *Divorced but not alone: A study of divorced women's social networks.* Paper presented at the annual meeting for the Society for the Study of Social Problems, Toronto.

Crittenden, P. M. (1981). Abusing, neglecting, problematic and adequate dyads: Differentiating by patterns of interaction. *Merrill-Palmer Quarterly, 27*(3), 201–218.

Crittenden, P. M. (1985). Maltreated infants, vulnerability and resilience. *Journal of Child Psychology and Psychiatry, 26,* 85–96.

Curtis, R. L., Jr., & Schulman, S. (1984). Ex-offenders, family relations, and economic supports: The "significant women" study of the TARP Project. *Crime and Delinquency, 30*(4), 507–528.

Danziger, S., & Weinberg, D. (1986). *Fighting poverty.* Cambridge, MA: Harvard University Press.

Daro, D. (November 1985). *Half-full/half-empty: An evaluation of nineteen child abuse and neglect demonstration projects.* Paper presented at Sixth Annual National Conference on Child Abuse and Neglect, Chicago.

Datesman, S., & Scarpitti, F. (1975). Female delinquency and broken homes. *Criminology, 13,* 33–55.

Davis, D. I., Berenson, D., Steinglass, P., & Davis, S. (1974). The adaptive consequences of drinking. *Psychiatry, 37,* 209–215.

Dean, A., & Lin, N. (1977). The stress-buffering role of social support: Problems and prospects for systematic investigation. *Journal of Nervous and Mental Disease, 165,* 403–417.

DeLeon, P. H., & VandenBos, G. R. (1980). Psychotherapy reimbursement in federal programs: Political factors. In G. R. VandenBos (Ed.), *Psychotherapy: Practice, research, policy.* Beverly Hills, CA: Sage.

de Shazer, S. (1982). *Patterns of brief family therapy.* New York: Guilford.

de Shazer, S. (1985). *Keys to solution in brief therapy.* New York: Norton.

de Shazer, S., Berg, I., Lipchik, E., Nunnally, E., Molnar, A., Gingerich, W., & Weiner-Davis, M. (1986). Brief therapy: Focused solution development. *Family Process, 25,* (207–222.

Dentler, R., & Monroe, L. J. (1961). Social correlates of early adolescent theft. *American Sociological Review, 26,* 733–743.

Disbrow, M. A., Doerr, H., & Caulfield, C. (1977). Measuring the components of parent's potential for child abuse and neglect. *Child Abuse and Neglect, 1,* 279–296.

Doane, J. A., West, K L., Goldstein, M. J., Rodnick, E. H., & Dones, J. E. (1981). Parental communication deviance and affective style. *Archives of General Psychiatry, 38,* 679–685.

Dreger, R. M. (1986). Does anyone really believe that alcoholism is a disease? *American Psychologist, 41,* 322.

Dumas, J. E., & Wahler, R. G. (1983). Predictors of treatment outcome in parent training: Mother insularity and socioeconomic disadvantage. *Behavioral Assessment, 5,* 301–313.

Durkeim, E. (1964). *The division of labor in society.* New York: Free Press.

Edgington, A., & Hall, M. (1982). *Dallas children and youth project: Child neglect demonstration.* Unpublished paper, Dallas, University of Texas, Health Science Center.

Egeland, B., Srouge, A., & Erikson, M. (1983). The developmental consequences of different patterns of maltreatment. *Child Abuse and Neglect, 7,* 459–469.

Elkin, M. (1984). *Families under the influence.* New York: Norton.

Eysenck, H. J. (1977). *Crime and personality.* London: Routledge and Kegan Paul.

Fagan, J., Piper, E., & Moore, M. (1986). Violent delinquents and urban youth. *Criminology, 24*(3), 439–472.

Falloon, I., Boyd, J. L., & McGill, C. (1984). *Family care of schizophrenia.* New York: Guilford.

Falloon, I., Boyd, J. L., McGill, G., Razoni, J., Moss, H. B., & Guilderman, H. M. (1982). Family management in the prevention of exacerbations of schizophrenia. *New England Journal of Medicine, 306,* 1437–1440.

Falloon, I. R. H., & Liberman, R. P. (1983). Behavioral family interventions in the management of chronic schizophrenia. In W. R. McFarlane (Ed.), *Family therapy in schizophrenia* (pp. 141–172). New York: Guilford.

Falloon, I. R. H., Boyd, J. L., McGill, C. W., Williamson, M., Razani, J., Moss, H. B., Gilderman, A. M., & Simpson, G. M. (1985). Family management in the prevention of morbidity of schizophrenia. *Archives of General Psychiatry, 42,* 887–896.

Farley, R. (1984). *Blacks and whites: Narrowing the gap?* Cambridge, MA: Harvard University Press.

Farrington, D. P., Gundry, G., & West, J. D. (1985). The familial transmission of criminality. In A. J. Lincoln & M. A. Strauss (Eds.), *Crime and the family* (pp. 193–206). Springfield, IL: Thomas.

Felix, R. H. (1967). *Mental illness: Progress and prospects.* New York: Columbia University Press.

Felt, S. K. (1983). The effects of neglect on children and implications for treatment. In C. M. Trainor (Ed.), *The dilemma of child neglect: Identification and treatment* (pp. 15–27). Denver: American Humane Association.

Fenwick, C R. (1982). Juvenile court intake decision making: The importance of family affiliation. *Journal of Criminal Justice, 10,* 443–453.

Fernandez-Pol, B., Bluestone, H., Missouri, C., Morales, G., & Mizruchi, M. S. (1986). Drinking patterns of inner-city Black Americans and Puerto Ricans. *Journal of Studies on Alcohol, 47,* 156–160.

Fisch, R., Weakland, J. H., & Segal, L. (1982). *The tactics of change: Doing therapy briefly.* San Francisco: Jossey-Bass.

Fischer, C. S. (1982). *To dwell among friends.* Chicago: University of Chicago Press.

Fishman, S. F., & Alissi, A. S. (1979). Strengthening families in natural support systems for offenders. *Federal Probation, 43,* 16–21.

Flanagan, T. J. (1980). The pains of long-term imprisonment. *British Journal of Criminology, 20*(2), 148–156.

Fonaroff, A., Falk, J., Kaplan, J., & O'Brien, C. P. (1980). Redemption of the overuser: An appraisal of plausible goals and methods for changing substance use practices. In D. R. Maloff & P. K. Levison (Eds.), *Issues in controlled substance use: Papers and commentary, conference on issues in controlled substance use.* Washington, DC: National Academy of Sciences.

Fox, M. R. (1985). *The Fox method.* Copyright 1985.

Fox, S. S. (1981). Families in crisis: Reflections on the children and families of the offender and the offended. *International Journal of Offender Therapy and Comparative Criminology, 25*(3), 254–264.

Freeman, H., & Simmons, O. (1961). Feeling of stigma among relatives of former mental patients. *Social Problems, 8,* 312–321.

Friedrich, W. N., Tyler, J. D., & Clark, J. A. (1985). Personality and psychophysiological variables in abusive, neglectful and low income control mothers. *Journal of Nervous and Mental Disease, 173*(8), 449–460.

Fritsch, T. A., & Burkhead, J. D. (1981). Behavioral reactions of children to parental absence due to imprisonment. *Family Relations, 30,* 83–88.

Froland, C., Pancoast, D. L., Chapman, N. J., & Kimboko, P. J. (1981). *Helping networks and human services.* Beverly Hills, CA: Sage.

Garbarino, J. (1977). The human ecology of child maltreatment: A conceptual model for research. *Journal of Marriage and the Family, 39,* 721–735.

Garbarino, J., & Stocking, H. (1980). *Protecting children from child abuse and neglect.* San Francisco: Jossey-Bass.

Garitano, W. W., & Ronall, R. E. (1974). Concepts of life style in the treatment of alcoholism. *International Journal of the Addictions, 9,* 585–592.

Garrett, C. J. (1985). Effects of residential treatment on adjudicated delinquents: A meta-analysis. *Journal of Research in Crime and Delinquency, 22*(4), 287–308.

Garrison, J. (1974). Network techniques: Case studies in the screening-linking-planning conference method. *Family Process, 13*(3), 337–353.

Garrison, V. (1978). Support systems of schizophrenic and nonschizophrenic Puerto Rican women in New York City. *Schizophrenia Bulletin, 4,* 561–596.

Gaudin, J. (1979). *Mothers' perceived strength of primary group networks and maternal child abuse.* Unpublished Ph.D. dissertation, Florida State University.

Gaudin, J. M., & Kirtz, D. P. (1985). Parenting skills training for child abusers. *Journal of Group Psychotherapy and Psychodrama, 38*(1), 35–54.

Gaudin, J. M., & Polansky, N. A. (1986). Social distances and the neglectful family: Sex, race and social class influences. *Children and Youth Services Review, 8,* 1–12.

Gelles, R. J. (1972). *The violent home.* Beverly Hills, CA: Sage.

Gendreau, P., & Ross, R. R. (1980). Effective correctional treatment: Bibliography for cynics. In R. R. Ross & P. Gendreau (Eds.), *Effective correctional treatment.* Toronto: Butterworths.

Gifford, C. D., Kaplan, F. B., & Salus, M. K. (1979). *Parent aids: In child abuse and neglect programs* (DHEW Pub. No. [OHDS] 79–30200). Washington, DC: National Center on Child Abuse and Neglect.

Giovannoni, J., & Billingsley, A. (1970). Child neglect among the poor: A study of parental adequacy in three ethnic groups. *Child Welfare, 49*(40), 146–204.

Giovannoni, J. M. (1971). Parental mistreatment: Perpetrators and victims. *Journal of Marriage and the Family, 33,* 649–658.

Gitlow, S. E. (1982). The clinical pharmacology and drug interactions of ethanol. In E. M. Pattison & E. Kaufman (Eds.), *Encyclopedic handbook of alcoholism.* New York: Gardner.

Gliksman, L., & Rush, B. R. (1986). Alcohol availability, alcohol consumption and alcohol-related damage. II. The role of sociodemographic factors. *Journal of Studies on Alcohol, 47,* 11–18.

Glueck, S., & Glueck, E. (1930). *Five hundred delinquent careers.* New York: Knopf.

Glueck, S., & Glueck, E. (1957). Working mothers and delinquency. In E. Wolfgang, L. Servitz, & N. Johnston (Eds.), *The sociology of crime and delinquency* (pp. 496–498). New York: Wiley.

Glueck, S., & Glueck, E. (1958). *Unraveling juvenile delinquency.* Cambridge, MA: Harvard University Press

Glueck, S., & Glueck, E. (1962). *Family environment and delinquency.* Boston: Houghton Mifflin.

Goffman, E. (1974). *Frame analysis.* New York: Harper & Row.

Gold, M. (1970). *Delinquency behavior in an American city.* Monterey, CA: Brooks/Cole.

Goldstein, A. P., Keller, H., & Erne, E. (1986). *Changing the abusive parent.* Champaign, IL: Research Press.

Goldstein, E. (1978). The influence of parental attitudes on psychiatric treatment outcomes. *Social Casework, 60*(6), 350–359.

Goldstein, E. (1987). Mental health and illness. *Encyclopedia of social work* (pp. 103–111). Silver Spring, MD: National Association of Social Workers.

Goldstein, M. J. (1985). Family factors that antedate the onset of schizophrenia and related disorders: The results of a fifteen year prospective longitudinal study. *Acta Psychiatrica Scandanavia,* Suppl. No. 319, *71,* 7–18.

Goldstein, M. J., Rodnick, E. H., Evans, J. R., May, P. R., & Steinberg, M. R. (1978). Drug and family therapy in the aftercare treatment of acute schizophrenia. *Archives of General Psychiatry, 35*(10), 1169–1177.

Goodwin, D. (1976). *Is alcoholism hereditary?* New York: Oxford University Press.

Gordon, D. A., Gustafson, K. E., & Arbuthnot, J. (1985, March). *Cost effectiveness analysis of a family therapy program with juvenile delinquents.* Paper presented at the Banff International Conference on Behavior Modification, Banff, Alberta, Canada.

Gottlieb, B. H. (1985). Assessing and strengthening the impact of social support on mental health. *Social Work, 30,* 293–300.

Gottlieb, B. H. (Ed.) (1981). *Social networks and social support.* Beverly Hills, CA: Sage.

Grad, J., & Sainsbury, P. (1963). Mental illness and the family. *Lancet, 1,* 533–547.

Greenwood, P. W., & Zimring, F. E. (1985). *One more chance: The pursuit of promising intervention strategies for chronic juvenile offenders* (Report #R–3214-OJJDP). Office of Juvenile Justice and Delinquency Prevention. U.S. Department of Justice. Santa Monica, CA: Rand.

Group for the Advancement of Psychiatry (1978). *The chronic mental patient in the community.* New York: Author.

Gurman, A. S., Kniskern, D. P., & Pinsof, W. M. (1986). Research on marital and family therapies. In S. L. Garfield & A. E. Bergin (Eds.), *Handbook of psychotherapy and behavior change* (pp. 565–624). New York: Wiley.

Hagedorn, J., Macon, P., & Moore, J. (1987). *Final report: Milwaukee gang project.* Milwaukee; Urban Research Center, University of Wisconsin–Milwaukee.

Hairston, C. R., & Lockett, P. (1985). Parents in prison: A child abuse and neglect prevention strategy. *Child Abuse and Neglect, 9*(4), 471–477.

Haley, J. (1963). *Strategies of psychotherapy.* New York: Grune & Stratton.

Haley, J. (1976). *Problem solving therapy.* San Francisco: Jossey-Bass.

Haley, J. (1980). *Leaving home.* New York: McGraw-Hill.

Hally, C., Polansky, N. F., & Polansky, N. A. (1980). *Child neglect: Mobilizing services* (DHSW Publication No. [OHDS] 80–30257). Washington, DC: U.S. Department of Health and Human Services.

Hammer, M. (1963). Influence of small social networks as factors in mental hospital admission. *Human Organization, 22,* 243–251.

Hammer, M. (1981). Social supports, social networks, and schizophrenia. *Schizophrenia Bulletin, 7,* 45–57.

Hammer, M., Makiesky-Barrow, S., & Gutwirth, L. (1978). Social networks and schizophrenia. *Schizophrenia Bulletin, 4,* 522–545.

Harding, C. M., & Strauss, J. S. (in press). The course of schizophrenia: An evolving concept. In M. Alpert (Ed.), *Controversies in schizophrenia: Changes and constancies.* New York: Guilford.

Hartman, A., & Laird, J. (1983). *Family centered social work practice.* New York: Free Press.

Hatfield, A. B. (1983). What families want of family therapists. In W. R. McFarlane (Ed.), *Family therapy in schizophrenia* (pp. 41–68). New York: Guilford.

Hatfield, A. B., & Lefley, H. P. (Eds.) (1987). *Families of the mentally ill: Coping and adaptation.* New York: Guilford.

Haynes, C. F., Cutler, C., Gray, J., Kempe, R. S. (1984). Hospitalized cases of nonorganic failure to thrive: The scope of this problem and short-term lay health visitor intervention. *Child Abuse and Neglect, 8*(2), 229–242.

Healy, W., & Bronner, A. (1926). *Delinquents and criminals.* New York: MacMillan.

Heath, D. B. (1975). A critical review of ethnographic studies of alcohol use. In R. J. Gibbins et al. (Eds.), *Research advances in alcohol and drug problems* (vol. 2). New York: Wiley.

Heider, F. (1958). *The psychology of interpersonal relations.* New York: Wiley.

Hennessy, M., Richards, P. J., & Berk, R. A. (1978). Broken homes and middle class delinquency. *Criminology, 15,* 505–528.

Herrenkohl, R. C., Herrenkohl, C., & Egolf, B. P. (1983). Circumstances surrounding the occurrence of child maltreatment. *Journal of Counseling and Clinical Psychology, 51*(3), 424–431.

Herz, M. I., Endicott, J., & Spitzer, R. L. (1976). Brief versus standard hospitalization: The families. *American Journal of Psychiatry, 133,* 759–801.

Hetherington, E. M., Cox, M., & Cox, R. (September 1976). *The aftermath of divorce.* Paper presented at the meeting of the American Psychological Association, Washington, DC.

Hill, S. Y. (1985). The disease concept of alcoholism: A review. *Drug and Alcohol Dependence, 16,* 193–214.

Hindelang, M. J. (1973). Causes of delinquency: A partial replication and extension. *Social Problems, 20,* 471–487.

Hinds, L. S. (1981). The impact of incarceration on low-income families. *Journal of Offender Counseling, Services and Rehabilitation, 5*(3/4), 5–12.

Hirsch, S. R., & Leff, J. P. (1975). *Abnormalities in parents of schizophrenics.* London: Oxford University Press.

Hirschi, T. (1969). *Causes of delinquency.* Berkeley: University of California Press.

Hirschi, T. (1983). Crime and the family. In J. Q. Wilson (Ed.), *Crime and public policy* (pp. 52–68). San Francisco: ICS Press.

Hoenig, J., & Hamilton, M. (1969). *The desegregation of the mentally ill.* London: Routledge and Kegan Paul.

Hoffman, E. (1980). Policy and politics: The Child Abuse Prevention and Treatment Act. In G. Gerbner, C. S. Ross, & E. Ziegler (Eds.), *Child abuse—An agenda for action* (pp. 157–170). New York: Oxford University Press.

Hoffman-Plotken, D., & Twentyman, C. T. (1984). A multimodal assessment of behavioral and cognitive defects in abused and neglected pre-schoolers. *Child Development, 53*(3), 794–802.

Hogarty, G. E. (1984). Depot neuroleptics: The relevance of psychosocial factors. *Journal of Clinical Psychiatry, 45*(2), 36–42.

Hogarty, G. E., Anderson, C. M., Reiss, D. J., Lornblith, S. J., Greenwald, D. P., Javna, C. D., & Madonia, M. J. (1986). Family psychoeducation, social skills training and maintenance chemotherapy in the aftercare treatment of schizophrenia. *Archives of General Psychiatry, 43,* 633–642.

Holahan, C. J., Wilcox, B. L., Spearly, J. L., & Campbell, M. D. (1979). The ecological perspective in community mental health. *Community Mental Health Review, 4*(2), 1–9.

Hornick, J., Patterson, C., & Clarke, M. (1983). *The use of lay therapists in the treatment of child abusers: A final evaluation report.* Waterloo, IA: Family and Children's Services.

Hraba, J., Warren, R. D., & Miller, G. (1979). A demographic diagnosis of delinquency. *Criminal Justice Review, 4*(2), 133–143.

Hull, J. G., & Bond, C. F. (1986). Social and behavioral consequences of alcohol consumption and expectancy: A meta-analysis. *Psychological Bulletin, 99,* 347–360.

Hurd, G., Pattison, E. M., & Smith, J. E. (1981, February). *Test, re-test reliability of social network self reports: The Pattison Psychosocial Inventory (PPI).* Paper presented to Sun Belt Social Networks Conference, Tampa, FL.

Jackson, A. M. (1984). Child neglect: An overview. In *Perspective on child maltreatment in the mid-80's* (DHSS Publication OHDS 84–30338, pp. 15–17). Washington, DC: National Center on Child Abuse and Neglect, Children's Bureau.

Jacob, T., Dunn, N. J., & Leonard, K. (1983). Patterns of alcohol abuse and family stability. *Alcoholism: Clinical and Experimental Research, 7,* 382–385.

Jacob, T., Favorini, A., Meisel, S. S., & Anderson, C. M. (1978). The alcoholic's spouse, children, and family interactions. *Journal of Studies on Alcohol, 39*(1), 1231–1251.

Jacob, T., & Leonard, K. (1986). Psychosocial functioning in children of alcoholic fathers, depressed fathers, and control fathers. *Journal of Studies on Alcohol, 47,* 373–380.

Jacobson, G. (1976). *The alcoholisms: Detection, diagnosis and assessment.* New York: Human Sciences Press.

Jellinek, E. M. (1952). Phases of alcohol addiction. *Quarterly Journal of Studies on Alcohol, 13* 673–684.

Johnson, D. (1986, February). *The family's experience of living with mental illness.* Paper presented at the National Alliance of the Mentally Ill—National Institute of Mental Health Colloquium, Rockville, MD.

Johnson, R. E. (1986). Family structure and delinquency: General patterns and gender differences. *Criminology, 24,* 65–80.

Johnson, V. E. (1980). *I'll quit tomorrow* (rev. ed.). New York: Harper & Row.

Joint Commission on Mental Health of Children (1969). *Crisis in child mental health: Challenge for the 1970's.* New York: Harper & Row.

Joint Commission on Mental Illness and Health (1961). *Action for mental health.* New York: Basic Books.

Jones, E. E., & Davis, K. E. (1965). From acts to dispositions: The attribution process in person perception. In L. Berkowitz (Ed.), *Advances in experimental social psychology* (vol. 2, pp. 219–266). New York: Academic Press.

Jones, J. M., & McNeely, R. L. (1980). Mothers who neglect and those who do not: A comparative study. *Social Casework* (November), 559–566.

Jones, R. S., & Schmid, T. J. (1987). *Prison partnerships: A coping mechanism for male and female inmates.* Paper presented at the annual meeting of the Midwest Sociological Society, Chicago.

Kamerman, S., & Kahn, A. (1978). *Family policy: Government and family in fourteen countries.* New York: Columbia University Press.

Katz, S. N., Howle, R. W., & McGrath, M. (1985). Child neglect laws in America. *Family Law Quarterly, IX,* 1.

Kellogg, T., & Hunter, M. (1986). Seeking balance and healthy moderation: The other side of adult children of alcoholics. *Focus on Family and Chemical Dependency, 9*(5), 24–29.

Kelly, J. G. (1966). Ecological constraints on mental health services. *American Psychologist, 21,* 535–539.

Kelman, H. (1964). The effect of a brain-damaged child on the family. In H. G. Birch (Ed.), *Brain damage in children.* Baltimore: Williams & Wilkins.

Kiesler, C. (1985). Mental hospitals and alternative care: Noninstitutionalization as potential public policy. In P. Brown (Ed.), *Mental health care and social policy* (pp. 292–315). Boston, London, Melbourne, Henley: Routledge and Kegan Paul.

Kiesler, C. A. (1987, May). *Testimony on the federal role in mental health.* United States House of Representatives, Subcommittee on Human Resources and Intergovernmental Relations. Washington, DC.

Klaus, P. A., & Rand, M. R. (1984). *Family violence.* Bureau of Justice Statistics Special Report. Washington, DC: Government Printing Office.

Klein, N. C., Alexander, J. F., & Parsons, B. V. (1976). Impact of family systems intervention on recidivism and sibling delinquency: A model of primary prevention and program evaluation. *Journal of Consulting and Clinical Psychology, 45*(3), 469–474.

Kopeikin, H. S., Marshall, V. and Goldstein, M. J. (1983). Stages and impact of crisis-oriented family therapy in the aftercare of acute schizophrenia. In McFarlane, W. R. (Ed.), *Family therapy in schizophrenia* (69–116). New York: Guilford Press.

Korsten, M. A., & Lieber, C. S. (1985). Medical complications of alcoholism. In J. H. Mendelson & N. K. Mello (Eds.), *The diagnosis and treatment of alcoholism* (2nd ed.). New York: McGraw-Hill.

Kratcoski, P. C. (1982). Child abuse and violence against the family. *Child Welfare, 61*, 445–455.

Kreisman, D., & Joy, V. (1974). Family response to the mental illness of a relative: A review of the literature. *Schizophrenia Bulletin, 10*(3), 241–248.

Kruttschmitt, C., & McCarthy, D. (1985). Family social control and pretrial sanctions. Does sex really matter? *The Journal of Criminal Law and Criminology, 76*, 151–175.

Lamb, H. R., & Oliphant, E. (1978). Schizophrenia through the eyes of families. *Hospital and Community Psychiatry, 29*, 803–806.

Lange, A. J., & Jakubowski, P. (1976). *Responsible assertive behavior.* Champaign, IL: Research Press.,

Lapp, J. (1983). A profile of officially reported child neglect. In C. M. Trainor (Ed.), *The dilemma of child neglect—Identification and treatment.* Denver: American Humane Association.

Lederer, W. J., & Jackson, D. D. (1968). *The mirages of marriage.* New York: Norton.

Ledingham, J., Schwartzman, A., & Serbin, L. (1984). Current adjustment and family functioning of children behaviorally at risk of schizophrenia. In A. Doyle, D. Gold, & D. Moskowitz (Eds.), *Children in families under stress.* San Francisco: Jossey-Bass.

Leff, J., & Vaughn, C. E. (1980). The interaction of life events and relatives' expressed emotion in schizophrenia and depressive neurosis. *British Journal of Psychiatry, 136*, 146–153.

Leff, J. P., Kuipers, L., Berkowitz, R., Eberlein-Vries, R., & Sturgeon, D. (1982). A controlled trial of social intervention in the families of schizophrenic patients. *British Journal of Psychiatry, 141*, 121–134.

Leff, J. P., Kuipers, L., & Berkowitz, R. (1983). Intervention in families of schizophrenics and its effects on relapse rates. In W. R. McFarlane (Ed.), *Family therapy in schizophrenia* (pp. 173–189). New York: Guilford.

Lehman, N. (1986a, June). The origins of the underclass. *The Atlantic Monthly,* pp. 31–55.

Lehman, N. (1986b, July). The origins of the underclass. *The Atlantic Monthly,* pp. 54–68.

Lieby, J. (1978). *History of social welfare and social work in the United States.* New York: Columbia University Press.

Levine, I. (1984). Homelessness: Its implications for mental health policy and practice. *Psychosocial Rehabilitation Journal, VIII*(1), 6–16.

Levitan, S. (1985). *Programs in aid of the poor* (5th ed.). Baltimore: Johns Hopkins University Press.

Lieber, L., & Baker, J. (1977). Parents anonymous and self-help treatment for child abusing parents: A review and evaluation. *Child Abuse and Neglect, 1*, 133–148.

Liem, J. H. (1980). Family studies of schizophrenia: An update and commentary. *Schizophrenia Bulletin, 6*, 429–455.

Lincoln, A. J., & Kirpatrick, J. T. (1985). Criminological theory and family crime. In A. J. Lincoln & M. A. Straus (Eds.), *Crime and the family* (pp. 46–64). Springfield, IL: Thomas.

Lipton, F. R., Cohen, C. I., Fischer, E., & Katz, S. E. (1981). Schizophrenia: A network crisis. *Schizophrenia Bulletin, 7*, 144–151.

Litwak, E., & Szelenyi, I. (1969). Primary group structures and their functions: Kin, neighbors and friends. *American Sociological Review, 34*, 465–481.

Lowenfels, A. B. (1979). Alcohol and cancer: A review and update. *British Journal of Alcohol and Alcoholism, 14*(3), 148–163.

Lutzker, J. R., Wesch, D., & Rice, J. M. (1984). A review of Project "12-Ways": An ecobehavioral approach to the treatment and prevention of child abuse and neglect. *Advances in Behavior Research and Therapy, 6,* 63–73.

Madanes, C. (1981). *Strategic family therapy.* San Francisco: Jossey-Bass.

Madanes, C. (1984). *Behind the one-way mirror.* San Francisco: Jossey-Bass.

Maloff, K., Becker, H. S., Fonaroff, A., & Rodin, J. (1980). Informal social controls and their influence on substance use. In D. R. Maloff & P. K. Levison (Eds.), *Issues in controlled substance use: Papers and commentary, conference on issues in controlled substance use.* Washington, DC: National Academy of Sciences.

Marlowe, H., Reid, J. B., Patterson, G. R., & Weinrott, M. (in press). Treating adolescent offenders: A comparison and follow up of parent training for families of chronic delinquents.

Marsh, R. L. (1983). Services for families: A model project to provide services for families of prisoners. *International Journal of Offender Therapy and Comparative Criminology, 27*(2), 156–162.

Martin, M., & Walters, S. (1982). Familial correlates of selected types of child abuse and neglect. *Journal of Marriage and the Family* (May), 267–275.

Martinson, R. (1974). What works? Questions and answers about prison reform. *Public Interest, 35*(22), 54.

Mas, C. H. (1986). *Attribution styles and communication patterns in families of juvenile delinquents.* Doctoral dissertation, University of Utah, Salt Lake City.

Mas, C. H., Alexander, J. F., & Barton, C. (1985). Modes of expression in family therapy: A process study of roles and gender. *Journal of Marital and Family Therapy, 11*(4), 411–415.

McCarthy, B. R. (1980). Inmate mothers: The problems of separation and reintegration. *Journal of Offender Counseling, Services and Rehabilitation 4*(3), 199–211.

McCord, J. (1978). A thirty-year follow-up of treatment effects. *American Psychologist, 33,* 284–289.

McCord, J. (1979). Some child-rearing antecedents of criminal behavior in adult men. In E. Bittner & J. Messinger (Eds.), *Criminology review yearbook* (vol. 2, pp. 121–136). Beverly Hills, CA: Sage.

McCord, W., & McCord, J. (1959). *Origins of crime: A new evaluation of the Cambridge-Somerville youth study.* New York: Columbia University Press.

McCrady, B. S. (1982). Marital dysfunction: Alcoholism and marriage. In E. M. Pattison & E. Kaufman (Eds.), *Encyclopedic handbook of alcoholism.* New York: Gardner.

McFarlane, W. R. (1982). Multiple family therapy in the psychiatric hospital. In H. Harbin (Ed.), *The psychiatric hospital and the family.* Jamaica, NY: SP Books.

McFarlane, W. R. (1983). Multiple family therapy in schizophrenia. In W. R. McFarlane (Ed.), *Family therapy in schizophrenia* (pp. 141–172). New York: Guilford.

McGarrell, F., & Flanagan, T. J. (1985). *Sourcebook of criminal justice statistics—1984.* U.S. Department of Justice, Bureau of Justice Statistics. Washington, DC: Government Printing Office.

McNeely, R. L., & Pope, C. E. (Eds.) (1981). *Race, crime and criminal justice.* Beverley Hills, CA: Sage.

Mead, G. H. (1934). *Mind, self and society.* Chicago: University of Chicago Press.

Mechanic, D. (1980). *Mental health and social policy* (2nd ed.). Englewood Cliffs, NJ: Prentice-Hall.

Mechanic, D. (1985). Mental health and social policy: Initiatives for the 1980's. *Health Affairs, 4,* 76–88.

Medinnas, G. R. (1965). Delinquents' perception of their parents. *Journal of Consulting Psychology, 29,* 592–593.

Meier, E. G. (1964). Child neglect. In N. E. Cohen (Ed.), *Social work and social problems* (pp. 153–199). New York: National Association of Social Workers.

Mendelson, J. H., Babor, T. F., Mellow, N. K., & Pratt, H. (1986). Alcoholism and prevalence of medical and psychiatric disorders. *Journal of Studies on Alcohol, 47,* 361–366.

Merton, R. K. (1968). *Social theory and social structure.* New York: Free Press.

Mezey, E. (1982). Effects of alcohol on the gastrointestinal tract. In E. M. Pattison & E. Kaufman (Eds.), *Encyclopedic handbook of alcoholism.* New York: Gardner.

Miklowitz, D. J. (1985). *Family interaction and illness outcomes in bipor and schizophrenic patients.* Unpublished doctoral dissertation, University of California at Los Angeles.

Miklowitz, D. J., Goldstein, J. J., & Falloon, I. R. H. (1983). Premorbid and symptomatic characteristics of schizophrenics from families with high and low levels of expressed emotion. *Journal of Abnormal Psychology, 92,* 359–367.

Miklowitz, D. J., Goldstein, M. J., Neuchterlein, I. H., Snyder, K. S., & Doane, J. A. (in press). Expressed emotion, affective style, lithium compliance and relapse in recent onset mania. *Psychopharmacology Bulletin.*

Miklowitz, D. J., Strachan, A. M., Goldstein, M. J., Doane, J. A., Snyder, K. S., Hogarty, G. E., & Falloon, I. R. H. (1986). Expressed emotion and communication deviance in the families of schizophrenics. *Journal of Abnormal Psychology, 95,* 60–66.

Miller, E. (1986). *Street women.* Philadelphia: Temple University Press.

Miller, W. B. (1958). Class culture as a generating milieu of gang delinquency. *Journal of Social Issues, 14,* 5–19.

Minuchin, S. (1974). *Families and family therapy.* Cambridge, MA: Harvard University Press.

Minuchin, S.. & Fishman, H. C. (1981). *Family therapy techniques.* Cambridge, MA: Harvard University Press.

Monahan, T. P. (1957). Family status and the delinquent child: A reappraisal of some new findings. *Social Forces, 35,* 250–258.

Mondale, W. (April 1977). Letter printed in *Children's rights report* (vol. 7). New York: Juvenile Rights Project of the American Civil Liberties Union Foundation.

Morris, S. B. (1986). *The effects of psychotherapeutic relabels on attributions, memory, and mood.* Doctoral dissertation, University of Utah, Salt Lake City.

Morris, S. B., Alexander, J. F., & Waldron, H. (in press). Functional family therapy: Issues in clinical practice. In I. R. H. Falloon (Ed.), *Handbook of behavioral family therapy.* New York: Guilford.

Morrissey, J., Goldman, H., & Klerman, L. (1985). Cycles of institutional reform. In P. Brown (Ed.), *Mental health care and social policy* (pp. 70–100). Boston, London, Melbourne, Henley: Routledge and Kegan Paul.

Moynihan, P. (1986). *Family and nation.* San Diego, CA: Harcourt Brace Jovanovich.

Murray, R., & Stabenau, J. (1982). Genetic factors in alcohol predisposition. In E. Pattison & E. Kaufman (Eds.), *Encyclopedic handbook of alcoholism* (pp. 120–150). New York: Gardner.

Myers, J., & Bean, L. (1968). *A decade later: A follow-up of social class and mental illness.* New York: Wiley.

Nagi, S. (1977). *Child maltreatment in the United States: A challenge to social institutions.* New York: Columbia University Press.

National Center on Child Abuse and Neglect (1981). *American Indian law: Relationship to child abuse and neglect* (OHDS 81–3032). Washington, DC: U.S. Department of Health and Human Services.

National Center on Child Abuse and Neglect (1985). *Selected annotated bibliography on child neglect* [Mimeograph]. Washington, DC: Government Printing Office.

National Council on Alcoholism (1972). Criteria for the diagnosis of alcoholism. *Annals of Internal Medicine, 77*(2), 249–258.

Nettler, G. (1984). *Explaining crime.* New York: McGraw-Hill.

Neuchterlein, K. H., & Dawson, M. E. (1984). A heuristic vulnerability/stress model for schizophrenic episodes. *Schizophrenia Bulletin, 10,* 300–312.

Neuringer, C. (1982). Alcoholic addiction: Psychological tests and measurements. In E. M. Pattison & E. Kaufman (Eds.), *Encyclopedic handbook of alcoholism.* New York: Gardner.

Norton, R. (1982). Soft magic. In C. Wilder-Mott & J. H. Weakland (Eds.), *Rigor and imagination: Essays from the legacy of Gregory Bateson.* New York: Praeger.

Nurse, A. R. (1982). The role of alcoholism in relationship to intimacy. *Journal of Psychoactive Drugs, 14*(1–2), 23–26.

Nye, F. I. (1958). *Family relationships and delinquent behavior.* Westport, CT: Greenwood.

Ortiz, M. (1985). Personal communication.

Pancoast, D. L. (1980). Finding and enlisting neighbors to support families. In J. Garbarino & S. H. Stocking & Associates (Eds.), *Protecting children from abuse and neglect* (pp. 109–132). San Francisco: Jossey-Bass.

Pancoast, D. L., & Collins, A. H. (1976). *Natural helping networks.* Washington, DC: National Association of Social Workers.

Paquin, H., Harris, P., Rothacker, J., & Warren, M. Q. (1976). Characteristics of youngsters referred to family court intake and factors relating to their processing. In H. J. Rubin (Ed.), *Juvenile justice.* Santa Monica, CA: Goodyear.

Parloff, M. (1979). Can psychotherapy research guide the policymaker? *American Psychologist, 34*(4), 296–306.

Parsons, B. V., & Alexander, J. F. (1973). Short term family intervention: A therapy outcome study. *Journal of Consulting and Clinical Psychology, 41*(2), 195–201.

Patterson, G. R. (1970). Behavioral intervention procedures in the classroom and in the home. In A. E. Bergin & S. L. Garfield (Eds.), *Handbook of psychotherapy and behavior change.* New York: Wiley.

Patterson, G. R. (1980). Children who steal. In T. Hirschi & M. Gottfredson (Eds.), *Understanding crime: Current theory and research.* Beverly Hills, CA: Sage.

Patterson, G. R. (1982). *Coercive family process.* Eugene, OR: Castalia.

Patterson, G. R. (1985). Beyond technology: The next stage in developing an empirical base for parent training. In L. L'Abate (Ed.), *Handbook of family psychology and therapy* (vol. 2, pp. 1344–1379). New York: Dorsey.

Patterson, G. R., Cobb, J. A., & Ray, R. S. (1973). A social engineering technology for retraining aggressive boys. In H. E. Adams & P. Unikel (Eds.), *Issues and trends in behavior therapy.* Springfield, IL: Thomas.

Patterson, G. R., & Reid, J. B. (1970). Reciprocity and coercion: Two facets of social systems. In C. Neuringer & G. L. Michael (Eds.), *Behavior modification in clinical psychology*. New York: Appleton-Century-Crofts.

Patti, P. (1976). *An analysis of issues related to child abuse and neglect as reflected in congressional hearings prior to enactment of the Child Abuse and Prevention Treatment Act of 1974*. Seattle: University of Washington, Center for Social Work Research.

Pattison, E. M. (1982a). Alcohol use: Social policy. In E. M. Pattison & E. Kaufman, (Eds.), *Encyclopedic handbook of alcoholism*. New York: Gardner.

Pattison, E. M. (1982b). The concept of alcoholism as a syndrome. In E. M. Pattison (Ed.), *Selection of treatment for alcoholics*. New Brunswick, NJ: Rutgers Center of Alcohol Studies.

Pattison, E. M., & Kaufman, E. (1982). The alcoholism syndrome: Definitions and models. In E. M. Pattison & E. Kaufman (Eds.), *Encyclopedic handbook of alcoholism*. New York: Gardner.

Pattison, E. M., Llamas, R., & Hurd, G. (1979). Social network mediation of anxiety. *Psychiatric Annals, 9*, 56–67.

Pattison, E. M., Sobel, M. B., & Sobel, L. C. (1977). *Emerging concepts of alcohol dependence*. New York: Springer.

Peele, S. (1984). The cultural context of psychological approaches to alcoholism. *American Psychologist, 39*, 1337–1351.

Pierce, F. (1854, 3 May). Veto message. *Congressional Globe*, 1061–1063.

Pinkney, A. (1984). *The myth of black progress*. New York: Cambridge University Press.

Polansky, N. A., Ammons, P. W., & Gaudin, J. M. (1985a). Loneliness and isolation in child neglect. *Social Casework, 66*, 38–47.

Polansky, N., Borgman, R. D., & DeSaix, C. (1972). *Roots of futility*. San Francisco: Jossey-Bass.

Polansky, N. A., Cabral, R. S., Magura, S., & Phillips, M. H. (1983). Comparative norms for the childhood level of living scale. *Journal of Social Service Research, 6(3/4)*, 45–55.

Polansky, N. A., Chalmers, M. A., Buttenweiser, E., & Williams, D. P. (1978). Assessing adequacy of child caring: An urban scale. *Child Welfare, 57(7)*, 439–448.

Polansky, N. A., Chalmers, M. A., Buttenweiser, E., & Williams, D. P. (1978). Assessing adequacy of child caring: An urban scale. *Child Welfare, 57(7)*, 439–448.

Polansky, N. A., Gaudin, J. A., Ammons, P. W., & Davis, K. S. (1985b). The psychological ecology of the neglectful mother. *Child Abuse and Neglect, 9*, 265–275.

Polansky, N. A., & Gaudin, J. M. (1983). Social distancing of the neglectful family. *Social Service Review, 57(4)*, 196–208.

Polansky, N. A., Hally, C., & Polansky, N. F. (1975). *Profile of neglect—A survey of the state of the knowledge of child neglect*. Washington, DC: U.S. Department of Education and Welfare, Community Services Administration.

Polich, J., Ellickson, R., Reuter, W., & Kohan, S. (1984). *Strategies for controlling adolescent drug use*. Santa Monica, CA: Rand.

Poole, E. D., & Regoli, R. M. (1979). Parental support, delinquent friends, and delinquency: A test of interaction effects. *The Journal of Criminal Law and Criminology, 70*, 188–193.

Pope, C. E., Feyerherm, W. H., & Toth, L. A. (1984). *Selection bias and juvenile court dispositions: The effects or race, gender and family status*. Paper presented at the annual meeting of the Midwest Criminal Justice Association, Chicago.

President's Commission on Mental Health (1979). *Final report*. Washington, DC: Author.

Rabkin, J. (1974). Public attitudes toward mental illness: A review of the literature. *Schizophrenia Bulletin, 10,* 9–33.

Regier, D., Goldberg, I, & Taucke, C. (1985). The de facto mental health service system. In P. Brown (Ed.), *Mental health care and social policy* (pp. 105–126). Boston, London, Melbourne, Henley: Routledge and Kegan Paul.

Reidy, T. J. (1977). The aggressive characteristics of abused and neglected children. *Journal of Clinical Psychology, 33,* 1140–1145.

Reiss, D., & Oliveri, M. E. (1980). Family paradigm and family coping: A proposal for linking the family's intrinsic adaptive capacities to its responses to stress. *Family Relations, 29,* 431–444.

Report of the President's Commission on Mental Health (1978). Washington, DC: Government Printing Office.

Riege, M. G. (1972). Parental affection and juvenile delinquency in girls. *British Journal of Criminology, 12,* 55–73.

Rogers, J. W. (1977). *Why are you not a criminal?* Englewood Cliffs, NJ: Prentice-Hall.

Rosen, L. (1985). Family and delinquency: Structure or function? *Criminology, 23,* 553–573.

Rosenquist, C. M., & Megargee, E. I. (1969). *Delinquency in three cultures*. Austin: University of Texas Press.

Ross, A. D. (1979). *Psychological disorders of children*. New York: McGraw-Hill.

Rozansky, P., & Chambers, P. (1982). *Project TIME for parents*. St. Louis: Family Resource Center.

Ruevini, U. (1979). *Networking families in crisis*. New York: Human Sciences Press.

Rush, B. R., Gliksman, L., & Brook, R. (1986). Alcohol availability, alcohol consumption and alcohol-related damage. I. The distribution of consumption model. *Journal of Studies on Alcohol, 47,* 1–10.

Salzinger, S., Kaplan, S., & Artemeyeff, C. (1983). Mothers' personal social networks and child maltreatment. *Journal of Abnormal Psychology, 92*(1), 68–76.

Sametz, T. (1980). Children of incarcerated women. *Social Work, 25*(4), 298–303.

Sample, A. S. (1984). *Racehoss: Big Emma's boy*. New York: Ballantine.

Satir, V. (1983). *Conjoint Family Therapy* (3rd ed.). Palo Alto, CA: Science and Behavior Books.

Scheff, T. (1985). Medical dominance: Psychoactive drugs and mental health policy. In P. Brown (Ed.), *Mental health care and social policy* (pp. 225–271). Boston, London, Melbourne, Henley: Routledge and Kegan Paul.

Scheflen, A. (1981). *Levels of schizophrenia*. New York: Brunner/Mazel.

Schene, P. (1986). National patterns in child neglect reporting. In M. McCabe, R. E. Cohen, & V. Weiss (Eds.), *Child abuse and neglect*. New York: Goldner.

Schorr, A. (1986). *Common decency*. New Haven, CT: Yale University Press.

Segal, R., & Sisson, B. V. (1985). Medical complications associated with alcohol use and the assessment of risk of physical damage. In T. E. Bratter & G. G. Forrest (Eds.), *Alcoholism and substance abuse: Strategies for clinical intervention*. New York: Free Press.

Segal, S. (1987). Deinstitutionalization. *Encyclopedia of social work* (vol. I, pp. 376–381). Silver Spring, MD: National Association of Social Workers.

Selvini-Palazzoli, M., Cecchin, G., Prata, G., & Boscolo, L. (1978). *Paradox and counter-paradox: A new model in the therapy of the family in schizophrenic transaction.* New York: Jason Aronson.

Shapiro, D. (1979). *Parents and protectors—A study of child abuse and neglect.* New York: Child Welfare League of America.

Shaw, C. R., & McKay, H. D. (1932). *Report on social factors and juvenile delinquency* (vol. II, No. 13). National Commission on Law Observance and Enforcement.

Silberman, C. E. (1978). *Criminal violence, criminal justice.* New York: Vintage Books.

Singer, M. T., Wynne, L. C., & Toohey, M. C. (1978). Communication disorders and the families of schizophrenics. In L. C. Wynne, R. L. Cromwell, & S. Matthysse (Eds.), *The nature of schizophrenia.* New York: Wiley.

Sluzki, C., & Veron, E. (1971). The double bind as a universal pathogenic situation. *Family Process, 10,* 397–407.

Smith, M. B., & Hobbs, N. (1966). The community and the community mental health center. *American Psychologist, 15,* 113–118.

Smith, P. (1955). Broken homes and juvenile delinquency. *Sociology and Social Research, 39,* 131–142.

Smith, T. E., & Bauer, M. (1986). *Alcohol misuse among general relief populations.* Unpublished manuscript.

Snyder, M., & Swann, W. B., Jr. (1978). Hypothesis testing processes in social interaction. *Journal of Personality and Social Psychology, 36,* 1201–1212.

Sobel, S. B. (1982). Difficulties experienced by women in prison. *Psychology of Women Quarterly, 7*(2), 107–117.

Speck, R., & Attneave, C. (1973). *Family networks.* New York: Vintage.

Speer, D. C. (1970). Family systems: morphotasis and morphogenesis, or "is homeostatis enough?" *Family Process, 9*(3), 259–279.

Spradley, J. P. (1980). Substance use: Context, meaning, and informal control. In D. R. Maloff & P. K. Levison (Eds.), *Issues in controlled substance use.* Washington, D.C.: National Academy of Sciences.

Stanton, M. D. (1980). A family theory of drug abuse. In D. Lettieri, M. Sayers, & H. Pearson (Eds.), *Theories on drug abuse. Selected contemporary perspectives* (National Institute on Drug Abuse Research Monograph Series No. 30). Washington, D.C.: U.S. Government Printing Office.

Stanton, M. D., Todd, T. C., Steier, F., Van Deusen, J., Mardern, L. R., Rosoff, R. J., Seaman, S. F., & Skibinski, E. (1979, October). *Family characteristics and family therapy of heroin addicts: Final report 1974–1976* (NIDA Grant No. RO1 DA 0119). Washington, DC: U.S. National Institute of Drug Abuse.

Staples, R. (1986). The masculine way of violence. In D. F. Hawkins (Ed.), *Homicide among black Americans* (pp. 137–153). Lanham, MD: University Press of America.

Steele, B. F. (1976). Violence within the family. In R. E. Helfer & C. H. Kempe (Eds.), *Child abuse and neglect.* Cambridge, MA: Ballinger.

Steinberg, H. R., & Durrell, J. A. (1968). A stressful social situation as a precipitant of schizophrenic symptoms. *British Journal of Psychiatry, 114,* 1097–1105.

Straus, M. A. (1985). Family training in crime and violence. In A. J. Lincoln & M. A. Straus (Eds.), *Crime and the family.* Springfield, IL: Thomas.

Straus, M. A., Gelles, R. J., & Steinmetz, S. K. (1980). *Behind closed doors: Violence in the American family.* Garden City, NY: Doubleday.

Straus, M. A., & Lincoln, A. J. (1985). A conceptual framework for understanding crime and the family. In A. J. Lincoln & M. A. Straus (Eds.), *Crime and the family* (pp. 5–23). Springfield, IL: Thomas.

Struckhoff, D. R. (1979). Toward a model of involuntary separation of families. *Offender Rehabilitation, 3*(4), 289–297.

Stuart, R. (1980). *Helping couples change.* New York: Guilford.

Sullivan, M., Spasser, M., & Penner, G. L. (1977). *Bowen Center Project for abused and neglected children.* Washington, DC: U.S. Department of Health, Education, and Welfare, Office of Human Development.

Swanson, J. F. (1980). Impact of parent aides in child neglect: An ecologically-oriented intervention approach. *Dissertation Abstracts International, 41*, 4166–A. (University Microfilms No. 81–06, 449.)

Szapocznik, J., Kirtines, W. M., Foote, F. H., Perz-Vidal, A., & Hervis, O. (1983). Conjoint versus one-person family therapy: Some evidence for the effectiveness of conducting family therapy through one person. *Journal of Consulting and Clinical Psychology, 51*, 889–899.

Talbot, J. (1978). Deinstitutionalization: Avoiding the disasters of the past. *Hospital and Community Psychiatry, 30*, 621–624.

Tarter, R. E., & Edwards, K. L. (1986). Multifactorial etiology of neuropsychological impairment in alcoholics. *Alcoholism: Clinical and Experimental Research, 10*, 128–135.

Taylor, J. R., Helzer, J. E., & Robins, L. N. (1986). Moderate drinking in ex-alcoholics: Recent studies. *Journal of Studies on Alcohol, 47*, 115–121.

Tecce, J. J., & Cole, J. O. (1976). The distraction–arousal hypothesis, CNV and schizophrenia. In D. I. Mostofsky (Ed.), *Behavior control and modification of psychological activity.* Englewood Cliffs, NJ: Prentice-Hall.

Terkelson, K. (1980). Toward a theory of the family life cycle. In E. Carter & M. McGoldrick (Eds.), *The family life cycle.* New York: Gardner.

Test M., & Stein, L. (1978). Community treatment of the chronic patient: Research overview. *Schizophrenia Bulletin, 4*(3), 350–363.

Tewari, S., & Carson, V. G. (1982). Biochemistry of alcohol and alcohol metabolism. In E. M. Pattison & E. Kaufman (Eds.), *Encyclopedic handbook of alcoholism.* New York: Gardner.

Toby, J. (1957). The differential impact of family disorganization. *American Sociological Review, 22*, 505–512.

Todd, T. C., & Stanton, M. D. (1983). Research on marital and family therapy: Answers, issues, and recommendations for the future. In B. B. Wolman & G. Stricker (Eds.), *Handbook of family and marital therapy.* New York: Plenum Press.

Tolsdorf, C. C. (1976). Social networks, support, and coping: An exploratory study. *Family Process, 15*, 407–415.

Tomasulo, P. A., Kater, R. M. H., & Iber, F. L. (1986). Impairment of thiamine absorption in alcoholism. *American Journal of Clinical Nutrition, 21*, 1340–1344.

Treating chronic neglect. (1984). *Preventive services: A technical assistance memorandum for line supervisors.* Chapel Hill: University of North Carolina, Group Child Care Consultant Services.

Turner, J., & Shifren, I. (1979). Community support systems: How comprehensive? In H. Lamb (Ed.), *New directions for mental health* (vol. 2, pp. 8–39). San Francisco: Jossey-Bass.

Twentyman, C. T., & Plotkin, R. C. (1982). Unrealistic expectations of parents who maltreat their children: An educational deficit that pertains to child development. *Journal of Clinical Psychology, 38,* 497–504.

Uyeda, M. K., DeLeon, P. J., Perloff, R., & Kraut, A. G. (1987). Financing mental health services: A comparison of two federal programs. *American Behavioral Scientist, 30*(2), 90–110.

Vaillant, G. E. (1983). *The natural history of alcoholism: Causes, patterns, and paths to recovery.* Cambridge, MA: Harvard University Press.

Vaughn, C. E., & Leff, J. P. (1976). The influence of family and social factors on the course of psychiatric illness. *British Journal of Psychiatry, 129,* 125–137.

Vaughn, C. E., & Leff, J. P. (1981). Patterns of emotional response in relatives of schizophrenic patients. *Schizophrenia Bulletin, 7,* 43–44.

Vaughn, C. E., Snyder, K. S., Jones, S., Freeman, W. B., & Falloon, I. R. H. (1984). Family factors in schizophrenic relapse: Replication in California of British research on expressed emotion. *Archive of General Psychiatry, 41,* 1169–1177.

Viken, R. J., Marlow, E. H., & Patterson, G. R. (in press). Is preventing serious delinquency possible? In S. Shah (Ed.), *Mental health and law: An overview of some major topics.* Rockville, MD: National Institute of Mental Health.

Vold, G. B., & Bernard, T. J. (1986). *Theoretical criminology.* New York: Oxford University Press.

Waldron, H. (1987). *Modifying blaming attributions in families with a delinquent member.* Doctoral dissertation, University of Utah, Salt Lake City.

Warburton, J. R., & Alexander, J. F. (1985). The family therapist: What does one do? In L. L'Abate (Ed.), *The handbook of family psychology and therapy.* Homewood, IL: Dorsey.

Warburton, J. R., Alexander, J. F., & Barton, C. (August 1980). *Sex of client and sex of therapist: Variables in family process study.* Paper presented at the annual convention of the American Psychological Association, Montreal.

Washburne, C. K. (Ed.) (1981). *Looking back, looking ahead: Selections from the Fifth National Conference on Child Abuse and Neglect.* Milwaukee.

Washington Cofo Memo (1986). December, VI, 4. Newsletter of the Coalition of Family Organizations. (Available from National Council on Family Relations, 1910 W. County Road B, St. Paul, MN 55113.)

Watson, E. L. (1972). *Trailor court: A daycare neighbor approach to protective service* [Mimeograph]. Portland, OR: Tricounty Community Council.

Watzlawick, P. (Ed.) (1984). *The invented reality.* New York: Norton.

Watzlawick, P., Beavin, J. H., & Jackson, D. D. (1967). *Pragmatics of human communication.* New York: Norton.

Watzlawick, P., Weakland, J., & Fisch, R. (1974). *Change: Principles of problem formation and problem resolution.* New York: Norton.

Waxler, N. (1979). Is outcome better for schizophrenics in nonindustrialized societies? *Journal of Nervous and Mental Disease, 167,* 144–158.

Weakland, J. H., Fisch, R., Watzlawick, P., & Bodin, A. (1974). Brief therapy: Focused problem resolution. *Family Process, 13,* 141–168.

Wegscheider, S. (1981). *Another chance.* Palo Alto, CA: Science and Behavior Books.

Weintraub, J. F. (1976). The delivery of services to families of prisoners. *Federal Probation, 40*(4), 28–31.

Wellman, B. (1979). The community question: The intimate networks of East Yorkers. *American Journal of Sociology, 84,* 1201–1231.

Wellman, B. (1981). Applying network analysis to the study of support. In B. H. Gottlieb (Ed.), *Social networks and social support* (pp. 171–200). Beverly Hills, CA: Sage

Welsh, R. S. (1978). Delinquency, corporal punishment, and the schools. *Crime and Delinquency, 24,* 336–354.

Werner, E. E. (1986). Resilient offspring of alcoholics: A longitudinal study from birth to age 18. *Journal of Studies on Alcohol, 47,* 34–80.

West, J. D. (1982). *Delinquency: Its roots, careers and prospects.* Cambridge, MA: Harvard University Press.

Westermeyer, J. (1982). Alcoholism and services for ethnic populations. In E. M. Pattison & E. Kaufman (Eds.), *Encyclopedic handbook of alcoholism.* New York: Gardner.

White, H. (1982). Sociological theories of the etiology of alcoholism. In E. Gomberg, H. White, & J. Carpenter (Eds.), *Alcohol, science, and society revisited.* Ann Arbor: University of Michigan Press.

Whittaker, J. (1987). Group care for children. *Encyclopedia of social work* (vol. I, pp. 672–682). Silver Spring, MD: National Association of Social Workers.

Wiatrowski, M. D., Griswald, B. D., & Roberts, M. K. (1981). Social control theory and delinquency. *American Sociological Review, 46,* 525–541.

Wilkinson, K. (1980). The broken home and delinquent behavior: An alternative interpretation of contradictory findings. In T. Hirschi & M. Gottfredson (Eds.), *Understanding crime: Current theory and research* (pp. 21–42). Beverly Hills, CA: Sage.

Wilkinson, K., Stitt, B. D., & Erickson, M. L. (1982). Siblings and delinquent behavior: An exploratory study of a neglected family variable. *Criminology, 20,* 223–239.

Willie, C. V. (1967). The relative contributions of family status and economic status to juvenile delinquency. *Social Problems, 14,* 326–335.

Wilson, J. Q., & Herrnstein, R. J. (1985). *Crime and human nature.* New York: Simon & Schuster.

Wilson, W. J. (1978). *The declining significance of race.* Chicago: University of Chicago Press.

Wing, J. K. (1978). Social influences on the course of schizophrenia. In Wynne, L. C., Cromwell, R. L. and Matthyse, S. (Eds.), *The nature of schizophrenia.* New York: Wiley and Sons.

Wiseman, J. P. (1980). The "home treatment": The first steps in trying to cope with an alcoholic husband. *Family Relations, 29,* 541–549.

Woititiz, J. G. (1985). *Struggle for intimacy.* Pompano Beach, FL: Health Communications.

Wolf, B. M. (1983). *Social network form: Information and scoring instructions.* Unpublished monograph. Temple University, Philadelphia.

Wolfgang, M. E. (1958). *Patterns in criminal homicide.* New York: Wiley.

Wolock, I., & Horowitz, B. (1979). Child maltreatment and material deprivation among AFDC–recipient families. *Social Service Review, 53,* 175–194.

Wolock, I., & Horowitz, B. (1984). Child maltreatment as a social problem: The neglect of neglect. *American Journal of Orthopsychiatry, 54*(4), 530–543.

Wyatt, R. J., Cutler, N. R., DeLisi, L. E., Jeste, D. V., Kleinman, J. E., Luchins, D. J., Potkin, S. G., & Weinberger, D. R. (1982). Biochemical and morphological factors in the etiology of the schizophrenic disorders. In L. Grinspood (Ed.), *The*

American Psychiatric Association Review. Washington, DC: American Psychiatric Association Press.

Wynne, L. C. (1981). Current concepts about schizophrenics and family relationships. *Journal of Nervous and Mental Disease, 169,* 82–89.

Yang, R. K., Brooke, F. L., & Powell, G. (1981). *Families at risk for child abuse: Increasing maternal skills in parent–child interaction.* Athens: Department of Child and Family Development, University of Georgia.

Yarrow, M., Clausen, J., & Robbins, P. (1955). The social meaning of mental illness. *Journal of Social Issues, 11,* 33–48.

Young, L. (1964). *Wednesday's children.* New York: McGraw-Hill.

Zimmerman, S. (1982). Confusions and contradictions in family policy developments: Applications of a model. *Family Relations, 31,* 445–455.

Zingraff, M. T., & Belson, M. J. (1986). Child abuse and violent crime. In K. C. Haas, & G. P. Alpert (Eds.), *The dilemmas of punishment* (pp. 49–63). Prospect Heights, IL: Waveland.

Zweben, A. (1986). Problem drinking and marital adjustment. *Journal of Studies on Alcohol, 47,* 167–172.

Zygarlicki, S. A., & Smith, T. E. (1986). *Marriage and family therapists; attitudes toward alcohol treatment.* Unpublished manuscript.

Index

About the Editors and Authors

James F. Alexander, Ph.D., is Professor of Psychology at the University of Utah. His clinical and research interests in juvenile delinquency, family therapy, and related research began over 20 years ago. As the field of family therapy has matured, Dr. Alexander has contributed with basic research projects, family therapy process and outcome research, and clinical model building. A recent recipient of the American Family Therapy Association Award for Distinguished Contributions to Family Therapy Research, he has produced over 75 convention presentations, published articles, reprinted articles, and chapters and has provided over 80 professional training workshops, consultations, colloquia, and invited professional lectures.

C. Christian Beels has for most of his professional life been concerned with the family and social care of severely ill, long-term patients. He founded and was the first director of the Family Service at Bronx State Hospital under Israel Zwerling and has taught family therapy at both Albert Einstein and Columbia. Dr. Beels is Associate Clinical Professor of Psychiatry at the Columbia University College of Physicians and Surgeons and formerly the Director of the Public Psychiatry Fellowship at the New York State Psychiatric Institute. He is now in the private practice of family and marital therapy in Manhattan.

Catherine S. Chilman, Professor Emeritus and part-time instructor at the School of Social Welfare, University of Wisconsin–Milwaukee, has her M.A. in social work from the University of Chicago and Ph.D. in psychology from Syracuse University. Her work experience includes direct service, administration, teaching, and research in the field of the family. Among other organizations, Dr. Chilman has served on the National Council on Family Relations, the Council on Social Work Education, the International Conference of Social Work, the American Psychological Association, and the Groves Conference on Marriage and the Family, of which she has been President. Her books include *Growing Up Poor, Your Child 6–12,* and *Adolescent Sexuality in a Changing American Society: Social and Psychological Perspectives for the Human Services Professions.*

Fred M. Cox is Dean and Professor of Social Work at the University of Wisconsin–Milwaukee School of Social Welfare. He earned the M.S.W. degree from the University of California in 1954 and the D.S.W. from the University of California at Berkeley in 1968. From 1954 through 1957 he was employed as a social worker with the Family Service Bureau in Oakland, California. His specialties are social welfare policy and community organization practice. He is principal editor of two works, *Strategies of Community Organization,* now in its fourth edition, and *Tactics and Techniques of Community Practice,* now in its second edition. He served as Secretary–Treasurer of the National Association of Deans and Directors of Schools of Social Work between 1985 and 1987 and was recently reelected to the Board of Directors of the Council on Social Work Education.

Steve de Shazer is Co-founder and Director of the Brief Family Therapy Center in Milwaukee, Wisconsin. He is the author of two books, *Patterns of Brief Family Therapy* and *Keys to Solution in Brief Family Therapy,* as well as various professional articles. Mr. de Shazer is on the editorial board of several journals and has presented, trained, and consulted widely in the United States, Europe, and Japan. He is currently working on Artificial Intelligence and a third book to be published by W. W. Norton in 1988.

Michael R. Fox earned his M.D. from the University of Iowa, received his pediatric and psychiatry training at the University of Maryland, and completed 5 years of psychoanalytic training at the Washington Psychoanalytic Institute. He was Medical Consultant for 6 years and supervisor for three years at the Family Therapy Institute of D.C. and currently holds the position of Clinical Assistant Professor in the Departments of Psychiatry at Johns Hopkins Hospital and the University of Maryland Hospital. He is also the Medical Director of the Woodbourne Residential Treatment Center for delinquent adolescents. Besides maintaining an active private practice, Dr. Fox is a geriatric consultant and conducts national workshops on family therapy.

James M. Gaudin, Jr., is Associate Professor at the School of Social Work, University of Georgia. He received his M.S.W. from the National Catholic School of Social Service, Catholic University of

America, and his Ph.D. in social work from Florida State University. He is currently Project Director for the Social Network Intervention Project, a research and demonstration effort with neglectful families in Georgia. Dr. Gaudin's research efforts over the past 10 years have concerned informal support networks, child maltreatment, and incarcerated mothers. His practice experience in social work over the past 20 years has included clinical practice, social welfare planning, administration, and teaching.

Alfred Kadushin has been on the faculty of the University of Wisconsin–Madison since 1950; in 1979 the regents of the University appointed him the Julia C. Lathrop Distinguished Professor of Social Work. The author of 12 books and over 50 articles in professional journals, Professor Kadushin has taught at Columbia University, Tulane University, San Diego State College, LaTrobe University in Melbourne, Australia, and Hebrew and Tel Aviv Universities in Israel. He has also been a Fulbright Lecturer in The Netherlands. In 1973 Professor Kadushin was named a Fellow at the Center for Advanced Studies in the Behavioral Sciences, Palo Alto, California.

Norman Liddle is currently enrolled in the doctoral program in clinical psychology at the University of Utah, where he also received his B.S. He has taught courses on abnormal psychology and has worked with autistic children and adolescents. His research interests include family therapy and adolescent psychopathology, and he is currently doing research on therapist variables and its effect on family therapy process.

William R. McFarlane is Director of the Biosocial Treatment Research Division of the New York State Psychiatric Institute and is an Associate Professor in the Department of Psychiatry, College of Physicians and Surgeons, Columbia University. He is Director of Family Therapy Training for the residency training program and Director of the Fellowship in Public Psychiatry at Columbia. A graduate of Earlham College, Columbia University College of Physicians and Surgeons, and the Albert Einstein College of Medicine, where he trained in social and community psychiatry, Dr. McFarlane is the editor of *Family Therapy in Schizophrenia*. His main interests are developing family and social treatments for major mental illnesses and their application in the public sector.

Elam W. Nunnally is a family life educator who is a co-designer of the (Minnesota) Couple Communication Program. He is also a marriage and family therapist who assisted in the development of solution-focused brief therapy at the Brief Family Therapy Center in Milwaukee, where he has his practice. He is Associate Professor in the School of Social Welfare, University of Wisconsin–Milwaukee, where he teaches marriage and family therapy, family development, and courses in parenting and parent education. During his summers he teaches Couple Communication and brief therapy in Scandinavia. He co-authored *Alive and Aware, Talking Together, Straight Talk,* and articles on communication and brief therapy.

Alice M. Newberry is currently a graduate student in clinical psychology at the University of Utah. She received her B.A. in philosophy and B.S. in computer science from Colorado State University and worked for the Eastman Kodak Company as a systems analyst until 1984 when she returned to school. Her professional interests include family therapy process research and the study of family interactions in general.

Carl E. Pope received his Ph.D. in criminal justice from the State University of New York at Albany and is currently Professor and Chair of the Criminal Justice Program at the University of Wisconsin–Milwaukee. He has published numerous articles, papers, book chapters, and manuscripts on the processing of both adult and juvenile offenders and issues pertaining to race and crime. Dr. Pope is currently engaged in historical research on ethnic patterns of confinement.

Thomas Edward Smith, Associate Professor at the School of Social Welfare, University of Wisconsin–Milwaukee, has his M.S.W. and Ph.D. in social welfare from the University of Washington in Seattle. He is a member of the Academy of Certified Social Workers and a Clinical Member of the American Association for Marriage and Family Therapy. Currently the Director of Training and Research for the Family Therapy Training Institute at Family Service in Milwaukee, Dr. Smith has a dozen publications in the area of treating adolescents and their families. His current research interest is in the brief systemic treatment of chemically dependent adolescents and their families.

Thomas C. Todd, Ph.D., is Chief Psychologist at Forest Hospital, Des Plaines, Illinois, and is on the faculties of the Illinois School of Professional Psychology and the Center for Family Studies/Family Institute of Chicago. Dr. Todd received his doctoral training in clinical psychology at New York University and postdoctoral training in psychotherapy research and family therapy at the University of Pennsylvania Department of Psychiatry and the Philadelphia Child Guidance Clinic. He developed, along with M. Duncan Stanton, a major research project on drug abuse and family therapy that culminated in the book *The Family Therapy of Drug Abuse and Addiction.*

Mary Uyeda is legislative representative for health at the National Association of Counties, Washington, DC. Prior to her work at NACo, she worked in the American Psychological Association's office of legislation where she was financial and reimbursement policy specialist. She has a master's degree in psychology from the University of Oregon and is currently completing a doctoral degree in health systems administration/public finance at George Washington University.

Holly B. Waldron, Ph.D., is a psychology resident at Rivendell Children and Youth Center, an inpatient psychiatric facility for emotionally disturbed children and adolescents. She received her B.S. from the University of Iowa and her M.S. and Ph.D. from the University of Utah. Her research interests in clinical psychology include marital therapy and family therapy process and the effects of therapeutic interventions on attributions in families with a delinquent member.

Carolyn Kott Washburne, who received her M.S.W. in community organization from the University of Pennsylvania School of Social Work, worked as a social worker for 15 years. She is now a freelance writer and editor and teaches English part time at the University of Wisconsin–Milwaukee.

Brian L. Wilcox is presently Director of the Office of Public Interest Legislation at the American Psychological Association. Prior to this he served on the faculty of the Community Psychiatry Program at the

University of Virginia. During 1984–1985 he was a recipient of the Society for Research in Child Development's Congressional Science Fellowship and served as an assistant to Senator Bill Bradley. He received his Ph.D. in 1979 from the University of Texas and has conducted numerous studies in the area of stress and coping.

NOTES

NOTES

NOTES

NOTES